VOLTAIRE REVISITED
BETTINA L. KNAPP

W9-ATP-431

Most famous for his philosophical novel *Candide* (1759)
and for his theoretical explorations in his *Philosophical
Dictionary* (1764) and *The Philosophical Letters* (1734),
Voltaire (1694-1778) came of age in France during the
reign of Louis XV, in a climate of strict censorship over
all publications that suggested injustices within the
monarchy. His very name is synonymous with the
Enlightenment and the Age of Reason, as exemplified in
his famous (and at the time incendiary) statement "Dare
to think for yourself." A philosopher, novelist, playwright, historian, and poet—and also an empiricist, a
polemicist, and pragmatist at heart—he also proved to
be an exceptional businessman. Despite his vast array of
talents, however, Voltaire wrote for a purpose: to teach
people how to transform a climate of war and poverty into
one of peace and prosperity, to inculcate a spirit of understanding among the religions, inclined as they were to
hatred and fanaticism, and to encourage broad-mindedness
where intellectual constriction had been the rule.

Stressing his life and work as an individual, Bettina L.
Knapp paints a vivid picture of Voltaire as a "freedom
fighter" and a "Promethean." To Knapp, Voltaire represents
the conscience of emerging modern man; as such, he is a
voice of moderation in a world full of fanatics and
murderers. She presents a provocative discussion of the
purely philosophical texts, with especially good coverage
of the questions of free will, religion, and faith. She
shows, in writing about his theoretical texts, how
Voltaire's admiration for the English and their form of
government influenced his later work. He contrasted the
monarchy there, held in check by the Parliament, with
the autocratic monarchy in France.

Knapp also writes at length about Voltaire's deism.
For him, God exists but functions like a clock. According
to this view, the deity is uninterested in people's lives but
does make sure that the sun rises and sets each day.
Knapp describes Voltaire's opposition to any form of
organized religion, which he equates with fanaticism. A
believer in God, Voltaire felt that morality, not dogma,
was important; he counseled to "use and enjoy" but to
do so always in moderation. He is ultimately depicted
as keenly aware of people's intellectual and spiritual
limitations; a person's best weapons, he suggested,

(Continued on back flap)

Voltaire Revisited

Twayne's World Authors Series

French Literature

David O'Connell, Editor

Georgia State University

TWAS 889

FRANÇOIS · DE · VOLTAIRE · COPIÉ · D'APRÈS · L[...]
[...]BLEAU · FAIT · PAR · LARGILIÈRE · EN · 1718 · ÉLU · EN · 174[...]

PORTRAIT OF VOLTAIRE (1694–1778)

Lusurier, Catherine (vers 1763–1781); Largillièrre, Nicolas de (1656–1746) (d'après). From a private collection exhibited in the Châteaux de Versailles. © Photo RMN.

Voltaire Revisited

Bettina L. Knapp

Hunter College and the Graduate Center,
City University of New York

Twayne Publishers
New York

Twayne's World Authors Series No. 889

Voltaire Revisited
Bettina L. Knapp

Twayne Publishers
1633 Broadway
New York, NY 10019

Library of Congress Cataloging-in-Publication Data

Knapp, Bettina Liebowitz, 1926–
    Voltaire revisited / Bettina L. Knapp.
      p. cm. — (Twayne's world authors series ; TWAS 889. French literature)
    Includes bibliographical references and index.
    ISBN 0-8057-1634-3 (alk. paper)
    1. Voltaire, 1694–1778—Criticism and interpretation. I. Title. II. Twayne's world authors series ; TWAS 889 III. Twayne's world authors series. French literature

PQ2122 .K63 2000
848'.509—dc21

                                    99-053756

This paper meets the requirements of ANSI/NISO Z3948-1992 (Permanence of Paper).

10 9 8 7 6 5 4 3 2 1

Printed in the United States of America

The more I advance in life, the more I find work necessary. It becomes, in the long run, the greatest of pleasures, and makes up for all the illusions one has lost.

—Voltaire, *The Age of Louis XIV*

Contents

Acknowledgments

I would once again like to express my gratitude to Norman Clarius and Jean-Jacques Strayer, librarians at Hunter College, for making certain important texts available to me.

Chronology

1694 François-Marie Arouet, who will take the name Voltaire in 1718, is born.

1704 Voltaire's mother dies. Enters the Jesuit Collège Louis-le-Grand.

1711 Begins his law studies.

1713 Goes to Holland, as secretary to the French ambassador. Affair with Pimpette, a Huguenot; is sent back to Paris.

1715 Becomes habitué of the Société du Temple. Louis XIV dies. Philippe d'Orléans becomes regent.

1716 Exiled for writings displeasing to the regent. Lives on the estate of the duke de Sully at Sully-sur-Loire.

1717 Incarcerated at the Bastille. Begins *The Henriade*.

1718 Released from the Bastille. Goes into exile at Châtenay, where his *Oedipus* will be performed.

1722 Voltaire's father dies. Leaves for Belgium and Holland with Mme de Rupelmonde. Writes *Epistle to Urania*. Has the first of many quarrels with the poet Jean-Baptiste Rousseau.

1723 Publishes *The Henriade* (first version entitled *The League*). Becomes ill from smallpox and is cared for by Adrienne Lecouvreur. The regent dies. Louis XV becomes king.

1725 Beaten by the lackeys of the chevalier de Rohan.

1726 Incarcerated in the Bastille. Exiled to England.

1727 Presented to the king of England, George I. Attends Newton's funeral. Writes *Essay on Epic Poetry*. Meets Swift, Congreve, Pope, and Gay.

1728 Publishes by public subscription revised version of *The Henriade* dedicated to the queen of England. Begins *History of Charles XII* and a play, *Brutus*.

1729 Returns to France. Given permission to live in Paris.

1753   Quarrel gains in intensity. Tries to leave Prussia and is arrested at Frankfurt with his niece Mme Denis.

1754   Stays in Geneva.

1755   Purchases an estate, Les Délices.

1756   Publishes *Essay on the Customs and the Spirit of Nations, Poem on Natural Law,* and *Poem on the Lisbon Earthquake.*

1757   Begins *History of Russia.* Scandal arises from publication in the *Encyclopedia* of d'Alembert's article "Geneva," inspired by Voltaire.

1758   Purchases an estate, Ferney, in France. Leases Tournay, also in France.

1759   Publishes *Candide* and *History of a Good Brahmin.*

1760   Quarrels with Jean-Jacques Rousseau.

1761   Has church built on his property at Ferney.

1762   Calas is executed. Publishes *Sermon of the Fifty* and *The Maid.*

1763   Publishes volume two of the *History of Russia.* Gibbon visits Ferney. Composes *Treatise on Toleration.*

1764   Publishes *Jeannot and Colin* and *Philosophical Dictionary.*

1765   Calas's name is cleared. Voltaire defends Sirven in a trial.

1766   Chevalier de La Barre and Count Lally-Tollendal are executed. Publishes *The Ignorant Philosopher.*

1767   Publishes *The Ingénu.*

1768   Publishes *The Princess of Babylon* and *The Man with Forty Crowns.*

1769   Publishes the *History of the Parliament of Paris.*

1771   The Sirven family is cleared.

1772   Composes *Questions on the Encyclopedia.*

1774   Louis XV dies. Louis XVI is coronated.

1775   Publishes *The Story of Johnny, Lord Chesterfield's Ears,* and *Complete Works.*

1778   Innumerable visitors come to Ferney. Publishes *The Bible Finally Explained.* Returns to Paris. Is apotheosized during performance of *Irene.* Meets Benjamin Franklin. Dies on May 30.

Introduction: *Voltaire the Promethean*

Ever since I began studying the works of Voltaire—and what a revelation they were!—I have frequently shared my thoughts with friends and colleagues. What we really need, I suggested, is a Voltaire in our time. As a catalytic agent, he would stir thought; as a peacemaker, he would transform a disparate and frequently conflictual society and polity into a harmonious whole. His incomparable wit, with its finely tuned sense of irony, at times arousing belly laughter, would open up new and viable directions to readers, enhancing their joy and quality of existence. Alas! my wish has not yet been granted. But rather than despair that there has been only one Voltaire, we may delight and learn from his writings and try once again, to whatever infinitesimal degree, to set our planet aright!

First and foremost, Voltaire was a *Promethean*. Bold, fearless, and earth-oriented, he unwaveringly attacked fanaticism, dogmatism, and censorship while also rejecting institutions such as the absolute monarchy and organized religion. In that Voltaire was so intimately linked with his times—and ours by extension—let us glance at the political, religious, socially volatile, and repressive climate of eighteenth-century France.

The king of France, Louis XV, was only five years old in 1715, when his great-grandfather, Louis XIV, died. Before his death, the aged monarch had appointed his nephew, Philippe d'Orléans, to carry on the affairs of state. Although aware of Philippe's debaucheries, Louis XIV considered him sufficiently competent to run the government during an interim period. France's virtually empty treasury and the penury of its people at the time may be largely attributed to the wars waged by Louis XIV during his reign and to his revocation in 1685 of the Edict of Nantes, resulting in the exodus of many prominent Protestant businessmen. To remedy economic matters somewhat, the regent accepted the finance system of the Scotsman John Law, who founded a bank in Paris in 1716. Commerce and industry were enormously stimulated by the institution of paper money and the credit system, but faulty judgment led Law to found the Occident Company for the exploitation of commercial possibilities in Louisiana and the Mississippi Valley. The linking of the fate of his bank with that of the French colonies in America sparked speculation and political intrigue that led to a dangerous economic situation. New highs and new lows were followed by a panic that broke out in 1719. Law fled France and died in Italy in poverty.

Voltaire was 21 years of age when Philippe d'Orléans became regent. Although the latter had a reputation for free thought and irreverence, in no way did he tolerate criticism, particularly from such an upstart as Voltaire, whose troubles with the government led to his imprisonment and to his banishment. Nonetheless, Voltaire proved to be an exceptional businessman—he speculated, lent money, made and lost it—and died a rich man.

When Louis XV came to the throne in 1723, the young king was known to be spoiled, opinionated, and completely disinterested in governmental problems and in anything intellectual. He ruled poorly. Not only did France become involved in the War of the Polish Succession (1733–1735), but also when Louis XV allowed some of his *favorites,* such as Mme de Châteauroux, to govern, the situation worsened. She encouraged the monarch to participate in the War of the Austrian Succession (1741–1748); the lettered marquise de Pompadour, a Maecenas whom Voltaire referred to as "one of ours," was in part responsible for the disastrous Seven Years' War (1756–1763), which divested France of both India and Canada. Mme Du Barry, known for her lavish spending as well as for her hirings and firings of those she favored or disfavored, fueled an already incendiary climate of outrage.

The combination of economic want with a rigid, conservative, and abusive theocratic government triggered riots, especially the fearsome one that broke out in the faubourg Saint-Antoine. To make matters worse, there were nearly continuous altercations between the religious right (the ultraconservative Jansenists, who controlled Parliament) and the intransigent Jesuits, who, although no longer dominating the government, sought frantically to reinstate the authority they had enjoyed during the previous century. A climate of strict censorship over all publications in which authors sought to point up the injustices of the time wrought havoc for many. With few exceptions, both the Jansenists and Jesuits were the declared foes of the forward-looking, freethinking, progressive, and enlightened *Encyclopedists*—and of Voltaire.

As an empiricist, the Promethean Voltaire made short shrift of politically vacuous speculations and of metaphysical theorizing: "All metaphysics contain two things: the first, everything that people with common sense already know; the second, what they will never know."[1] Nor did Voltaire shy away from controversies. *"Dare to think for yourself,"* he wrote in his *Philosophical Dictionary.*[2] He always took a stand against injustice or bigotry—albeit sometimes out of spite or jealousy—whatever the consequences. A polemicist and pragmatist at heart, he wrote for a purpose: to teach people how to transform a climate of war and poverty into one of peace and prosperity; to inculcate a spirit of understanding among the religious, inclined as they were to hatred and fanaticism; and to encourage broad-mindedness where intellectual constriction had been the rule. To follow the adage "dare to think for yourself" in eighteenth-century France could lead to one of several types of punishments: exile, imprisonment, or death. Because he practiced what he preached, Voltaire was constantly in trouble with the government (a monarchy that ruled by divine right with the ruling faith, Roman Catholicism).

Addressing the notion of travel in space and the concept of relativity in his philosophical tale *Micromégas,* he derided the idea of absolutes. With an acute sense of irony and mockery in such philosophical tales as *Zadig, Candide,* and *The Ingénu* he denounced humankind's hubris in its regard of reason as an instrument capable of leading to perfection and divining nature's infinite secrets.

Voltaire was what Jean-Paul Sartre would have called *un homme engagé.* He wrote with purpose as a historian, as a fighter for religious toleration, and as a proponent of virtue and enlightenment. As a pragmatist, he pointed to the ravages of war as opposed to the prosperity of peace. In his *History of Charles XII,* he attempted to instill a love for peace by showing how the king of Sweden had begun his reign with a productive and happy land and how his passion for war had led to his demise and his nation's economic impoverishment. The life of Charles XII "should teach kings how far superior a pacific and happy government is to one which searches for great glory."[3] No longer a matter of God's will, as Bossuet claimed in *Discourse on Universal History,* politics, economics, and military events were strictly human affairs; hence, wars, treaties, and defeats should be recounted accurately by the historian. Source material must be used, facts must be analyzed, and a moral must be drawn from great historical events so that human beings may learn from previous mistakes. In Edward Gibbon's *History of the Decline and Fall of the Roman Empire (1776–1788)* and in Montesquieu's *Considerations on the Greatness and Decadence of the Romans,* arguments were based on man's ideas and actions, not on divine intervention in worldly affairs. In *The Age of Louis XIV,* Voltaire enlarged the historical vision by pointing out not merely the wars waged but the artistic, literary, and scientific achievements of the seventeenth century under the reign of the Sun King. In his *Essay on Customs,* Voltaire dealt in a comparative manner with world history from ancient to contemporary times.

A believer in God, Voltaire adored this "Supreme Artisan" as the "Architect of the world." Morality, not dogma, was important to him. Organized religions he regarded as breeders of bloodshed, corruption, and hatred. Their systems were dangerous because they encouraged an ossification of thought, intransigence, and fear. Mysteries and ceremonies, inherent in almost all religions, were not only useless but the dangerous outcome of superstition and ignorance. They systematized what should be spontaneous, muddled what should be clear, and hid what should be apparent. Prayer was an act of arrogance: it revealed humankind's attempt to make God a function of an individual's own will. Voltaire's God was an impersonal deity—omniscient, immanent, unknowable. To ask him for aid in worldly matters was to reduce his infinite nature to man's size. The proof of one's love for God, Voltaire suggested, was the virtuous life one led. All else was hypocrisy. The function of religion should serve men and women to better their earthly condition, expand their understanding of and compassion for others, and lessen their intransigence. As a Deist, Voltaire believed that life on earth counted—the here and now, and not the hereafter. Therefore, he counseled, use and enjoy, but always in moderation.

Freedom of thought in Voltaire's time—and in ours in some areas of the globe—was considered dangerous by regressive governments and repressive church leaders. Such liberty could lead to objectivity and independence of spirit—a danger to institutions that sought to hold their flock in check. In his pertinent satire *The Horrible Danger of Reading,* he underscored with perfectly logical arguments the calamities that could befall state and religious institutions if freedom of thought and speech were granted to individuals and the collective.

Voltaire's struggle for religious tolerance took on Promethean proportions in his play *Mohammed,* in which he derided fanaticism. In *Philosophical Letters* he wrote, "An Englishman as a free man chooses whatever path he wishes to go to heaven." In his play *Oedipus,* the hero was transformed into a protester, a man who struggled to lead a virtuous existence but was crushed by the dictates of the gods and was therefore sinless. Understandably, then, does Oedipus cry out in anger and desperation: "Pitiless Gods, my crimes are yours!"

Imbued with the skeptical tradition of Montaigne, Bayle, Fontenelle, and the English empiricists, Voltaire accepted the ills of humanity and believed that no amount of reason could cure them all. Indeed, he considered that life was made up of a series of obstacles that had to be perpetually overcome. He lived with a sense of doubt that he considered beneficial. Doubt, he said, fosters wisdom and action. To reject doubt is to accept placebos such as institutionalized religion.[4]

Voltaire was not a negativist. He was a realist, holding to the notion of progress principally mostly in the domains of science and mathematics, where knowledge was gained through experimentation and observation. He was aware of people's intellectual and spiritual limitations, and cognizant as well that for every two steps forward there was an inevitable step backward. A person's best weapons, he suggested, were enthusiasm, energy, and a desire to concretize his or her ideals. Voltaire despised, and perhaps feared, the self-satisfaction implicit in what he deemed to be the complacent notions of Leibniz and Pope. In his *Essay on Man,* Pope had written: "Whatever is, is Right"; "all partial Evil" is intended for universal Good. If these concepts were true, insisted Voltaire, then why not accept life as it is in all of its wretchedness? Why strive to better one's lot? Voltaire admired Locke, who, unlike many metaphysicians and theologians, never claimed to have knowledge of the nature or of the function of the soul. Locke advocated searching and learning without a display of arrogance concerning humankind's ultimate nature and certainly not with regard to godly design.

Voltaire did not subscribe to the concepts of Christian goodness and Christian charity because he felt they bred attitudes of helplessness and inertia. Those who retreated from worldly matters, and refused to enter debates or fight to improve conditions, were of no use to the pragmatic Voltaire. Monks and nuns in their monasteries were guilty of escapism. For his part, Voltaire neither shunned worldly distress by throwing himself into the arms of the Church nor avoided it by creating systems.

Voltaire's energy, his thirst for knowledge, his need to enter situations to right a wrong, his humorous—frequently sidesplitting—diatribes and ironies point to his Promethean temperament. He did not live in a vacuum, nor in an ivory tower. He put his beliefs into practice as had Prometheus and found pleasure in life's struggle by furthering his own ideas and belittling those of his enemies. He could be cutting, merciless, prejudiced, and bigoted in his attacks, but he was also experienced in sorrow. The very human Voltaire was a man of action, but not a maker of systems. Never passive, he worked courageously and fought, because virtue was his goal.

Why are we in need of a Voltaire today? To sustain a climate in which freedom of thought and freedom from injustice, intolerance, bigotry, and fanaticism—and, certainly, freedom to do good for others!—are allowed to flourish.

Chapter One
Voltaire Dared to Think

François-Marie Arouet, trickster-thinker and *enfant terrible* of his day, was painfully small and weak at birth on November 21, 1694. Rather than die, as had been medically prognosticated, he surprised family and doctors alike by not only surviving but living to the ripe old age of 83! Nonetheless, he was sickly throughout his life, given for the most part to severe intestinal problems. Hypochondriacal, he worried over the slightest passing inconvenience or fever.

Astonishingly, this feeble infant developed a sparkling personality and an arresting wit, as well as a passion for scholarship and for polemics. Traditional, systematic, and structured forays into history, philosophy, and literature were not for him; his incursions were impulsive, irregular, and unsystematic. His humor added to the effectiveness of his writings: it was unique, redolent with sarcasm and ribaldry. Laughter saw him through the complexities of situations and served as well to expand his vision and diversify his perspectives.

It is understandable that François's bourgeois parents—his mother, Marguerite Daumard, and his father, François Arouet, a Parisian notary—looked askance at their little son's antics. After his mother's death, when he was ten, these antics became even more frightening and embarrassing. Saint-Simon, the great memorialist of the age, in a moment of compassion for François's father, exclaimed: "He was never able to do anything with his libertine (free-thinker) son."[1]

Had the young man's innate outspokenness been encouraged by the company he kept? In part, certainly, and especially by that of the irreverent libertine abbé Châteauneuf, François's godfather and lover of the famous courtesan Ninon de Lenclos. Not only had he taught him La Fontaine's provocative *Fables* when François was only three years old, but he would become his spiritual adviser. It was through the abbé Châteauneuf that François met the Deist abbé de Chaulieu, the noted poet from whom the young man was to learn the art of versification.

Two other children were to be born to the Arouet parents: Marguerite-Catherine and Armand. François was deeply attached to his sister who, like their mother, died early. No love was lost between François and his brother, especially after the latter turned into what Voltaire considered a religious fanatic and bigot.

From 1704 to 1711 François was sent to the Collège Louis-le-Grand, a Jesuit boarding school in Paris. His business-oriented father reasoned correctly that such a school would give him entry to the socially well-placed and moneyed classes. It was at the Collège that François met Pierre Robert Cideville, future counselor to the parliament of Rouen and his lifelong friend; and Charles Augustin d'Argental, counselor to the parliament of Paris and devoted confidant during Voltaire's exiles and periods of stress.

Although fashionable, François led a no-frills existence at the Collège Louis-le-Grand. A scarcity of food coupled with cold and damp buildings wrought havoc with his frail constitution. Yet it was during his years at the Collège that François, the recipient of an extraordinary education, discovered his love for poetry, history, theater—learning in general—and his propensity for creating uproars. On the one hand, then, his Jesuit education left him with an extensive and deeply rooted passion for the classics; on the other hand, it stirred in him an overt opposition to all institutionalized religions.

When the bon vivant abbé Châteauneuf took François to visit the 90-year-old but still delightfully charming Ninon de Lenclos, she was so impressed with his brilliance, wit, and bent for poetry that in her will she bequeathed him a thousand francs to buy books.

It was the abbé Châteauneuf as well who first invited François to the Société du Temple, a group of freethinkers and high livers, who loved not only the finest foods but the pleasures of carousing.[2] Rejecting most of Christian thought, they believed neither in the biblical Fall nor, consequently, in the need for redemption. Rather than flagellating themselves for past sins and indulging in protracted repentances to be assured of future heavenly beatitude, many of the habitués of the Société du Temple reveled in life at its fullest in the here and now. Placing their faith in *humanism*, these morally independent freethinkers felt confident in nature's bounty, and they accepted humans with their foibles and their qualities. From the members of the Société du Temple François learned the meaning of impiety, elegance, gallantry, and brilliance in speech and manner.

Although he began to study law to please his father, François did so in a desultory manner, knowing that he wanted to become a poet. To dissuade his son from following what he considered a sycophantic career,

M. Arouet decided to send François to Holland. He reasoned that in the service of the French ambassador to the Hague, the marquis of Châteauneuf, brother of the abbé, François would spend his time working in an office and change his ways. Illusion! His son made the most of his stay in this land of refuge for persecuted Huguenots and for philosophers such as Pierre Bayle and René Descartes. The governmental entourage stilled neither François's love of learning nor his love of life.

Before long François met an expatriate, Mme Dunoyer, a victim of French religious intolerance, whose daughters, particularly Olympe, suited his fancies. To her were destined his earliest madrigals. When M. Arouet was apprised that François desired to marry a Huguenot, he summarily ordered the "wayward" youth home.

Although François returned to law studies in Paris, his passion for poetry and theater overcame any scruples he might have had with regard to pleasing his father. Determined to fulfill what he believed to be his mission in life, he continued to write poetry and plays. That he failed to win the prize of the French Academy for his verses *Veau de Louis XIII* in no way weakened his decision to shine in his chosen career. By 1715 his connections at the Société du Temple made it possible for him to meet the prestigious Duchess Du Maine at her estate at Sceaux, a small court in its own right. Invited to read his play *Oedipus* to her and her entourage, he did so in true thespian manner.

Gifted and alert, a marvelous conversationalist and entertainer at dinners and gatherings, the now-urbane François had become an expert at networking.

A Propensity for Scandal

During the long reign of Louis XIV (1643–1715), his once glowingly creative and exciting court had grown austere and retrograde following his second marriage to the ultradevout Mme Françoise d'Aubigné de Maintenon. After his death, Philippe, duke of Orléans, was named regent of France, a post he kept until 1723, when he died of his debaucheries.

Aware of the fact that the regent was a member in good standing of the Société du Temple, François reasoned that acquaintance with him would play in his favor. Although correct in his logic, he was wrong in his overly optimistic assessment of the impact his stinging remarks might have on the hedonistic regent.

Not entirely to blame for the events that followed, François participated in what had become a stylish pastime during the Regency: the lampooning of powerful figures in couplets and satires. Failing to contain his zest for saying the wrong things about the wrong people in his verses, François implied that an incestuous relationship was taking place between the regent and his daughter, the duchess de Berry. Although denying its authorship, stating that the verses were too poor to have been written by him, François added, "One may accuse me of everything, but not of being a poor writer."[3] Although the regent seemed to have taken the innuendo lightheartedly, François was required to leave Paris.

Fortunately for the outspoken young man, the duke de Sully, a highly influential friend from the Société du Temple, invited him to stay at his estate on the Loire River. Not only had a theater been built on the grounds, but everything about the place and its environs seemed to enchant the nascent poet. Occupying his time with writing, he also accepted invitations to visit the homes of the rich and the titled living in the vicinity. So charmed were they by François's wit, humor, and talent as a *raconteur* that he was asked to grace many evening get-togethers. In time, however, François tired of country life and longed for Paris. He wrote to the regent in December 1716, asking him to lift his ban. Obligingly his request was granted.

Had François learned his lesson? Seemingly not, since almost a year later he composed a poem, *J'ai vu* (I have seen), a violent attack on the regent and his regime, in which the poet listed the scandals he had ostensibly witnessed. For these infractions the regent sent him to a place he had—mimicking the title of his verses—"never before seen": to the Bastille.

Not one to bemoan his fate, François turned what could have been a negative experience—his incarceration from May 16, 1717, to April 11, 1718—into a productive one. He devoted many of the long hours during his imprisonment to writing what was to become one of his most celebrated poems, *The League,* later known as *The Henriade.* An epic commemorating the compassionate and wise leadership of Henry IV (1589–1610) during France's harrowing wars between Catholics and Protestants, it also verbalized the heroic qualities François truly admired in an individual. Henry IV was a stalwart fighter against superstition and fanaticism; greatest perhaps among his achievements was the promulgation of the Edict of Nantes in 1598, granting freedom of worship to all French citizens. Much to his discredit, Louis XIV abrogated the edict a century later, in 1685, thereby restoring a climate of overt religious antagonism in France.

Seven months after his release from the Bastille, François's *Oedipus* was performed on November 18, 1718, at the Comédie-Française. It earned not only a resounding success, but substantial receipts from the box office as well. Knowledgeable about the stringent rules of French classical theater, including Aristotle's dicta that tragedy must incite fear and pity in the hearts of audiences, François knew just how to play up to his own audiences. He chose an ancient myth, dramatized by, among others, Sophocles and Corneille, involving suspenseful themes such as incest and patricide.

Fame and fortune might now have enveloped the young poet in their pleasurable grip had it not been for his inability to desist from polemics, evident in *Oedipus* in his impious references to the ancient Greek gods and in his mockery of their oracles and priests—mockery that cast, by extension, a similar cloud on the clerics of his own day, divesting them of authority and sacrality. Perhaps unconsciously at the time, he was emphasizing what was to become one of his lifelong goals: the destabilization of religious institutions.

François-Marie Arouet, working frenetically as always, came into his own in February 1719 when he changed his name to Arouet de Voltaire and then, not long thereafter, simply to Voltaire. Despite the failure of his next play, *Artémire,* he was not one to wallow in despair. Instead, he looked forward to a positive future and to more productions that would be—of this he would make certain—more palatable to his audiences.

The following year, in 1720, Voltaire visited the English statesman, philosopher, and writer Lord Bolingbroke, himself an exile who had been living with the marquis de Villette at the Château de La Source near Orléans since 1717. It was to this cultured man that Voltaire read fragments of his again-reworked *Henriade*. Although Lord Bolingbroke was favorably impressed, when Voltaire attempted to have his poem printed, the French authorities refused to grant him a permit for its publication. Relying on his own resources and ingenuity, he had it printed clandestinely in Rouen in 1723. When word spread of the event, freethinkers rejoiced at the prospect of copies being brought to Paris secretly.

Voltaire's reputation was growing. Ebullient, excited by the first flush of success, he wrote rapidly and adroitly: theater pieces, such as *Mariamne, The Indiscreet One,* and a poem, *Epistle to Urania,* the latter serving to shock the devout by its flagrant disregard for organized religions. Indeed, he sang his adoration of a universal, impartial, and nonsectarian God, in such lines as "I am not a Christian that I may love thee [God] more."

Humor, as previously mentioned, was one of Voltaire's best drawing cards. The rich and the famous now vied for the pleasure of entertaining this 30-year-old celebrity at their homes; he received gifts and accolades. The king of England sent him a gold watch; the new French monarchs, Louis XV and his queen, Marie Leszczyńska, granted him an annuity. Although not a businessman by profession, Voltaire discovered in himself a propensity for moneymaking, which, despite some important setbacks, he successfully developed throughout his life.

Even the death of his father in 1722, and his own almost fatal bout with smallpox the following year, did not hamper his zest as an achiever. That he was cared for during his illness by the celebrated actress Adrienne Lecouvreur, with whom he had had a liaison and to whom he had dedicated some poems, in no small way added to his love for and gratitude toward her.

Voltaire's Exile: 1726–1729

In December 1725 Voltaire met the chevalier de Rohan-Chabot at the Comédie-Française in Adrienne Lecouvreur's loge. Even after the rupture of their liaison, Lecouvreur and Voltaire remained deeply attached to each other. When the chevalier de Rohan realized that she was paying more attention to Voltaire, a commoner, than to him, a nobleman, his rage was translated into arrogance. Doing his best to confuse the name Voltaire with that of Arouet, the chevalier smiled maliciously and asked: "Arouet? Voltaire? Do you really have a name?" And Voltaire replied with utmost poise: "Voltaire! While I am setting out to make a name, you are ending yours" (Orieux, 168).

Three days later, when Voltaire, a regular guest at the duke de Sully's home, was called from the dinner table to be told that a messenger awaited him in the street, he stepped outside in good faith. Upon hearing a man's voice from within one of the two carriages stationed in front of the duke's home asking him to come closer, he did just that. No sooner had he begun walking toward the carriage than lackeys began beating him. During the melee, he heard a voice resembling that of the chevalier de Rohan from within the carriage: "Don't beat him on his head, something good might come out" (Orieux, 169).

Minutes later, the bruised Voltaire rushed back into the duke de Sully's home to recount the event. Since the beating had taken place in front of his host's home while he was a guest, he asked the duke to lodge a complaint with the authorities. Neither he nor any of his guests came forward to help Voltaire—a bitter lesson for a young man to learn, but necessary for someone who still had faith in so-called friendship. He realized as well that he was vulnerable in every way, regardless of his talents as dramatist, poet, or storyteller. Having lost confidence in his erstwhile friends, Voltaire also seemed incapable of shrugging off increasingly corrosive feelings of humiliation. He experienced mood swings, and his high-strung nervous system was seemingly incapable of restraining his volatility. He was beset by a need for revenge. He felt compelled to challenge his enemy to a duel. The pusillanimous chevalier de Rohan-Chabot, however, declined the request, giving as an excuse the fact that Voltaire was a commoner and he was a nobleman. In reality, the chevalier was benumbed with the fear of being killed, since rumor had it that Voltaire was sporting a pistol. Upon being informed by secret agents of the goings-on, the chevalier's family, fearing for his life, used their influence to have Voltaire summarily arrested. Sent to the Bastille on April 7, 1726, Voltaire requested self-exile in England, which was granted on May 5. With the exception of a brief secret return to the continent, ostensibly to provoke the chevalier to a duel, Voltaire remained in England until March 1729.

His exile in England proved to be a thrilling and positive learning experience. The highest British circles extended invitations to him. His audience with King George I buoyed him, as did his meetings with Lord Bolingbroke, who had himself returned from his exile in France. Ranking highest on the list of people Voltaire sought to meet was the mathematician and natural philosopher Sir Isaac Newton. Unfortunately, the great man had been ailing for some time and Voltaire was present only at his funeral. That his meeting with Jonathan Swift, the author of *Gulliver's Travels,* was an inspiration for Voltaire became evident when years later he composed *Micromégas,* a philosophical tale about a giant and a dwarf who made their way around the universe. Alexander Pope's *Essay on Man* impressed Voltaire for its optimistic approach to life. *The Way of the World,* by the Restoration dramatist William Congreve, and John Gay's *The Beggar's Opera* also made inroads on Voltaire's writings. Samuel Clarke, metaphysician, moralist, defender of rational theology, militant Deist, and author of *A Discourse Concerning the Unchangeable Obligations of Natural Religion,* was to play a role in Voltaire's philosophical development. It was, however, John Locke's *Essay Concerning Human Understanding* that became Voltaire's most important intellectual and spiritual guide during the years to come. Another major influence, which would reverberate in Voltaire the dramatist throughout his life, was his discovery of the *real* Shakespeare—as performed by British actors and actresses, rather than the pallid French versions to which he had grown accustomed.

It was during his stay in England that Voltaire's sister, Mme Mignot, perhaps the only member of his family he had truly loved, died. On another level, he was distressed by the loss of considerable sums of money to a moneylender who declared bankruptcy the day before he was to reimburse Voltaire. Taking pity on the young man's strained circumstances, King George sent him 100 guineas. A rich merchant, M. Falkener, invited him to stay at his home near London. Voltaire also visited Lady Churchill, the duchess of Marlborough, and spent three months at Lord Peterborough's home. Lord Bath, Lord Walpole, and others extended invitations to him as well.

An inveterate worker, Voltaire realized that to really experience his exile to the fullest he would have to learn English. Applying his usual authorial zest in his writing to the development of his linguistic skills, he learned to speak and write English so well that he composed the *Essay on Civil Wars* and the *Essay on Epic Poetry* and sketched out his new play, *Brutus,* in this foreign tongue. Time was also allotted to another revisioning of *The Henriade,* which he now dedicated to the English queen. To his delight, the poem was brought out in a new deluxe edition by public subscription. With his usual fervor and excitement, Voltaire now turned his energies to the writing of a *History of Charles XII* of Sweden. By introducing the element of suspense to his political, social, religious, and topographical narrative, the future historian invited readers not only to enhance their knowledge of the times, but to better understand the motivations of his royal protagonist.

Voltaire's two-and-a-half-year stay in England enabled him to enjoy intellectual and spiritual freedom for the first time and enlarged as well his worldview via his studies of the works of Newton and Locke. He now yearned to return to France, and did so secretly.

France Again: 1729 –1734

Wisdom prevailed after Voltaire set foot in France on March 15, 1729. Voltaire made it a policy, at least temporarily, to stay out of sight. After first thinking he might live with friends near Paris, fear of entrapment by the authorities dominated, and he moved about the country until he was granted permission at the end of April to remain in Paris.

Although yearning to pursue his poetic and dramatic endeavors, Voltaire also realized that he needed some semblance of financial security to realize his inclinations. A sharp financier and shrewd businessman, as previously mentioned, he was also the beneficiary of luck: he won 500,000 pounds in a government lottery, bought gold in Nancy, tripled his investment, and then returned to Paris.

One of Voltaire's lifelong characteristics—his extreme loyalty to friends—became manifest after he learned of Adrienne Lecouvreur's death in 1730. His ire took poetic form when he found out that the clergy had decided to refuse her burial privileges in sanctified ground because she had been an actress. He accused the French of hypocrisy and pusillanimity—of adulating Lecouvreur while she was alive for her genius as a performer but blackening her reputation now that she was dead. Underscoring the contradictions existing between the mores of the French and their laws, he accused them of being "asleep under the dominion of superstition."

Although Voltaire would miss Lecouvreur deeply, he began training Mlle Gaussin to play the female lead in *Brutus*—another success, much to the irritation of mediocre detractors such as Alexis Piron. A host of other plays by the budding dramatist followed suit, among these *Eriphyle* and *Zaïre*.

A different fate, however, awaited Voltaire's *Philosophical Letters* or *English Letters,* a collection of groundbreaking essays on Locke, Newton, Bacon, Descartes, Shakespeare, the Quakers, Presbyterians, Anglicans, and smallpox vaccination, to mention but a few. Most deeply appreciated by Voltaire were the freedoms accorded to the English people by their enlightened monarchs. No sooner did the *Philosophical Letters* appear in France, however, than Voltaire's publisher was imprisoned in the Bastille and the book was publicly burned.

The publication of Voltaire's *The Temple of Taste* created another set of enemies for the author. Most generously did he express his thoughts on art and literature, but most foolhardily did he also offer his judgments on the worth of contemporary poets. Referring to the trifling writings of Jean-Baptiste Rousseau, Antoine Houdar de La Motte, and other inferior authors, how could Voltaire expect anything but vitriolic reprisals? To rid themselves of this troublemaker, Voltaire's multiplying ill-wishers resurrected in 1732 his poem, *Epistle to Urania,* originally written 10 years earlier. Once again the establishment was scandalized, but experience had taught Voltaire the art of eluding his attackers. Rather than waiting to be served with another *lettre de cachet* for what censors considered his atheistic, Anglophile, and insurrectionary writings, Voltaire decided to leave Paris. Happenstance favored him, for he came into contact with the most fascinating and brilliant woman of the time: Mme Emilie Du Châtelet, an extraordinary mathematician, physicist, and metaphysician, who also ran her own chemistry laboratory and knew Latin, Italian, and English. Her works included *Institutions of Physics, Principles of Newton,* papers for the Academy of Science, and translations of Newton's *Principia* and a portion of Mandeville's *Fable of the Bees.*[4]

Ironically, Voltaire had met her years before, when she was still a child. Her father, the baron de Breteuil, had been helpful to the young man in acquiring his release from the Bastille. It was at this juncture in Voltaire's life, however, that love between the two blossomed. For the next 17 years Emilie Du Châtelet and Voltaire lived together, their relationship spanning two phases: a love period and one of deep friendship.

Cirey and the "Divine Emilie": 1734–1749

In 1734 Voltaire moved to the estate of his "divine Emilie," at Cirey, in northern Champagne. Love was not the only focus of their lives, since, even more importantly, they studied together and learned from each other. (That she was 10 years younger than he, the mother of three children, and the wife of a broad-minded man in no way impeded the closeness of their relationship.)

Although Voltaire was not a devotee of the optimistic philosophy of G. W. Leibniz (1646–1716), he was intrigued by his companion's profound understanding of the ideas of this German thinker. It was her knowledge of the sciences that enabled Voltaire to gain increased access to Newton's more difficult scientific writings. She, on the other hand, learned history from Voltaire. Both studied astronomy and the Bible, the latter not for the literalism of its religious doctrines but for the possibilities of metaphorical interpretation. Like Voltaire, Mme Du Châtelet loved the performing arts, poetry, and music. At Cirey—the "small paradise," as Voltaire referred to it—he had the leisure to compose tracts, poems, essays, and plays, performing in and directing them in a theater constructed on the property. Who better than he could have couched his relationship with his "divine Emilie" in a blending of wit and truth: "Madame Du Châtelet possesses all the virtues of a great man with the graces of her sex."[5]

Not all their days were spent at Cirey. Both loved socializing, and they traveled to Paris, Versailles, Holland, Belgium, and Lunéville, the animated court of the deposed Polish king Stanislaw Leszczyński, who also happened to be the father-in-law of Louis XV.

Nonetheless, Voltaire's life was never without anxiety. Betrayals by erstwhile friends and deleterious criticisms by his enemies were virtually continuous. Nor was he free from a desire to avenge himself! Fortunately, Mme Du Châtelet was there to restrain him from castigating the many malevolent people who had scoffed at him. Not that his derisive comments at times did not warrant such treatment. To these vexations could be added his own frequent stomach indispositions, the problematics of his diet, and his moments of irritability and brusqueness. Although Voltaire was not given to morosity, it has been suggested that he suffered from a mild form of manic depression, giving some people the impression that he was cold and unfeeling (Torrey 1938, 37). In reality he felt deeply for others throughout his life, and increasingly so as he grew older. Whenever periods of sadness intruded, they exited through arduous work. He minimized their impact by making plans, by writing, and even more pressingly as time went on, by his profound yearning to help the less fortunate.

Deprived of a mother since his 10th year, Voltaire graciously accepted Mme Du Châtelet's mothering. It was she who judged that some of his books could be safely released to publishers but hid his *dangerous* writings under lock and key until the time would come—if ever—that the upheavals of ultraorthodoxy, fanaticism, and bigotry should subside.

During his stay at Cirey, Voltaire worked diligently on such plays as *Mohammed* and *Mérope,* on scientific writings (*Elements of Newton's Philosophy*), on histories (*The Age of Louis XIV* and *Essay on Customs*), on antibiblical works (*Sermon of the Fifty*), on philosophical poems (*The Man of the World, Discourses in Verse on Man*), and on tales (*Micromégas, Memnon,* and *Zadig*). His *Treatise on Metaphysics,* considered subversive at the time, was safely ensconced in a hiding place by Mme Du Châtelet, together with his epic-drama, *The Maid* (*La Pucelle*), a sidesplitting satire on Joan of Arc.

Mme Du Châtelet, aware of Voltaire's deep yearning to be recognized at court, astutely went about promoting his reputation. Thanks to her tireless networking and to his genius, Voltaire became the royal historiographer, Gentleman in Ordinary to the King, and—one of the most coveted of honors—member of the French Academy.

Certain indiscretions on Voltaire's part may have served to diminish his welcome in the capital. A verse in his play *Sémiramis,* for example, complimenting Mme de Pompadour, the king's mistress, had offended the queen. On another occasion, while Mme Du Châtelet was playing cards and losing, Voltaire informed her in English in what he thought to be quiet tones, but was in fact a stage whisper, that she was playing with cheats. Little did he realize that the highly placed individuals to whom he was referring had heard and understood the insults!

More significant events intruded into what had formerly been an ideal relationship. Voltaire had fallen in love and begun a liaison with his widowed niece, Mme Denis. His letters to her not only revealed his great tenderness for her but also made references to their relationship. Perhaps seeking diversion from her sorrow, Mme Du Châtelet found consolation with a young and handsome officer, Saint-Lambert, in 1748. When Voltaire found out, he was angry and hurt. But as Mme Du Châtelet rightly questioned, hadn't he chosen someone else for his pleasures? The case rested. The two remained fast friends until the birth of Saint-Lambert's baby girl. Tragically, Mme Du Châtelet died six days later of puerperal fever. The loss of his great love and partner caused Voltaire no end of sorrow.

The Courtier in Frederick II's Prussian Court: 1750–1753

Frederick II, the would-be "philosopher poet" and "philosopher king" with whom Voltaire had been corresponding since 1736, became ruling monarch of Prussia in 1740. Although he had admired Voltaire for many years and had invited him to shine at his court in Potsdam on previous occasions, only after Mme Du Châtelet's death, in 1749, did Voltaire leave for Frederick the Great's court, reputed to have been transformed into a miniature Versailles.

Other celebrities had also been chosen to participate in what was known as the king of Prussia's Berlin Academy. They included, among others, the scientist-explorer Pierre-Louis Moreau de Maupertuis, president of the Berlin Academy of Sciences; the atheist physician and author Julien Offroy de La Mettrie; and Count Francesco Algarotti, a Newtonian who had visited Voltaire and Mme Du Châtelet at Cirey.

As long as he received respect and admiration from Frederick, Voltaire found his stay most rewarding. At court he enjoyed freedom of expression, particularly on religious issues, but he felt constrained in other areas. While his wit and brilliance made him the center of attraction at Frederick's intimate dinners, what he had not anticipated was the dullness of having to correct Frederick's French verses—a task he had previously agreed to perform. More important were his quarrels with a young poet, Baculard d'Arnaud, who had, Voltaire suspected, been one of Mme Denis's lovers; and the lawsuit that he brought against the banker Hirschel. King Frederick, annoyed by these quarrels, forbade Voltaire to see him until he could calm down and live *en philosophe*.[6] To add insult to injury, La Mettrie indiscreetly repeated in Voltaire's hearing what the king had said about him: "I shall need him [Voltaire] another year at most; you squeeze the orange and you throw away the peel" (Mason 1981, 61). Although Voltaire was traumatized by this revelation, he had been working diligently on *The Age of Louis XIV*, and now that his magnum opus was in press he had no intention of leaving until its publication. To this end, he maintained his calm, at least on the surface.

Voltaire's departure, however, was accelerated by a quarrel between two members of the Berlin Academy of Science: Maupertuis, who had also been a former lover of Mme Du Châtelet, and Samuel König, librarian to the princess of Orange at the Hague and Mme Du Châtelet's former tutor. Maupertuis claimed to have been able "to establish as fundamental a principle to the laws of movement in the universe as had Newton" (Mason 1981, 63). König had found these laws to be nugatory, basing part of his refutation on a letter by Leibniz in which Maupertuis's principle had already been stated. But König was unable to furnish the letter in question that would have proven his assertion. Since König had been Mme Du Châtelet's tutor, Voltaire understandably sided with him, while Frederick, having named Maupertuis head of the Berlin Academy, supported his appointee.

Leaving Prussia being no simple matter at the time, Voltaire conveyed his concern for his own safety to Mme Denis.

> You and your friends are perfectly right to urge my return, but you have not always done so by special messengers: and what goes through the post is soon known.
>   . . . These are my circumstances: Maupertuis has certainly spread the report that I think the King's writings very bad: he accuses me of conspiring against a very dangerous power—self-love: he gently insinuates that, when the King sent me his verses to correct, I said, "Will he never stop giving me his dirty linen to wash?" He has whispered this extraordinary story in the ears of ten or a dozen people, vowing each of them to secrecy. At last I am beginning to think the King was one of his confidants. I suspect, but cannot prove it. This is not a very pleasant situation: and this is not all.[7]

Rather than restraining himself, Voltaire again resorted to the written word to avenge his hurt. In his *Diatribe of Doctor Akakia,* an acerbic satire of Maupertuis, he told of Akakia's trial by an Inquisitor for having proven God's existence based on an incomprehensible formula: "Z = BC divided by A + B. . . ." So outraged was Frederick by Voltaire's *Diatribe* against his protégé, which amounted in his mind to a challenge to his authority, that he had it burned in Berlin on December 24, 1752. Although a brief reconciliation seemingly took place, Voltaire left for France on March 26, 1753, taking Frederick's *oeuvre de poésie* with him. Fearing what Voltaire might do with it, the Prussian monarch had him detained at Frankfurt until his luggage had arrived. Even after the manuscript had been retrieved, Voltaire, his secretary, Collini, and Mme Denis, who had gone to meet him, were obliged to remain in Germany until the reception of Frederick's written authorization to leave. When it was discovered that Voltaire and his party had attempted to flee, they were placed under house arrest in a seedy inn. A little over two weeks later, they were allowed to leave (Mason 1981, 65).

"Les Délices" and Patriarch of Ferney (1753–1778)

Fear of other incarcerations motivated Voltaire to settle in what he considered to be the safety of Protestant Switzerland. Although Catholics were forbidden to own property in this land, thanks to the good offices of some pastor friends of Voltaire, the existing law was circumvented. He and Mme Denis moved into his new and beautiful estate in Geneva, which he named "Les Délices" (The Delights). During the winter months they lived in another residence near Lausanne.

Located at the gates of Geneva, Les Délices not only overlooked the Rhône River, but had a superb view of Mont Blanc. While in the process of remodeling his house, Voltaire also refurbished the makeshift theater located in a barn adjoining the living room of his home. It was there that *Zaïre,* one of his most popular plays, was performed in February 1755. Wagnière, Voltaire's secretary, noted how emotionally drained his master had been following the event.

> When he had his plays rehearsed in his presence he was beside himself, so entirely was he seized by the different emotions. . . . At a showing of *Zaïre,* in which he played the part of Lusignan, at the moment of recognition of his children, he melted so completely into tears that he forgot what he was to say; the prompter, who was weeping too, could not give him the cue. (Torrey 1938, 39)

After the performance, the now-relieved Voltaire, smiling wryly, was purported to have said that never had so many tears been shed in a Calvinist country.

True to form, Voltaire continued his enormous literary production, including thousands of letters to admirers, well-wishers, and even enemies. As a humanist and universalist, he was drawn to events occurring in all parts of the globe. Upon hearing of the Lisbon earthquake of 1755, and of the thousands who had perished as a result, he was so emotionally torn that he verbalized his profound distress in his *Poem on the Lisbon Earthquake* (1756). Striking out at those who contended that this catastrophe was sent by God to punish sinners, he questioned the entire concept of divine benevolence: "What crime, what sin, had those young hearts conceived / That lie, bleeding and torn, on mother's breast?" In his *Poem on Natural Law,* written the same year, Voltaire forwarded the notion of a universal morality independent not only of organized religions but of all concepts and systems relating to the Supreme Being. Again he decried the evils of fanaticism, as witnessed in the Spanish and Portuguese inquisitions organized by the Catholic Church, where Moors and Jews were burned at the stake in an auto-da-fé, or "act of faith."[8]

Meanwhile, Voltaire was contributing essays to the *Encyclopedia,* the giant venture that Denis Diderot was directing and for which the mathematician d'Alembert had written "The Preliminary Discourse." D'Alembert also wrote the article "Geneva"—seemingly urged to do so by Voltaire, who may even have written part of it —in which it was lamented that this city lacked a theater. The writer also extolled the pastors for their Socinianism (profession of a belief in God and in Christian Scriptures, but denial of the divinity of Christ and, consequently, the Trinity). No sooner had these statements been made public than Voltaire realized that the pastors, several of whom he knew and liked, would take umbrage. And they did. Jean-Jacques Rousseau also expressed his anger in narrow moralistic terms at the very thought of allowing a theater to open in Geneva. In his "Letter to M. d'Alembert on Theatrical Performances," Rousseau explained that theatergoing should be forbidden because it encourages both immorality and idleness. His opposition to performance was contradictory, particularly in view of the fact that he himself had authored several operas. After Geneva's Church body met, it was decreed that all theatrical performances were to be forbidden. No longer feeling secure or free to air his ideas, the now wealthy Voltaire decided that prudence was the better part of valor: in 1758 he bought a property, Ferney, in France, approximately four miles from Geneva, and leased another at Tournay, also in France, with a little theater in which he could satisfy his love for drama.

As "Patriarch of Ferney," as he was to be known until his death 20 years later, Voltaire continued his multiple activities: writing poems, philosophical tales, histories, burlesques, and diatribes; and producing and performing in plays. A plethora of new works and revised editions of old ones also appeared in print: *History of Russia, History of the Paris Parliament,* the *Philosophical Dictionary, Tancred, Candide, The Ingénu,* and so forth.

Although the Empress Catherine the Great of Russia had begun reading Voltaire's works in 1744, it was the *Philosophical Dictionary* that most specifically impressed her. After completing his *History of the Russian Empire under Peter the Great* in 1762, Catherine began looking upon its author as a sage from whom she could learn the real meaning of enlightenment, its philosophic ideas and ideals, its right principles. A fascinating correspondence began between the two, which concluded only with Voltaire's demise. Catherine's feelings about Voltaire were shown by her purchase (through an agent in the French art market) of a copy of Houdon's famous statue of the seated Voltaire, which now garnishes the Comédie-Française.[9]

As polemicist and humanist, Voltaire worked steadily for the cause of toleration and justice, his lifelong preoccupation. To this end, he spent long hours attempting to reverse several court judgments: in the cases of Calas (1762), Sirven (1764), de La Barre (1766), and Lally-Tollendal (1768).

Calas, a Protestant accused of murdering his son because of the latter's conversion to Catholicism, had been tortured on the wheel and executed in Toulouse. The family had maintained all the while that their son had been depressed and had committed suicide. After studying the documents in question, Voltaire decided in favor of the parents' assertion and worked hard to prove that the court's indictment of Calas had been a travesty of justice. He succeeded in having the decision reversed and the name of Calas cleared in 1765.

Equally insidious were the legal actions taken against the Protestant Sirven, whose simpleminded daughter, after converting to Catholicism, entered a convent where she went insane. Leaving the convent to return home, one night she vanished. Following the discovery of her body some time later, both parents were accused of murder and sentenced to be hanged. In despair, Sirven came to see Voltaire, and getting down on his knees before him, begged the aged writer to take his case. He accepted and won a court reversal in 1771, but not before Mme Sirven had died of heartache.

Even more harrowing was the fate of the 19-year-old chevalier de La Barre. Not only had he been accused of blaspheming and of mutilating a crucifix, but most shockingly of all, said his persecutors, they had discovered a copy of Voltaire's *Philosophical Dictionary* among his belongings. Accused of complicity in the affair, Voltaire, although fearing for his own life, spoke out courageously in the young man's favor. Despite his actions, the chevalier was decapitated on February 28, 1766, to the lusty satisfaction of huge bloodthirsty crowds. So emotionally and physically disturbed was Voltaire by the proceedings that he was unable to contain his outrage.

> The atrocity of this deed [he wrote] seizes me with horror and anger. I am sorry that I have ruined myself in buildings and improvements on the border of a country where, in cold blood, and on the way to dine, barbarities are committed which would make drunken savages tremble with horror. And that's what you call a gentle, light, and gay people! Cannibalistic harlequins! may I never hear of you again! Run from the stake to the ball, from execution grounds to the Comic Opera; put Calas on the wheel, hang Sirven, burn these five unhappy youths, who deserved, as you say, six months in the prison of St. Lazare; may we never breathe again the same air! (Torrey 1938, 43)

The embittered writer was again asked to serve the cause of righteousness. This time it was the count de Lally-Tollendal who asked Voltaire to clear his father's name. After the French were defeated by the English in India, the father was accused by the French of treason and executed in 1766. Voltaire's enormous work on this and the other cases again led to exoneration, but again after the fact. His unrelenting fight for the causes of justice, toleration, and freedom of thought and of speech fueled his ire even more powerfully against all institutionalized religions because of the mainly destructive power they exercised over the people's minds.

It was in 1762, while Voltaire was working on the Calas affair, that his *Extracts of the Sentiments of Jean Meslier* appeared. He had written this most flagrant attack on the Church and Christian theology in reaction to a manuscript left by a country curate, Meslier, who asked to be pardoned for having preached for so many years what he looked upon as an "absurd, intolerant, and oppressive religion" (Torrey 1938, 109). Henceforth, Voltaire's concerted battles against the "infamous superstition" and "the infamous spirit of religious persecution" began. His *Treatise on Toleration* (1763), among other works of this vintage, followed. "Theology amuses me," he declared, "for the folly of the human mind is therein contained in all its fullness."

As "Patriarch of Ferney," Voltaire devoted long hours enhancing the welfare of the inhabitants of the community and seeing to its smooth running. Assailing the social hypocrisies, vanities, and ingratitude of the powerful, he worked hard to relieve the peasants of the Jura from the hardships of burdensome taxes imposed upon them by the government and the Church.

As governor of Ferney and certain surrounding areas, Voltaire ruled with equity, his vast wealth allowing him to recompense workers for their good work habits and fine deeds. He lent money without interest to nearby communities. He attended also to the revivifying of formerly unyielding vineyards, to the improvement of roads, the draining of swamps, the reclaiming of land, and the building of more than a hundred houses, a church, school, and hospital; he created and refurbished such industries as tanning, production of silk, pottery, and "blond" lace, and watchmaking. His dream to build an agricultural community, "to make two blades of wheat grow where only one had grown before" was realized (Torrey 1938, 189), and his enormous efforts on behalf of the natives was instrumental in furnishing them with a modicum of pleasure in *this world*. In return, they organized a fete on his name day, and as in the old days, they paid homage to their great seigneur in rejoicings and revels. A statue of Voltaire was even erected in his honor.

Voltaire's *Treatise on Toleration* (1763) may in some small sense sum up the multisided personality of a man whose outspokenness against persecution and for freedom of thought, coupled with his extreme compassion for the suffering of others, set him apart—for he not only verbalized his feelings, he acted upon them.

A Glorification

When Voltaire's plays *Irene* and *Nanine* were to be staged on April 7, 1778, at the Comédie-Française, its author was invited to the gala performance. Urged by Mme Denis to return to a city he had not visited in nearly 30 years, and learning that the queen, Marie Antoinette, had wept during one of his plays and would like to meet him, Voltaire left Ferney for Paris.

Received in Paris with awe, admiration, and respect, he was feted as a fighter for the oppressed, for tolerance, for freedom of thought, for equity in the workplace. Although he was 83 and extremely thin, his energy seemingly remained very nearly as it had always been. His mind was active, his memory clear, his thoughts concise, and his will for justice obdurate. Among the multitude of people he saw were Diderot and d'Alembert and, at a gala affair, Benjamin Franklin. The latter had brought his grandson to be blessed by the great Deist with the words "For God and Liberty." Voltaire now enjoyed renown the world over for his courage, integrity, and acerbic humor (Torrey 1938, 203).

Unforgettable to Voltaire were the multitudes who turned out to greet him on his way to the Comédie-Française and the warmth of their prolonged ovations.

> His carriage was surrounded all the way by a double row of the curious. Having arrived in the courtyard of the Tuileries, his carriage had the greatest difficulty in getting through the crowd which overwhelmed him with applause, and the whole of the French guard had to make the greatest efforts to find a way for him to the box of the first gentleman [of the bedchamber]. You can imagine the applause he received when he appeared in the theatre! Nothing like it has ever been seen or heard. There has never been so flattering a triumph.[10]

Once in the theater, Voltaire was again deeply touched when an actor came to his box to place a crown of laurel leaves on his head. When, during the intermission, a bust of himself was placed onstage, and then crowned and kissed by the entire cast, virtual hysteria broke out.

The emotional strain must have proven too great for the aged Voltaire, who died in Paris on May 30, 1778.

D'Alembert, who had visited him in Paris a few days prior to his death, described him as tense, fearing he would never return to Ferney alive.

A former Jesuit, the abbé Gaultier, "a good imbecile" as Voltaire was purported to have called him, had written to him, begging him to receive him and to think about his salvation. The writer agreed. After some discussion concerning his imminent death, Voltaire signed a confession of faith of his own manufacture. It stated that he died a Catholic, hoping that "divine mercy . . . will deign to pardon all my faults, and that if I have ever caused scandal to the Church I ask pardon for that from God and the Church."[11] Voltaire not only did not take communion at this or any other time, but in the document in question he made no reference to the divinity of Christ, nor did he disavow his own writings (Mason 1981, 148). It is surmised that he signed the document to make certain that his body would not be cast into a dump, as had been the

fate of countless artists, including Adrienne Lecouvreur, who did not
receive the last rites.

Voltaire's precautions were to no avail. Near the time of his death, the
abbé Gaultier and another abbé from Saint-Sulpice arrived. The latter,
dissatisfied with the confession of faith Voltaire had signed, asked the
now-delirious writer: "Do you recognize the divinity of Jesus Christ?" to
which Voltaire replied: "In the name of God, don't talk to me about that
man" (Pomeau 1969, 454). With that, the men of the cloth departed.

Following Voltaire's demise, the Church refused to bury him in holy
ground. Nor would the authorities agree that his body be taken to Ferney. Thus Voltaire's carefully laid plan for burial at Ferney—his body
was to lie in a tomb half in and half out of the church built on his property—was thwarted. His nephew, the abbé Mignot, taking matters in
hand, had the body embalmed, dressed it in a nightshirt and cap, then
placed it in a sitting position in a carriage that was then conveyed to the
monastery of Scellières in Champagne under his jurisdiction, where
Voltaire was buried in accordance with church ritual. His remains, however, were disinterred in July 1791 and brought back to Paris, where
they were transferred to the Pantheon and buried with the veneration a
great revolutionary and freedom fighter deserved!

Voltaire's real confession of faith revealed his true convictions as the
Deist he had always been. He gave the signed document to his secretary
Wagnière, who, under Mme Denis's orders, returned to Ferney.

I die adoring God, loving my friends, not hating my enemies and detest-
ing superstition." (Pomeau 1969, 453).

Chapter Two

The Unsystematic Philosophical Polemicist

Voltaire's highly developed religious and social *conscience* and *consciousness* was instrumental in sparking what was to become his extraordinary talent for disputation. His continuous involvement since early youth in attempts to right a wrong led to a behavioral pattern of outspokenness and intellectual warfare. All too frequently his goal of transforming the values and comportment of individuals whom he considered perpetrators of unrighteousness brought on dire results. The brandishing of "Dare to think for yourself" in a regressive, theocratic, monarchical system eventuated in his imprisonment in the Bastille, in exile, and in virtually continuous houndings by his enemies. Understandably, the authorities kept an eagle eye on his writings, clandestine or not, and unhesitatingly burned and/or trashed some of them in literary auto-da-fés. He vented his spleen against the concerted efforts of what he deemed to be France's regressive monarchy and its equally repressive Catholic Church, but he failed to diminish their efforts to silence him.

One of the many spokespersons energizing the anti-Voltaire and anti-Encyclopedist camp was Elie Fréron, editor of the influential *Année littéraire,* advocate of Christian absolutism. Voltaire's feud with Fréron lasted his entire life. The mediocre poet Lefranc de Pompignan, siding with authority and intellectual enslavement, also attacked the philosophes en masse and Voltaire in particular. No matter their scurrilous assaults, not one succeeded in stilling or even dimming Voltaire's verbal onslaughts. His argumentations against war, fanaticism, intolerance, and harassment were direct, simple, swift, and, at times, one might add, faulty and even duplicitous. For Voltaire, the end always justified the means.

Voltaire's *Philosophical Letters, Treatise on Metaphysics, Philosophical Dictionary, Questions on the Encyclopedia,* and *The Ignorant Philosopher* are paradigms of his fearless openness, his stalwart perseverance in fighting for the causes in which he believed. Although frequently foolhardy, his verbal lynchings were launched under the banner of *reason, scientific experimentation,* and *compassion* toward humanity.

Philosophical Letters (1734)

So explosive a document was Voltaire's *Philosophical* or *English Letters* (*Lettres Philosophiques* or *anglaises*) that the critic Gustave Lanson alluded to it as "the first bomb dropped on the Old Regime."[1] Daring, perhaps even brash, it may also be considered one of Voltaire's key works. Within its pages are contained, explicitly or implicitly, the seeds of many of his future writings. The publication of the *Philosophical Letters* also marked the birth of Voltaire the polemicist, the propagandist, the philosopher, and the freethinker.

His aim in his satiric but highly informative *Philosophical Letters* was to teach the French a serious lesson. Religious, scientific, political, and artistic freedom, he indicated, had served to enrich England economically as well as artistically and spiritually. The repression existing in his native land, to the contrary, had fomented discontent, had palled on the people, and had brought about a condition of penury.

As mentioned in chapter 1, Voltaire's two-and-a-half year stay in England in self-exile was the direct consequence of the beating incident in 1725 involving the chevalier de Rohan-Chabot. Released from the Bastille on May 3, 1726, he left France shortly thereafter, disembarking near London; he returned to France in February 1729.

Drawn to England, a land bursting with creativity in the sciences, philosophy, and literature, Voltaire was determined to make the most of his exile. He was already the author of a successful play, *Oedipus,* and of an epic poem, *The Henriade,* about Henry IV of France, which some of his admirers considered an even greater work than the *Iliad.* He had great plans for the future. To initiate himself in a new, albeit unsystematic, but highly successful methodological direction in his philosophical pursuits was on his agenda. He was convinced that a comparative method based on logical and factual argumentation would succeed in opening up his readers to cogitation, disputation, and, most importantly, to *doubt.* For Voltaire, "doubt was the beginning of wisdom" (Torrey 1938, 3). One might venture to say that Voltaire "learned to think" during his stay in England.

To study English was also on his list. Not only would it enable him to communicate with those he would meet, but also it would help him draw new ideas based on the assessment of the works he was to read. To acquire fluency in English, he reasoned, was also crucial for his theatrical ventures. In addition to his friend Lord Bolingbroke, the Tory politician, writer, and philosopher whom Voltaire had met in France prior to his exile, and with whom he was to exchange many an idea during his stay in England, he met such notables as Jonathan Swift, Alexander Pope, William Congreve, Colley Cibber, John Gay, Joseph Butler, George Berkeley, and members of the nobility, King George I, the Prince and Princess of Wales, and the Duchess of Malborough.

Voltaire's Self-Imposed Mission

Voltaire's long-standing curiosity and admiration for the English way of life served the utilitarian purposes of setting his *Philosophical Letters* against a background of the religious, political, and artistic freedom enjoyed under England's enlightened monarchy as opposed to repression in France. By juxtaposing such extremes, the retrogradation of his native land became the butt of ridicule. Invited to compare the two, the readers were then urged to draw their own conclusions.

By opposing the way the French had disregarded and condemned the strivings of their nationals, Voltaire awarded accolades to the English for the manner in which so many of their writers and artists had been honored and rewarded for their efforts. To be sure, status was a factor for the British, but only insofar as merit was concerned. England was, in Voltaire's words, a land "where men think free and noble thoughts without any of [the] fears of servile restraint."[2]

Philosopher, Prober, Reformer

Not a *philosopher* in the strict sense of the term, as were Plato, Aristotle, Descartes, Spinoza, Leibniz, and Kant, Voltaire was nonetheless a searcher, a *philosophe* in the manner of Diderot, d'Alembert, and Baron d'Holbach, whose critical, experimental, and rational method he shared. Similarly, he was a prober who believed in progress and sought to rectify injustices through reform.

Rather than waxing in systematic and theoretical arguments, Voltaire put his vast knowledge to work by facing problems empirically, relativistically, comparatively, and synoptically. Naturally intuitive and armed with a swift repartee, he unabashedly lashed out with method and vigor at those who sought to stifle the great freedoms. Certainly he was not the first to do so, but it may be said that he was instrumental in calling repressiveness to the public's attention. The skeptic Pierre Bayle, author of a *Historical and Critical Dictionary* (*Dictionnaire historique et critique*, 1697), believed that organized religion had destroyed "all natural ideas of justice." Fontenelle, in his *History of Oracles* (*Histoire des oracles*, 1687), had ridiculed belief in the supernatural nature of oracles. Montesquieu's ironies in his *Persian Letters* (*Lettres persanes*, 1721) had assaulted intolerance, despotism, vanity, and other assorted ills.

The juggling of difficult ideas, explaining them clearly while also adding zest via light banter, was the hallmark of Voltaire's style. His apparently unsystematic blend of merriment with a spirit of wonderment and absurdity seemed spontaneous. Nonetheless, his deep-rooted sense of logic pressured him to substantiate each of his statements with appropriate factual data and each generalization with examples drawn from multiple sources. His technique included the downgrading of certain ideas of French philosophers and scientists, especially of Descartes and Pascal, while lauding the innovativeness of Locke, Newton, and Bacon as freethinkers.

Philosophy and Science

John Locke

Voltaire intimated that his compatriots were in urgent need of an intellectually fearless empiricist such as Locke to offset the stranglehold on the French of many of Descartes's worn concepts.[3] Focusing on the vastness of human knowledge, Locke rejected Descartes's "I think therefore I am," his notion of "innate ideas" (i.e., that concepts are present in the mind at birth), and his theory of vortices. In contrast, in his *Essay Concerning Human Understanding* (1690) Locke declared that the mind, like that of a newborn, was like a blank sheet of paper, a *tabula rasa,* knowledge being acquired through the experience of the five senses (sense impressions) and perfected by mental reflection through a process of association and recollection.

> Having done away with [Descartes's] innate ideas, having altogether renounced the vanity of believing that we are always thinking, Locke proves that all our ideas come to us through the senses, examines our ideas both simple and complex, follows the human mind in all its operations, and shows the imperfections of all languages spoken by man, and our constant abuse of terms.[4]

Voltaire admired Locke for humbly suggesting that humankind might "possibly . . . never be able to know whether any mere material being thinks or no" (*PL*, 55). Theologians, however, had taken umbrage at Locke's argument concerning the soul. By declaring it to be material, he implied that it was mortal, such a judgment being anathema to them. When Voltaire took up the cudgel, he pointed out with his usual pith and point that "theologians have a bad habit of complaining that God is outraged when someone has simply failed to be of their opinion" (*PL*, 55). Moreover, he asserted:

> Men have been wrangling for a long time over the nature and immortality of the soul. As for its immortality, that is impossible to prove since we are still arguing over its nature, and since, in order to determine whether something that exists is immortal or not, we surely must first be thoroughly familiar with it. The human reason is so little capable of proving by its own means the immortality of the soul that religion has been obliged to reveal it to us. (*PL*, 56)

In accordance with Locke, Voltaire was convinced that answers to general or specific problems were not possible. Doubt was implicit in everything. Locke "dares to doubt," wrote Voltaire, doubt paving the way for inquiry—and wisdom. Rather than indulge in metaphysical speculations, Locke sought to *know*.

Eminently significant for Voltaire was Locke's empirical understanding of the place accorded to *mystery* in religion. Thinkers who considered themselves to be unable to explicate Deity's unfathomable nature or inclinations were neither to be labeled atheists nor antireligious. To the contrary, their point of view was a sign of humility. They acknowledged that the entire question "lay outside the pale of scientific investigation and could be met only by hypotheses" (Torrey 1938, 13).

Both Locke and Newton believed in the existence of God and in his mystery. Voltaire asserted that religionists, however, must not impinge on natural philosophy, nor on an experimental approach to science. They must cease to constrain thought.

Sir Isaac Newton
By the time Voltaire arrived in England, Newton was on his deathbed. Rather than wallowing in regret, Voltaire set about studying the works of this great mathematician and natural philosopher, and discussing his readings with the scientists of the day. Most significant for Voltaire was Newton's deductive method of investigation, which, he was convinced, not only had destroyed the Ptolemaic understanding of the universe but also had paved the way for a new era of scientific investigation the world over.

In his *Principia* (1687), for example, Newton had not resorted to occult means to prove his theory of universal gravitation. Let us note en passant that it was Voltaire who first acquainted the French with the Newtonian apple anecdote. The year was 1666. While Newton was walking in his garden he saw fruits falling from a tree. He allowed himself to meditate on this weighty subject, as others had before him. Rather than resort to the notion of a religious "mystery," he computed the event mathematically and in keeping with the laws of mechanics— thus giving birth to the theory of gravitation.

The same may be said for the confirmation of his theory of optics: "with the help of nothing more than a prism, [Newton] opened our eyes to the fact that light is an agglomeration of colored rays which, all together, produce the color white" (*PL*, 76). Similarly, he had offered conclusive evidence that, among other things, the earth was "flattened on both sides," that light came "from the sun in six and a half minutes," that matter "is solidity," that "planets revolve in ellipses," and, in passing, he discovered the basis for modern calculus (*PL*, 67). Voltaire did not fail to mention Newton's importance as the inventor of integral and differential calculus.

Impressive for Voltaire was Newton's forthrightness in conveying his disbelief in the Trinity as well as his belief in the existence of a Supreme Being. The conclusions of his discoveries—attraction, optics, and calculus—were not based on the concatenations of metaphysicians but on hard facts. He rejected the notion of an intelligible universe and claimed not to have been able to explain the word *attraction* other than as an effect that he had discovered in nature: "the certain and indisputable effect of an unknown principle, a quality inherent in matter," for which "cleverer men" than he would eventually find the cause, if possible. Humans should be aware of their limitations, Newton posited: "Attraction . . . is a reality, since its effects are demonstrated, and proportions calculated. The cause of that cause is in the bosom of God" (*PL*, 74).

Newton's concepts answered Voltaire's needs. For both men the universe was a "clock" kept in running order by a "clockmaker" who would see to its continued course despite certain irregularities that occurred but were rectifiable. According to Newton, God was a necessity in the scheme of things: he set this world in motion and created its immutable natural laws, after which he withdrew into a remote sphere whence he continued to keep his mechanism going. Because machines do break down, it stood to reason that the earth as well as other planetary forces would be destroyed and God's machine would come to an end. If this occurred, its creator would reorder it; in so doing, however, the universe as humankind knows it would alter in shape and substance.

Although Voltaire wrote favorably of Newton's system in his *Philosophical Letters* and in his poem *On Newton's Philosophy* (1736), detractors of this Englishman's beliefs were not in short supply. In *Principles of Human Knowledge* (1710), George Berkeley suggested that Newton had so mechanized the universe that God was absent from it. In the second edition of his *Principia,* however, Newton assuaged the fears of believers by explaining that his mechanistic system was limited to the visible world and that God was very much part of it. The "great machine" that was Newton's universe had to have a prime mover to set it in motion, and such a force had to be God. Moreover, if God did not take things into his own hands every now and then, who would restore the universe's continuously depleting force and energy? The beautiful arrangement of sun, planets, and comets could only have been designed and ordered by an intelligent and powerful Being.

Newton's and Voltaire's shared view is conveyed most concisely by Richard Brooks:

> Like Newton, Voltaire did not consider the world eternal, but, impressed by the increasing irregularities of the planets, he believed the universe would either perish or be reordered by its creator. Leibniz had reproached Newton for making a rather bad machine of the world. But Voltaire thought it clear that God made machines to be destroyed, so why should not the same be true of the world?[5]

Newton's influence on Voltaire led him to believe that fanaticism was as incompatible with the notion of Deity as it was with fraternity. How would Newton, Locke, and Leibniz have fared in France, Rome, and Lisbon? Voltaire wondered. Without a doubt, they would have been persecuted in France, imprisoned in Rome, and burned in Lisbon.[6]

Sir Francis Bacon

Voltaire admired Bacon, "the father of experimental philosophy," because his writings were designed to teach rather than simply appeal to his readers. Let it be known, Voltaire noted, that of "all the physical experiments that have been made since his time, hardly one was not suggested in his [Bacon's] book" [*Novum scientiarum organum,* 1620] (*PL,* 49). Bacon went so far as to construct pneumatic machines himself, even while also encouraging the discovery of "some kind of magnetic power which operates between the earth and heavy bodies, between the moon and the ocean, between the planets, etc." Voltaire further noted that shortly after the publication of Bacon's magnum opus, "experimental physics suddenly began to be cultivated in almost all parts of Europe at once" (*PL*, 49).

Medicine

Voltaire also ventured into the domain of medicine. He believed that if he could convince the French to adopt the concept of the smallpox vaccine—the insertion of smallpox blisters into the skin—he might be instrumental in helping to prevent the spread of a disease that had already devastated Europe. Despite the gravity of his subject, Voltaire's words bubbled over with humor, attracting the reader's attention by the utter absurdity of his reasoning process.

> In Christian Europe people gently aver that the English are fools and madmen: fools because they give their children smallpox to keep them from having it; madmen because they lightheartedly communicate to these children a disease that is certain and frightful, with a view to preventing an evil that may never befall them. (*PL*, 41)

In his polemic, Voltaire intended that his argument in favor of the use of the smallpox vaccine be considered a medical declaration of his freedom as a philosopher.

Religion

Voltaire's epic poem, *The Henriade,* was written, as has been mentioned, in honor of Henry IV, the promulgator of the Edict of Nantes in 1593, a document granting freedom of worship to his people. The dire economic effects of its abrogation in France in 1685 convinced Voltaire that one of his missions in his *Philosophical Letters* was to awaken his readers to certain realities: namely, the role played by political and religious fanatics in stirring hatred and triggering wars, thus leading to the depletion of the treasury. Voltaire was persuaded as well that to allow multiple religions to flourish in a nation not only would enrich it economically but also would serve to instill a climate of mutual understanding and trust in its citizens. Having himself been victimized by the clergy and the monarchy, he well understood that hatred, once activated, traveled like fire, at full speed.

In England, a multiplicity of religions—Quakerism, Anglicanism, Presbyterianism, Unitarianism, Methodism, and so forth—were allowed to coexist, which served indubitably to improve the country's economic situation and living standards. Voltaire imaginatively used the image of the London Stock Exchange—a gathering place of multicultural and multireligious groups—to make his point. A symbol of harmonious interchange, it eminently represented unity in diversity. To reinforce the strength of his not-always-objective arguments, Voltaire was sufficiently astute to refrain from alluding to the acrimonious battles occurring between various religious sects in England.

Quakers

Voltaire admired the Quakers—the Society of Friends—for their humility, integrity, spirit of toleration, and pacifism. To convey the absurdity of organized religions filled with complicated dogmas, ritual, and hierarchized clericalism, Voltaire described his visit to a Quaker who lived simply and unassumingly in a small house outside of London. Feigning shock at the Quaker's forthrightness and simplicity, which differed drastically from the guiles of the normal money-hungry businessman, Voltaire commented on the fact that the Quaker, after working hard as a linen draper for 30 years, had "set a limit to his fortune and to his desires, and [retired] to a comfortable house near London" (*PL*, 3). After his insinuating comments on the Quaker's highly moral ideology and the materialism of the acquisitive businessman, Voltaire, to be fair, made a point of depicting the Quaker's slight eccentricities as well. He underscored his peculiar dress, "a coat without pleats in the side . . . without buttons in either pockets or sleeves, and . . . a large hat with the brim turned down" (*PL*, 3). That he neither removed his hat when Voltaire entered, nor bowed before him in greeting, would, he noted, have been considered ill-mannered to the extreme in France.

Broaching matters of religion, Voltaire asked the Quaker if he had been baptized. "No," he replied, nor had any Quaker. "Then you are not Christians?" Voltaire said categorically. The Quaker's retort: "We are Christians and try to be good ones; but we do not think that Christianity consists in throwing cold water on the head, with a little seasoning." Pretending to be shocked to the extreme, Voltaire cried out that Jesus Christ had baptized John. "Christ received baptism from John, but he baptized no one; we are the disciples not of John but of Christ" (*PL*, 4). Nor did they take communion, the Quaker asserted.

During a Sunday service, Voltaire noticed that there was no priest.

God forbid that we should presume to ordain anyone to receive the Holy
Ghost on Sunday to the exclusion of the rest of the faithful. . . . We do
not give money to men dressed in black to take care of our poor, bury our
dead, and preach to the faithful; these sacred duties are too dear to be
passed on to the shoulders of others. (*PL*, 9)

With notable pleasure, his interlocutor mentioned to Voltaire the
names of the great Quakers: John Fox, Robert Barclay, as well as
William Penn, who had established Quakerism in Pennsylvania.

Anglicans, Presbyterians, Socinians

With his usual verve, Voltaire labeled England a "land of sects," each
citizen having the freedom of going "to heaven by whatever road he
pleases" (*PL*, 22). Each sect in its own way—Anglican, Presbyterian,
Socinian, Methodist, or Quaker—neutralized the effects of the others by
its very presence in the society. Thus did England's pluralism offer protection against tyranny. Were there only two sects, Voltaire noted, "they
would cut each other's throats; but there are thirty, and they live happily together in peace" (*PL*, 26). To avoid giving the impression of lauding one sect to the detriment of another, Voltaire noted that Presbyterianism to some extent resembled Calvinism in that not only were priests
poorly paid, but also on Sunday, a holy day, all forms of entertain-
ment—operas, plays, concerts, and cards—were forbidden.

Although the Anglicans dominated in England and the Presbyterians
in Scotland, Voltaire pointed out, "All others are welcome there and live
pretty comfortably together, though most of their preachers detest one
another almost as cordially as a Jansenist damns a Jesuit" (*PL*, 26).

Always provocative, Voltaire ostensibly poked fun at the Anglicans
the better to castigate the French clergy. The former were ordained as
young men, studied at Oxford or at Cambridge far from the corrupt
capital, married early, and rose in rank only after lengthy service; the
French clergy, many of whom were debauched, rose in the hierarchy
with ease, thanks to the intrigues of women and to the "exquisite supper
parties" they attended, following religious functions "to beseech the
light of the Holy Spirit." And, Voltaire added with muted shock, they
"call themselves the successors of the Apostles" (*PL*, 24).

Blaise Pascal

Although not related to his English sojourn, Voltaire's lengthy letter
"On the *Thoughts* of Mr. Pascal" was added to his *Philosophical Letters*

after his return to France. On the one hand, Voltaire singled out for praise both this mathematician's genius and the magnificence of his poetic prose. On the other hand, he attacked this "sublime misanthrope" for depicting humankind in an "odious light" (*PL*, 119). For Pascal, humankind, living in a state of perpetual dread, was a conglomerate of unfathomable contradictions, understandable only through the Christian dogma of Original Sin.

Why despair, Voltaire questioned, over the unsolvable mystery that is humankind? "Who is the wise man who will be ready to hang himself because he does not know how to see God face to face, and because his reason cannot unravel the mystery of the Trinity? One might as well despair over not having four feet and two wings" (*PL*, 124).

Unlike Pascal who found refuge in Jansenism, a sect that awarded God's grace only to the *predestined* while condemning the rest of humanity to eternal damnation, Voltaire, like other eighteenth-century philosophes, believed in working for and with people in an attempt to rectify society's many evils. Neither an ascetic nor a mystic in the true sense of the word, Voltaire chose to participate fully and vigorously in the battles *of this world.*

He considered Pascal's claim that people's need for diversion and their "aversion . . . for repose" stemmed from a fundamental "unhappiness [with] our weak and mortal condition" to be morbidly introspective. To yield to such behavioral patterns, Pascal maintained, was nothing more than a facile and temporary way of escaping from their wretched earthly lot (*PL*, 132). Voltaire affirmed the opposite by deriding what he considered Pascal's negative and distorted approach to life. By innuendo he castigated those who spent their days in self-indulgent contemplation of their sad existence, hoping all the while that forms of self-chastisement such as flagellation would help them earn redemption for their sins. "Man is born for action as the sparks fly upward and as stone is earthbound," contended Voltaire (*PL*, 133).

As a man of action and purpose, Voltaire was unable to accept what he looked upon as Pascal's tortured, disturbed, and sickly worldview. Still young and optimistic, Voltaire reviled organized religions based on complex dogmas, as previously mentioned, particularly those relating to the doctrine of Original Sin. Rather than sowing a sense of well-being, love, and freedom—qualities so cherished by Voltaire—Pascal's self-imposed torture, be it physical or mental, disseminated in the hearts of individuals feelings of terror, oppression, and sometimes hatred as well. Pascal, stated Voltaire, is dead set on painting us all wicked and miserable. He writes against human nature . . . as he wrote against the Jesuits. . . . He eloquently insults the human race. I venture to take the side of humanity against this sublime misanthropist; I dare assert that we are neither so wicked nor so miserable as he says. (*PL*, 119)

Both men looked upon life as an arduous struggle, Pascal blaming it on humankind's misery and wretchedness (the aftermath of Original Sin), Voltaire seeing it, at this period in his life, in terms of the competitive and friction-gathering nature of the life process itself (bestowed by a beneficial Providence).[7]

Why make us hate our nature? Our existence is not so unhappy as they try to make us think. To look upon the universe as a dungeon, and all mankind as criminals who are going to be executed, is the idea of a fanatic. To believe that the world is a place of delight, where one should experience nothing but pleasure, is the dream of a Sybarite. To think that the earth, men, and animals are what they must be, according to the law of Providence, is, I believe, the part of a wise man. (*PL*, 125)

Tormented to the extreme by the notion of Original Sin as well as by his own illnesses, Pascal found no rest either within or withdrawn from the world. The panic that haunted him throughout his brief earthly trajectory compelled him not only to wager on God's existence but also to plead until his very last breath—"May God never abandon me!"

Voltaire had difficulty understanding how Pascal's terror of the life experience and agony over his destiny could be equated with his belief in and love of God. In no way, Voltaire implied, had such a credo been instrumental in assuaging Pascal's anguish. Unlike Pascal, rather than arouse morbid fear in his readers by depicting humankind "in an odious light," Voltaire sought, through his understanding of life mainly as a sequence of adaptations, to usher in a positive and confident outlook on humanity.

Government

Whereas France's absolute monarchy was medieval, sclerotic, unworkable, and nonadaptable to the political, economic, or social needs of the time, enlightened despotism was not more expedient in Voltaire's opinion. Hostile always to the close alliance between government and church, he denounced such bedfellowing outright as one of the most precipitous causes for war. Religious institutions should therefore, he maintained, be divested of *all* political power.

While democracy in the eighteenth century seemed like a utopian fantasy, the English brand of controlled or enlightened monarchy headed by an elite was, to a great extent, Voltaire's ideal. To set a healthy administrative corps in place, and to encourage the production of material resources in an equitable fashion, would both reinforce peace and discourage war.

Voltaire's letter "On the Parliament" conveyed his admiration for the English parliamentary system, with its checks and balances that ensured civil and religious freedom. "The House of Lords and that of Commons are the arbiters of the nation, and the king is umpire" (*PL*, 31). Interestingly, the most repugnant aspect of the *Philosophical Letters* for the French authorities was the author's assessment of English freedom:

> The English are the only people on earth who have managed to prescribe limits to the power of kings by resisting them, and who by long endeavor have at last established that wise form of government in which the prince, all-powerful to do good, is restrained from doing evil; in which the nobles are great without insolence or feudal power, and the people take part in the government without disorder (*PL*, 31).

In Voltaire's letter "On the Government," he briefly traced England's historical and political evolution up to the creation of the "happy mixture in the government of England, this union of commons, lords, and king" in the parliamentary system (*PL*, 34).

Literature

As a writer who had been sent to the Bastille and exiled for his anti-establishment declarations, Voltaire stressed—but in exquisitely poised terms—the ignominious manner in which many thinkers and creative artists were treated in French society. A diplomat at heart when need be, he countered his negative assessments by expressing his gratitude to Louis XIV for not only founding the academies but also providing men of letters and of sciences with subventions, thus encouraging them in their endeavors. He noted with favor seventeenth-century France's system of subsidization of people of letters either by the king or by wealthy aristocrats, if they were not themselves born to means. As the power of the monarchy declined in the eighteenth century, however, and writers concentrated more on the world of ideas, or on aiming darts against the government to correct political and religious abuses, they fell out of favor, were deprived of subsidies, and were persecuted as well.

A comparative approach served to bolster Voltaire's arguments: for example, William Congreve, a master of the Restoration comedy of manners and author of *The Way of the World,* is praised for his urbane and provocative wit; and Restoration dramatist, William Wicherley, author of *The Country Wife,* is lauded for his mordant satires, realism, and provocative ironies. How fortunate were the English dramatists, Voltaire adds coyly, for not being exempt from the tightly knit rules and regulations dominating the French theater.

Shakespeare, abhorred in France for his violence, brutality, and lack of refinement and elegance, although not fully understood by Voltaire, nonetheless caught his attention and admiration. He depicts the English dramatist as

> a fecund genius, full of vigor, ranging from simple naturalness to the sublime, without the least glimmer of taste or the slightest knowledge of the rules. . . . There are such beautiful scenes, such grand and terrible passages scattered throughout those monstrous farces of his called tragedies, that these plays have always been put on with great success. Time, which alone makes the reputation of men, in the end makes their faults respectable. Most of the crude whimsy and the enormous extravagance of this author has, after two hundred years, acquired the right to pass for sublimity. (*PL,* 85)

Accolades are due to Voltaire for having been one of the earliest Frenchmen to have discerned and addressed Shakespeare's genius. His own future plays, *Zaïre, Brutus, Caesar's Death,* and others, reveal the influence on him of Shakespeare's powerful characterizations and theatrical techniques.[8]

Alexander Pope, whom Voltaire visited after having absorbed his essays and poems—*Essay on Criticism, Essay on Man,* and *The Rape of the Locke*—also made his mark on Voltaire. Indeed, he considered him "the most elegant, the most correct, and—which is in itself a great deal—the most harmonious poet England has had. He turned the harsh wheezings of the English trumpet into the sweet sounds of the flute" (*PL,* 106).

Jonathan Swift, whom Voltaire knew and whose *Gulliver's Travels* he praised, was to inspire in part the cosmic and relativistic outlook Voltaire adopted in his philosophical tale *Micromégas.* Indeed, he considered Swift to be England's Rabelais.

Rabelais in his right mind and living in good company; it is true he has not the gaiety of the older man [Rabelais], but he has all the delicacy, the rationality, the selectivity, the good taste that are wanting in our Curé de Meudon. The style of his verses is unusual, almost inimitable; true wit and humor are his province in verse and in prose. (*PL*, 106)

Praise was also accorded to John Milton and John Dryden. Although Voltaire noted the poor taste of many English writers, whose frequently "overblown" styles were removed from nature, he nonetheless admired the ease and power of their imaginations and the creativity of their thought, which were more valued in England than were the thematics and talents of comparable writers in France. As always, Voltaire gave his readers examples of his assertions. He noted that whereas Addison had become secretary of state, and Newton, Congreve, and Swift had held places of honor, most French writers, including himself, were neither respected, nor given freedom of expression, nor awarded positions.

Nor was the lot of theater people any better. A case in point was Adrienne Lecouvreur, considered by Voltaire to be one of the great stage stars of all time, and whom he picked to play Jocasta in his very popular *Oedipus*. Denied a religious burial by the Catholic Church, her body at death was simply thrown into a lime pit, as has been mentioned. In England, Voltaire mused, she would have been buried in Westminster Abbey.

Impressed by the state funeral accorded to Newton, in contrast to the shabby treatment accorded to French scientists, in life and in death, in their native land, Voltaire stingingly rebuked French governmental and ecclesiastical authorities for their "gothic barbarity" in denigrating the works of creative spirits. Many imaginative and talented French works, condemned for their so-called impiety, frequently reduced their authors—writers or scientists—to impecuniosity.

Five years after his return to France, in April 1734, Voltaire's *Philosophical Letters,* explosive and revolutionary for its time, was published without his permission. Although enjoying great success with a certain class of French readers, it was condemned by the Jansenist parliament in France on June 10, 1734. Considered as an endangerment to religion, morals, and civil order, the volume was burned and its publisher arrested. An order of imprisonment awaited Voltaire, who had now been declared an enemy of the state. Wisely, he fled to Lorraine, to the Marquise Du Châtelet's castle of Cirey-sur-Blaise. Situated on the frontier

between France and Lorraine, Voltaire was able to pass in relative safety
from one state to another.

The Cirey Experience

A mental giant, "Lady Newton," as some called Mme Du Châtelet,
although shying away from social functions where she would have had
to engage in dull and idle chatter, was not wanting in lovers. Her husband, the marquis who lived at Cirey but was frequently absent, had no
misgivings when she became Voltaire's mistress, nor Richelieu's, nor
Saint-Lambert's, nor Maupertuis's, and a host of others. Or, perhaps, he
simply never knew what she was about!

It was at Cirey (1734–1749) that Voltaire had the opportunity to
deepen his understanding of Deism, a natural religion that dates back to
Creation, and study its course throughout the centuries in the works of
many thinkers, including Democritus, Confucius, Socrates, and Cicero.
So legion are the definitions of Deism that it may be in order to quote
Norman L. Torrey's words on the subject:

> as consisting in the acceptance of a natural religion based on common
> ideas of morality and including the worship of an impersonal deity, whose
> laws are plain and engraved in the hearts of all men, as opposed to
> revealed religions with their supernatural doctrines and specific religious
> duties. (Torrey 1938, 228)

While attempting better to understand the Deistic connections—if
any—among God, soul, matter, and thought, Voltaire spent long hours
and days probing the sciences, metaphysics, philosophy, and history. To
this end, he listened to and discoursed with Mme Du Châtelet, as well as
with her visitors, including mathematicians such as Pierre-Louis Moreau
Maupertuis and Samuel König, the historian and president of the Paris
parliament Charles J. F. Hénault, and the Italian critic and poet Francesco
Algarotti. The atmosphere was conducive to laying the groundwork for
Voltaire's seminal writings during this period: *Treatise on Metaphysics, Elements of Newton's Philosophy,* and *History of Louis XIV.*

Treatise on Metaphysics (1734)

Voltaire's *Treatise on Metaphysics* disclosed his very deep preoccupation
with moral and spiritual matters, which he broached empirically and

polemically, exploring such questions as the existence of God, the immortality of the soul, the essence of matter, the origin of the human species, and free will. His highly reasoned and logical method of argumentation having, under Mme Du Châtelet's tutelage, become increasingly rigorous, he presented both sides of an argument as objectively as possible, transforming his pyrotechnical treatise into a virtual tour de force.

Like Locke, Newton, Samuel Clarke, and French rationalists as well, Voltaire, though marveling at the universe's apparent order, comparable to a clock, as Newton had forwarded, maintained that no human being *really knows* anything about the nature of this higher intelligence identified as God. Such reasoning inferred the existence of "a *higher intelligence* [that] had arranged the springs of this machine, so that the hands would mark the hours." In like manner, Voltaire posited, did the "springs" in the human body function, "in all probability an intelligent being [had] arranged these organs so that they might be received and nourished for nine months in the womb," giving eyes made to see, hands made to grasp, and so forth. Such reasoning, he observed, suggested that "an intelligent and superior being [had] prepared and fashioned matter with expertise."[9]

Voltaire realized, however, that pursuant to the preceding argument, he could not claim that this intelligent being had fashioned matter from nothing (ex nihilo), nor that "he [was] infinite in every way." The problematic of his thesis allowed him only to predicate the following: "I probably am the product of a more powerful being than I, thus this being existed for all eternity, thus he created everything, thus he is infinite" and timeless. Since he was incapable of perceiving the links leading to this conclusion, Voltaire maintained: "I see only that there is something more powerful than I, and nothing more" (*Mélanges,* 162).

The next step in Voltaire's contention was more complex.

> I exist, therefore something exists. If something exists, something must have existed for all eternity, for what is, or is by itself, or has received its being from another. If he is by himself, he is necessarily, and has always been necessarily, and he is God; if he received his being from another, and the second from a third, the one from whom the last received his being must necessarily be God. (*Mélanges,* 163)

Broaching the subject of evil, Voltaire pointed to the existing imperfections of this intelligence's design. To indulge in such speculation, however, would be to remove the notion of perfectibility from God. Nor, arguing against the materialists, would it be possible, he asserted, to consider nature and not God as the infinite and eternal being. "It is just as absurd to say of God in this connection that God is just or unjust as to say that God is blue or square" (Besterman, 353).

Voltaire concluded—although his conclusions were always subject to change—that to believe in the existence of God was the most plausible answer to an unprovable question. He had also become aware, as he had not been when composing his refutation of Pascal in his *Philosophical Letters,* that God's existence or nonexistence cannot be proven via rational means, nor can human intelligence understand the purpose of things.

Restating Locke's concept that ideas are acquired from sense impressions, he, like him, questioned the existence or nonexistence of a soul, or "incorporeal essence," immortal or not, disposing of the issue by denying the availability of proof. He concurred with Locke that God gave matter the property of thought, in contradiction to Descartes's view that matter was an extension in space. The question of free will given by God, if it exists at all, was at best for Voltaire "limited," "feeble," and "ephemeral." In time, his understanding became increasingly deterministic: everything is decided by natural law, divested of human or divine intervention.

In summing up, we may say that Voltaire believed neither in a supernatural guide nor in moral relativism (virtue and vice reflecting the utility or nonutility of a particular society). Although humans may indulge in generous or selfish actions, morally responsible individuals will be motivated to act by an inner understanding and by feelings of warmth toward their fellow beings.

> Those who need the help of religion to comport themselves honorably are to be greatly pitied; they must be society's monsters not to be able to discover in themselves the feelings necessary to society, and feel obliged to borrow them from a different source, other than from our own nature. (*Mélanges,* 202)

Protective of Voltaire, Mme Du Châtelet applied to the fate of his writings the wisdom and common sense that he sometimes so sorely lacked. It was she who secreted under lock and key his *Treatise on Metaphysics,* which he dedicated to her.

That the Academy of Sciences failed to award Voltaire a single prize for his papers on physics and metaphysics written during his stay at Cirey may have contributed to a desire on his part to broaden his interests. Meanwhile, travel was on his agenda: Brussels, Paris, Potsdam, Berlin. . . .

The Philosophical Dictionary (1764)

Voltaire undertook his *Philosophical Dictionary* with the express purpose of inciting his readers to at least suppress, if not obliterate, notions of persecution and fanaticism. Some scholars have suggested that its composition had been generated by the preparation in 1746, and the publication in 1751, of the first volume of the *Encyclopedia.* Voltaire, however, himself a contributor to the *Encyclopedia,* asserted that the *Dictionary* had not been written to compete with d'Alembert's and Diderot's monumental undertaking. Others have asserted that because the parliament had blocked the publication of the *Encyclopedia* (1758–1760), Voltaire took advantage of the opportunity to fill the vacuum with his own concentrated and convenient portable dictionary.[10]

Tradition suggests that the idea for Voltaire's portable *Philosophical Dictionary* was the subject of conversation on September 28, 1752, during the course of a dinner at Potsdam, at which La Mettrie, Maupertuis, d'Argens, Voltaire, and Frederick the Great were present. Voltaire cleverly and in a most businesslike and perceptive manner foresaw that "twenty folio volumes will never make a revolution. It is the little portable volumes of thirty *sous* that are to be feared. Had the gospel cost twelve hundred sesterces the Christian religion would never have been established" (Besterman, 434).

Whatever the facts, Voltaire's work was to be a short, concise, and readable compendium of knowledge. As a composite of empiricism, skepticism, and philosophical and scientifically deterministic Deism, it would serve as a springboard to disclose his "dangerous" ideas.

The first edition of the *Philosophical Dictionary* consisted of only 73 articles—a single octavo volume—thus meeting the requirements of a portable, convenient, and relatively accessible work. By 1769 it had been expanded to two octavo volumes, thus no longer answering its initial needs. Many more articles were added to the posthumous edition, the collection we know today.

Voltaire's Methodology

Although alphabetically arranged—beginning with Abraham and ending with Virtue—Voltaire's work was neither a dictionary nor an encyclo-

pedia in the true sense of the word (Naves 1938, 9). He saw his *Philosophical Dictionary* rather as "a series of essays on a wide variety of subjects,"
presented at times "under deliberately misleading or even provocative
catchwords" (Besterman, 433). As for the word *philosophy* (Gr. *philo,* love;
sophia, wisdom), both as implied in the title of Voltaire's dictionary and in
eighteenth-century parlance, it referred to "free thought" in the rational
pursuit of empirical wisdom and the search for understanding.

   In his *Philosophical Dictionary,* Voltaire sought to make complex philosophical, scientific, and religious notions accessible to many. He believed
that by establishing certain relatively simple criteria, he could more
readily prove the truth or falsity of his assertions. Clarity, then, was
Voltaire's tool; detailed erudition, his method of proof. His *Elements of
Newton's Philosophy* had already demonstrated his agility in translating
difficult concepts into terms comprehensible to those with little or no
scientific background. His goal of explaining new trends and ideologies
required him to furnish his readers with exact definitions of terms, precise documentation, even summaries if need be rather than elaboration,
and most importantly, pleasurable reading for the purposes of instruc-
tion (Naves 1938, 101–15). He pursued his goal with the help of many
historical and moral theses, including those of such Church fathers as
Thomas Aquinas, and with the *Commentaries on the Bible,* which he prized
highly, by his Benedictine friend Dom Calmet.

Voltaire's Empirical Purpose

As usual, Voltaire's *Philosophical Dictionary* was marked with whimsy,
skepticism, and irony and was empirical in purpose. It aspired to rid the
concept of God of all the barnacles that religious dogma had affixed to it
throughout the centuries. Religion, which should be in concord with
universal morality, often was not, Voltaire asserted, as evidenced by the
carryings-on of such archbishops as Dubois and Tencin. Power plays and
material acquisitiveness among Church sects and the institutions each
sought to aggrandize left the individual unable to believe in and love
God freely, openly, and wholeheartedly.

   Most of the essays in the *Philosophical Dictionary* were philosophical,
theological, and ethical in intent, no matter the entry's title: Abraham,
Soul, Friendship, Self-love, Baptism, Beauty, Good, Chain of Created
Beings, the Heaven of the Ancients, Circumcision, Body, Chinese Catechism, Japanese Catechism, Catechism of the Clergy, Christianity, Destiny, God, Hell, Fanaticism, Idol, Free Will, Luxury, Messiah, Miracles,
Moses, Peter, Prejudices, Religion, Resurrection, Dreams, Superstition,

Tolerance, Virtue, and so forth. Pointing up specific inequities in behavioral patterns, thought, and action, Voltaire flagrantly underscored the viciousness and violence of the intolerant, the persecutory, the fanatic, and the warmongering (Besterman, 436).

Voltaire permitted himself all the liberties he needed to topple the very foundations of hero worship. Under the rubric "Abraham," for example, he wrote:

> Abraham is one of the names famous in Asia Minor and in Arabia, like Thoth among the Egyptians, the first Zoroaster in Persia, Hercules in Greece, Orpheus in Thrace, Odin among the northern nations, and so many others whose fame is greater than the authenticity of their history. (*PD* 1972, 16)

Although many were offended by what they considered to be the author's crassness in placing the sacred name Abraham alongside those of so-called heathens and idolaters, Voltaire had resorted to such drastic tactics to shock his readers into a state of awareness. They had to be taught to *think,* to appraise the worth of all statements, biblical or otherwise, made in the name of religion. People must become attentive to the contradictions, dichotomies, and fantasies inherent in religious credos and shun blind acceptance of what is served to them by their spiritual guides. No longer should worshipers simply mouth the miracles and fabulations heard from others. An idea implanted in the mind, Voltaire claimed, should catalyze the reader's own thought patterns, perhaps even elicit new mental trajectories and increase discernment, thereby paving the way for enlightenment.

Not only did Voltaire put into doubt the actual existence of Abraham as well as of other biblical figures in both Testaments, he also cast into uncertainty the many carefully enunciated miracles those biblical works transcribed. In addition, he disbelieved the veracity of Koranic teachings; notably, its claim of the Arabs' descent from Abraham. Underscoring the many errors and contradictions in the Bible as well as in other religious texts, he noted ironically, "They are all written by delicate wits and discerning minds, excellent philosophers, unprejudiced, no pedants" (Besterman, 438).

Are Pagans the Only Idol Worshipers?

Taking his argument to the forefront, Voltaire spared no one's feelings in his article "Idol," in which he traces the etymology of the word from the

Greek (*eidolon,* phantom; *eidos* form); lists its many meanings in Latin, suggesting adoration; and then gives a brief history of its use in ancient times, noting that the word is found neither in Homer nor in Hesiod, nor in Herodotus (*PD* 1972, 238).

By basing his argumentation on etymological and historical facts as far as these were verifiable, Voltaire intended to alter the conviction held by many Christians that they were superior to pagans, since the latter alone, they believed, had been and still were idol worshipers. One of several examples Voltaire brought to prove his point was the signing of a peace treaty between the Romans and Carthaginians. By invoking their gods "as witnesses and judges" to the event, and contending that "it was certainly not the simulacrum that constituted the divinity," Voltaire disculpated them of any and all forms of idol worship (*PD* 1972, 239).

Rather than take a categorical stand, Voltaire sought to probe the actual role played by statues of gods in ancient societies. Ingenuously posed, his question invites him to compare the feelings of other ancients on the subject of veneration with Christian interpretation.

> Their error lay, not in worshiping a piece of wood or marble, but in worshiping a false divinity represented by the wood and marble. The difference between them and us is not that they had images and we don't: the difference is that their images represented the fantastic beings of a false religion, and that ours represent the real beings of a true religion. The Greeks had a statue of Hercules, and we have one of saint Christopher; they had Aesculapius and his goat, and we saint Roch and his dog: they had Jupiter armed with thunder, and we saint Anthony of Padua and saint James of Compostella . . . .
>
> Neither the most recent nor the most distant ages of paganism offer a single fact from which we could conclude that they worshiped an idol. . . .
>
> The Romans and the Greeks knelt before statues, gave them crowns, incense, flowers, paraded them in triumph in public places. But we too have sanctified these practices, and we are not idolators.[11]

By associating and comparing Christian with pagan customs, Voltaire not only underscored humanity's need of manufactured idols since the beginning of time, but pointed to the identical practices carried on by Christians. To broaden his argument, he brought to light the role played by shamans and/or clergy of all religions in fostering and manipulating conditions of emotional dependency on objects intended to assuage humankind's anxieties.

Voltaire's comparative method allowed him to explore, and in so doing, to clarify the specific point he had set out to prove. He pointed out, for instance, that as soon as individuals realize how powerless they are—"subject to every accident, to illness and to death"—they attempt to win the favor of gods/God in any way possible, including the use of idols, prayers, promises, and punishments, to help them through their ordeals (*PD* 1972, 245). He made a connection between the ancients' feelings of awe for the Almighty, and his own belief in the *reality* of a living Deity.

> They have readily recognized that there is something more powerful than they. They have felt a power in the earth that supplies their nourishment, one in the air that often destroys them, one in the fire that consumes and in the water that submerges. What more natural than to revere the invisible power that makes the sun and the stars shine in our eyes? And, as soon as man sought to form an idea of these powers superior to him, what even more natural than to represent them in a visible manner? (*PD* 1972, 245)

To further underscore the tenets of his argument, Voltaire again had recourse to history: the overrunning of Asia Minor, Syria, Persia, India, and Africa by the Muslims, who "called the Christians idolators *giaours* because they believed that the Christians worshipped images." After smashing some of the statues in Santa Sophia (the cathedral in Constantinople) and in other churches, the Muslims proceeded to convert these buildings into mosques. Voltaire continued, tongue in cheek: "appearances [had] misled them as they always mislead mankind, and [had] led them to believe that temples dedicated to saints who had once been men, images of these saints revered on bended knee, miracles performed in these temples, were invincible proof of the most complete idolatry." Of course this was not so, Voltaire noted wryly, because "Christians in fact worship only one god, and revere in the blessed only the quality of god itself operating in his saints. Iconoclasts and Protestants have levelled the same reproach of idolatry against the church, and have been given the same answer" (*PD* 1972, 244).

While encouraging his readers to separate the "religion of the wise from that of the vulgar," Voltaire assured them that by reading the Orphic hymns and the maxims of Epictetus and Marcus Aurelius, they would not be following idolatrous behavior, but practicing Deism in its purest form (Naves 1938, 138).

Although Voltaire had sought to destabilize unprovable certitudes in his article "Idol" by having recourse to ancient history, he noted a stumbling block in this kind of scholarly pursuit: for, beyond the existence of artifacts, works of art, and ancient writings, what evidence remained to prove anything, except perhaps the most rudimentary type of argument? Moreover, how much weight can be given to ancient writings? Weren't they for the most part simply stories—*fables*—that fathers told their children? And didn't those *fabulous tales* expand in wondrousness with the passing of generations? (Naves 1938, 137).

Voltaire, a true descendant of Pyrrho (the fourth-century Greek skeptic), questioned the very fundaments of being. A dangerous course, indeed! Never, however, did he question the existence of God.

God the Clockmaker et al.

Not only did Voltaire not doubt the existence of God; when it came to proving his existence rationally and empirically, he recoiled from basing his arguments on absolute mathematical certainty. His belief in God, formulated in his *Treatise on Metaphysics,* was, as previously mentioned, grounded on the evidence of "design" and the "clock" analogy. The inference was that God existed as "Clockmaker," that is, as a supreme intelligence who ordered and regulated the world and saw to the immutability of the laws of the universe. Further proof of Voltaire's belief in a supreme intelligence—reminiscent to a certain degree of Descartes's *cogito ergo sum*—was the fact that humankind possessed the ability to think, feel, imagine, and perceive their bodies. Equating the physical with the mathematical, he asserted:

> I exist, I think, I feel grief—is all that as certain as a geometrical truth? Yes, sceptical as I am, I avow it. Why? It is that these truths are proved by the same principle that it is impossible for a thing to exist and not exist at the same time. I cannot at the same time feel and not feel. A triangle cannot at the same time contain a hundred and eighty degrees, which are the sum of two right angles, and not contain them.[12]

Voltaire's studies and probings into rational and empirical evidences of God as cosmic Clockmaker had influenced him to the point of transforming his former concept of free will into what has been alluded to as a kind of scientific determinism. How could one even begin to conceive of an event, he questioned, without discerning its determining cause? He now asserted that the notion of free will operated in consort with that of a motive, itself dependent on the nature of the individual involved.

> Every effect evidently has its cause, ascending from cause to cause, into the abyss of eternity; but every cause has not its effect, going down to the end of ages. I grant that all events are produced one by another; if the past was pregnant with the present, the present is pregnant with the future; everything is begotten, but everything does not beget. It is a genealogical tree; every house, we know, ascends to Adam, but many of the family have died without issue. (*PD* 1988, 4.1:60)

Since motive precedes *choice,* how can anyone "want without a reason"? It follows, then, that neither he nor she possesses free will. In a sense that is true, is Voltaire's response, and he explains: "Your will is not free, but your actions are. You are free to act when you have the power to act." Furthermore, discussions on free will are absurd. "There is no indifferent free will. This is a term without sense invented by people who had little" (*PD* 1972, 277). Nor, he further posits, has free will succeeded in liberating humanity of its hatreds, prejudices, and passions.

Belief in God Is Not a Matter of Faith

In his article "God, Gods," Voltaire posited that his belief in God was *not* a matter of faith, for were it so, it would indicate a belief on his part in *the traditional doctrines of religion,* which he rejected. Unable to prove God's existence based on reason, as already noted, Voltaire used instead the "argument of design," warning readers that he had not written his *Philosophical Dictionary* simply to repeat what others had already posited. Speaking out courageously as always, he declared that

> we have no adequate idea of the Divinity, we creep on from conjecture to conjecture, from likelihood to probability. We have few certainties. There is something; therefore there is something eternal; for nothing is produced from nothing. Here is a certain truth on which the mind reposes. Every work which shows us means and an end, announces a workman; then this universe, composed of springs, of means, each of which has its end, discovers a most mighty, a most intelligent workman. Here is a probability approaching the greatest certainty. But is this supreme artificer infinite? Is he everywhere? Is he in one place? How are we, with our feeble intelligence and limited knowledge, to answer these questions? (*PD* 1988, 5.1:214)

Nor, as previously mentioned, had Voltaire ever wavered in his belief in God, proof of his existence being evident in cosmic design. Taking yet a further step, he also noted that motion cannot come into being from a condition of stasis, design from no design, intelligence from no intelligence, or ex nihilo nihil. To try to define God's nature, his powers, or anything else about him, would be to enter into metaphysical speculations that, in the last analysis, would be to no avail. God is beyond human understanding; God is beyond good and evil. Rather than attempt to figure out the impossible, Voltaire recommended that people be more realistic, conduct themselves in a moral and ethical manner in the empirical world, enjoy the fruits of this life, and "adore the Eternal Being."

Never did Voltaire suggest, however, that one should believe in God as a panacea to assuage one's sense of insecurity and anxiety, nor as a means of gaining feelings of well-being. "There is no safety in uncertainty," he wrote; there is no guarantee of anything in life. He counseled a believer not to "go to Mecca to instruct yourself by kissing the black stone, take hold of a cow's tail, muffle yourself in a scapulary, or be imbecile and fanatical to acquire the favor of the Being of beings." On the other hand, he did advise people to

> continue to cultivate virtue, to be beneficent, to regard all superstition with horror, or with pity; but adore, with me, the design which is manifested in all nature, and consequently the Author of that design—the primordial and final cause of all; hope with me that our monad, which reasons on the great eternal being, may be happy, through that same great Being. (*PD* 1988, 5.2:241)

In his entry "Idea," Voltaire used the dialogue form, as he frequently did, to broach the question of God's nature. First defining his term, as was his custom, Voltaire noted that an *idea* was "an image that paints itself in my brain." As the nameless interlocutor asked him whether he saw everything in God, Voltaire retorted:

> I'm quite sure at least that if we don't see things in god himself we see them in his all-powerful action.
> And how does this action operate?
> I've told you a hundred times in our conversation that I haven't the slightest idea, and that god hasn't told his secret to anyone. I don't know what makes my heart beat, and my blood run in my veins; I don't know the cause of all my movements. (*PD* 1972, 237)

Over and over again in all ways and forms did Voltaire, the Deist, attempt to expand people's understanding of an infinite God by showing them that they need not have recourse to dogma, to artifacts, idols, houses of worship, or anything else to win God's affection, since God was everything.

Primacy Goes to Ethics

Under the rubric "Chinese Catechism," which has nothing to do with anything Chinese, Voltaire broached the notion of ethics, which he considered not only far more important than dogma, but the key to life. He fleshed out his point in a fictitious dialogue between Prince Koo, son of the King of Lou, and an equally fictitious interlocutor, Ku-Su, a disciple of Confucius.

KU-SU: Since you have virtue, how will you practise it when you are king?

KOO: By being unjust neither to my neighbours nor to my peoples.

KU-SU: It is not enough to do no evil, you will do good. You will feed the poor by employing them in useful work, and not by endowing idleness. You will beautify the highways, you will dig canals, you will erect public buildings, you will encourage all the arts. You will reward merit of every kind. You will forgive involuntary misconduct.

KOO: That's what I mean by not being unjust; these are all duties.
. . .

KU-SU: But how will you behave to your enemies? Confucius recommends us in twenty texts to love them. Doesn't that seem to you a little difficult?

KOO: Love one's enemies! Great heavens! Nothing is more common . . . . Whenever one of the enemy was wounded and fell into our hands we took care of him as if he were our brother. We often gave our own beds to our wounded and captured enemies, and we slept next to them on tiger-skins spread on the ground. We waited on them ourselves. What more do you want? that we should love them as one loves one's mistress?

KU-SU: I'm very edified by everything you tell me, and I wish that all the nations could hear you; for I am assured that there are peoples so impertinent that they dare to say that we don't know true virtue, that our good actions are only splendid sins. (*PD* 1972, 91)

Voltaire aimed his darts at Christian teachings in general, but especially at the teachings of Saint Augustine, for he had been the one to declare "that the good actions of pagans could at most be *peccata splendida*" (PD 1972, 92).

What of Atheism?

Having been accused so many times of atheism by those who sought to denigrate him or, worse, to have him cast into prison or exile, Voltaire, believing the best defense to be an offense, declared that atheists were everywhere. Only the ill-informed would deny this fact (PD 1972, 51).

He furthermore asserted that not only do atheists have the right to exist, but that there is no correlation between morality, ethics, and religious beliefs. Many great philosophers had been unbelievers—Anaxagoras, Aristotle, Socrates, Spinoza, and others—but their comportment was exemplary. Hobbes, Voltaire argued, was considered an atheist and "he led a calm and innocent life: the fanatics of his time deluged England, Scotland and Ireland with blood" (PD 1972, 56).

Which is more dangerous, questioned Voltaire, "fanaticism or atheism"? His answer: "Atheism does not inspire bloody passions, but fanaticism does; atheism does not discountenance crime, but fanaticism causes crimes to be committed." As an example, Voltaire denounced the Saint Bartholomew Massacre, the killing of Protestants by Roman Catholics (to which Voltaire seemingly reacted so powerfully that he became ill every year on the anniversary—August 23, 1572—of this "official massacre"). The atheist philosopher Spinoza, according to Voltaire, had not been the one to assassinate Johan Olden Barneveldt (1619) or Johan and Cornelius de Witt (1672), nor "tore to pieces the two brothers de Witt and ate them on the grill" (PD 1972, 56).

Indeed, Voltaire concluded: "Most of the great ones of this earth live as if they were atheists." Still, neither atheist nor believer has influenced humankind's propensity for war, ambition, or enjoyment (Besterman, 207; see also Moland, 17:456).

Is There a Soul?

By tracing the varied definitions of or allusions to the soul by the Chaldeans, Egyptians, Greeks, Hebrews, and Christians, Voltaire, with his usual penchant for irony, heaped more and more confusion onto an already ambiguous subject. Paradigmatically, he writes that some ecclesiastics and philosophers claim that the soul of man is part of the substance of god himself; another, that it is part of the great whole; a third, that it is created from all eternity; a fourth, that it is made, and not created; others assert that god forms them as they are needed, and that they arrive at the moment of copulation. "They lodge in the seminal animalculae," cries one. "No," says another, "they occupy the fallopian tubes." (PD 1972, 23)

Gassendi, Locke, among a host of others were less arrogant in their affirmations concerning the soul than were intransigeant believers.

We repeat that we rely on the word of god; and you, enemies of reason and of god, you who blaspheme the one and the other, you treat the humble doubt and the humble submission of the philosopher as the wolf treated the lamb in Aesop's fables; you tell him: "You spoke ill of me last year, I must suck your blood." Such is your conduct. As you know, you have persecuted wisdom because you thought that the wise men despised you. It is well known that you have said so, you have felt your own merit, and you wanted to avenge yourself. Philosophy takes no revenge; she laughs peacefully at your vain efforts; she gently enlightens mankind, whom you want to brutalize so that they should become like you. (PD 1972, 28)

In the final analysis, the soul is a vague term, an unknown principle that has been defined as that "which animates. We know little more about it, our intelligence being limited" (PD 1972, 21). Since no verification of the existence of what metaphysicians have alluded to as the soul can be evidenced in the physical being, nor described, nor even imagined, to state categorically that this "immaterial substance" exists is impossible. To speak of this unknowable entity as immortal or mortal is therefore a fiction. Nor is it really a matter of concern either way (PD 1972, 21). The lesson to be drawn from such a cogitation, Voltaire indicated, was to suggest that people accept their limitations and recognize the concept of the unknowable truth.

Are Miracles Believable?
Or Should Judgment Be Suspended?

Delving in his entry on "Miracles" into the Egyptian, Babylonian, Greek, Hebrew, and Christian pantheon of gods—the latter a "thornier" matter—Voltaire presents an intentionally naive conundrum to draw attention to the absurdities. "Could several equally powerful gods survive at the same time?" Approaching the question of miracles in a similarly pithy (and for nonquestioning believers, destabilizing) manner, he asserted:

A miracle, in the full meaning of the word, is an admirable thing. In this
sense everything is miraculous. The prodigious order of nature, the rota-
tion of 100 million globes around a million suns, the activity of light, the
life of animals are perpetual miracles. (*PD* 1972, 311)

By claiming that miracles were a violation of mathematical, divine,
immutable, and eternal laws, Voltaire was again deriding Christian
philosophers whose belief in their religion's "saintly" miracles was un-
questioning.

A miracle is the violation of the divine, immutable, eternal laws of mathematics. By this very definition a miracle is a contradiction in terms. A
law cannot be at once immutable and violated. But, they are asked, cannot god suspend a law established by himself? They have the hardihood
to answer that it cannot, that it is impossible for a being infinitely wise to
have made laws in order to violate them. He could disturb his machine,
they say, only to make it function better. (*PD* 1972, 311)

A freethinker in the same dialogue on miracles was asked what he
would say were he to see incredible happenings, such as the termina-
tion of the earth's movement around the sun, the resurrection of the
collapse of mountains into the ocean. "I would turn Manichean; I
would say that there is one principle which undoes what the other has
done" (*PD* 1972, 317).

"Dare to Think"

One of the most significant entries, "Freedom of Thought," argues in
dialogue form in favor of each person's right to think for himself or herself. While Count Medroso, a tipstaff (constable) of the Dominicans and
familiar of the Inquisition, is taking the waters, he meets Boldmind, an
Englishman. Admitting that he would have favored being the valet of
the Dominicans rather than their "victim," he admits as well that he
would have preferred "the misfortune of burning my neighbour to that
of being roasted alive." What "horrible alternative," Boldmind retorts,
indicating in no uncertain terms that his life would have been happier
under Moorish rather than Christian rule, for the former allowed their
people and others under their dominion "to wallow freely in [their]
superstitions." Nor did they "arrogate to themselves the unheard-of
right of keeping the mind in chains" (*PD* 1972, 279).
   Confronted with the notion of freedom of thought, Medroso laments:
"We aren't allowed to write, nor to talk, not even to think" (*PD* 1972,

279). Without freedom of thought, Boldmind explains, there would
have been no Christianity. Still not fully aware of the *real* meaning of
freedom of thought, Boldmind informs Medroso that there are hundreds
of religions in England, "all of which damn you if you believe in your
dogma, which they call absurd and impious" (*PD* 1972, 280). Boldmind
then suggests that Medroso examine his dogma:

> It's up to you to learn to think. You were born with intelligence. You're a
> bird in the cage of the inquisition. The holy office has clipped your wings,
> but they can grow again. He who knows no geometry can learn it. Every
> man can educate himself. It's shameful to put one's mind into the hands
> of those whom you wouldn't entrust with your money. Dare to think for
> yourself. (*PD* 1972, 280).

Dare to think for yourself, always one of Voltaire's bywords, took on
even greater meaning for him with the passage of years.

In keeping with Locke's formula, Voltaire made it a practice of obliterating misconceptions by first defining his terms, then reviewing the
appropriate facts as consistently as possible, while remaining, but not
always, skeptical and clearminded in the process. Such a method would
serve, he hoped, to enlighten his readers so that they might recognize
the absurdity of specific religious beliefs and credos.

That Voltaire turned to historical and religious texts from both Eastern and Western traditions in many of his works, and especially in his
Philosophical Dictionary, underscored not only the vastness of his knowledge but also the importance of a comparative approach in dealing with
religious, philosophical, and ethical studies. It also offered him the pleasure of ridiculing and ironizing certain beliefs—of using humor as a
vehicle for educational purposes.

Questions on the Encyclopedia (1770–1772)

Although the idea of free will still had some validity for Voltaire when
he composed his *Philosophical Letters* and his *Treatise on Metaphysics,* he
distanced himself from the concept in his *Philosophical Dictionary.* In his
Questions on the Encyclopedia (1770–1772), he again approached the subject of free will, linking it indelibly with, among other thematics, "miracles" and "superstitions." The magnitude of this nine-volume work was
all the more impressive given Voltaire's age and the fact that he had
composed it virtually single-handedly (Naves 1938, 97).

Although humankind was certainly at liberty to *want* or to *will* to choose one direction or another in life, Voltaire insisted that in no way must this notion be associated with the religious concept of free will. Because God's ways, as Voltaire envisioned them, were vast and general, and not specific, to believe that people had free will and were master of their thoughts was to yield to illusion. He made his point in his entry on "Providence," citing with his typical humor the case of Sister Fessue. Her sparrow had been very ill and would have died, she told Sister Confite, had she not said her Ave Maria nine times to obtain a cure. "God has restored my sparrow to life; thanks to the Holy Virgin" (*PD* 1988, 7.1:28). A metaphysician (Voltaire's spokesperson) proceeds to illuminate her:

> Sister, there is nothing so good as *Ave Marias,* especially when a girl pronounces them in Latin in the suburbs of Paris; but I cannot believe that God has occupied Himself so much with your sparrow, pretty as he is; I pray you to believe that He has other matters to attend to. It is necessary for Him constantly to superintend the course of sixteen planets and the rising of Saturn, in the centre of which He has placed the sun, which is as large as a million of our globes. He has also thousands and thousands of millions of other suns, planets, and comets to govern. His immutable laws, and His eternal arrangement, produce motion throughout nature; all is bound to His throne by an infinite chain, of which no link can ever be put out of place! (*PD* 1988, 7.1:28)

Aghast at such heretical pronouncements, Sister Fessue informs the metaphysician that she will tell her confessor of their conversation and that he will surely conclude that this man does not believe in Divine Providence. Notwithstanding, he has faith neither in personal revelation nor in intercessory prayer, and he replies:

> I believe in a general Providence, dear sister, which has laid down from all eternity the law which governs all things, like light from the sun; but I believe not that a particular Providence changes the economy of the world for your sparrow or your cat. (*PD* 1988, 7.1:29)

The Ignorant Philosopher (1766)

In *The Ignorant Philosopher,* a kind of review of his past philosophical probings, Voltaire again broached such imponderables as providence, free will, reason, doubt, thought, intelligence, eternity, matter, the infinite, the finite, people's feebleness, and most importantly, their all-encompassing ignorance with regard to the cosmos. Nonetheless, there was one type of religious experience that, commented upon in works such as his philosophical tale *Zadig,* became more important to him as the years passed. The incommensurability of the mystical experience, which Voltaire sensed through the contemplation of the universe, took on increasing actuality and viscerality for him.

In no way may this kind of mysticality be looked upon as an escape mechanism—a yearning to be wafted off onto the lap of God! Rather, these feelings filled him with an ineffable joy that served to strengthen him and succeeded in empowering him to focus more forcefully on the causes of humanity.

Although Voltaire most probably wrote *The Ignorant Philosopher* during the course of a physically taxing winter, his mystical experiences must not be confused with those of a doctrinaire like saint Teresa of Avila or saint Francis of Assisi. His emotive reactions to the spectacle of nature before him were free of all canons. Nonetheless, it may be said that an affinity existed between his own encounters with the vastness of the universe and those of Democritus, Newton, Spinoza, and even Plato and Pascal, although he mocked the latter two because they "mistook their visions for truths" (Torrey 1938, 258).

Describing his extraordinary encounters with nature to the intellectually oriented Mme Du Deffand, who invited the philosophes to her home, Voltaire noted emotively:

> So, in the midst of eighty leagues of snowy mountains, besieged by a very hard winter and my eyes refusing me their service, I have passed all my time meditating. Don't you meditate, too, madame? Don't there come to you, too, sometimes, a hundred ideas on the eternity of the world, on matter, on thought, on space, on the infinite? I am tempted to believe that we think of all these things when our passions are spent and when everybody is like Matthew Garo, who is trying to find out why pumpkins don't grow on the tops of oak-trees. (Torrey 1938, 258)

Never completely abandoning himself of his identity during a cosmic experience, Voltaire acknowledged both the existence of the sublime and the awareness of his own fallibility.

> I find myself suddenly stopped short in the pursuit of my vain curiosity. Miserable mortal, if I cannot fathom my own intelligence, if I cannot know by what I am animated, how can I have any acquaintance with

that ineffable intelligence which visibly presides over matter in its entirety? There *is* one, as everything demonstrates, but where is the compass that will guide me toward its unknown and eternal abode? (Torrey 1938, 251)

Voltaire continuously enriched many of his monumental works by rewriting them, making deletions or appending a host of new ideas. Such accretions reflected the nature of his ever-evolving thoughts, gropings, yearnings, and critical attitudes to ethical and moral problems. In his philosophical and polemical writings, his approach was scientific: whatever was claimed had to be verified, scrutinized, and evaluated on ethical and reasonable grounds. His condemnation of fanaticism, intolerance, persecution, and other abuses was unstinting. Not surprisingly, his *Philosophical Dictionary* was an indictment of Christianity and the Church—the "Infamous," as he referred to it: a religion and an institution that had to be crushed so that Enlightenment could radiate. An indictment of the French monarchy as well, the *Philosophical Dictionary* was looked upon as one of the most important of Voltaire's works—and so dangerous that it was publicly burned.

Nor was it surprising to learn that fanatics, bigots, and obsessively religious individuals backed by their regressive institutions should have so feared the impact of Voltaire's arguments. What had they to offer as rebuttals to each of his sparrings in the *Philosophical Dictionary,* the *Treatise on Metaphysics,* or the *Questions on the Encyclopedia?* In response to Voltaire's verbal clarity, intellectual honesty, open-mindedness, with blendings of irony and sprinklings of humor on the side, they offered book burnings and trashing ceremonies. What better way was and is there to abolish free thought and free speech once and for all?

His struggle against despondency and the encroaching diseases of old age did not deflect Voltaire from his desire to help those in distress. To add balance and pleasure to his existence were the moments of jubilation he experienced during what could be referred to as instances of expanded consciousness. He described one of these in his *Philosophical Dictionary,* under the rubric "Religion":

> I was meditating last night; I was absorbed in the contemplation of nature; I admired the immensity, the course, the harmony of those infinite globes which the vulgar do not know how to admire. I admired still the intelligence which directs these vast forces. I said to myself: One must be blind not to be dazzled by this spectacle; one must be stupid not to recognize the author of it; one must be mad not to worship Him. (Torrey 1938, 257)

Chapter Three
A Poet Laureate Then

Considered one of the finest poets of his age, Voltaire is today remembered not for the greatness of his verses, but for their philosophical, satiric, and whimsical import. An admirer of classical writers—Nicolas Boileau, for his biting ironies and his literary and moral counsel, and Racine, to whose genius and purity of language he bowed in admiration—when it came to content, Voltaire preferred to combine classical rigor and depth with the spirit of the Enlightenment. An inquiring mind, free thought, and experimentation were crucial to Voltaire the creative artist, and especially to Voltaire the humanist and humanitarian.

In his poetics Voltaire favored the autonomy and spontaneity of ideas as well as the pleasures of aestheticism, but he also sanctioned the constraints imposed by classical regulations, considering them safeguards against inexactitudes and errors, and guardians of good taste. Rather than wax lyrical in his poetry, therefore, he aimed at clarity and precision of terminology. To give weight to his philosophical inquiries and arguments on questions of Deism, fanaticism, love, morality, and so forth, he had recourse to specific historical and scientific facts. Aesthetics also played an important role in his poetic constructs. To heighten moods and add tonal and rhythmic modulations to his work, like some of the painters of his day (Jean-Etienne Liotard, Antoine Watteau, Nicolas de Largillière), he used vibrant but also mat and nuanced colorations in his imagery. Voltaire's figures of speech—metaphors, similes, onomatopoeias, and repetitions: tools common to poets—accentuated the drama of a situation, created a particular atmosphere, or highlighted a special individual. Voltaire was also sensitive to music, and the harmonic distillations of a Lulli, Rameau, and Grétry nourished his verse with that sentient factor buried so deeply within his volatile personality. His language was always controlled and consciously articulated, tuned and toned to the mood or effect he sought to achieve. A classicist, his alexandrines and his octo- or decasyllables were, with few exceptions, tastefully, elegantly, and nobly fitted out, adding to the pleasures, but also to the realities and responsibilities, of a century given to gracious living.

It must be kept in mind that Voltaire, the rationalist, was also highly emotive. Given to moments of great jubilation followed by periods of severe despondency, he sometimes responded so impulsively, openly, and unabashedly to catastrophes (the Saint Bartholomew's Day Massacre, the Lisbon earthquake) that he actually became ill, even taking to his bed. Whereas some writers might simply be plagued by issues such as free will, evil, determinism, responsibility, humanitarianism, fanaticism, and intolerance, Voltaire, the thinker/feeler, Deist, took human suffering, no matter its origin, to heart—deeply and powerfully.

Understandably, Voltaire's Deism, antibigotry, and antimilitarism were at the root of many of his philosophical poems. Cases in point were his *Epistle to Urania, The Henriade, Discourses in Verse on Man, Poem on Natural Law,* and *Poem on the Lisbon Earthquake.* Allied to his concern for magnanimity, humanitarianism, morality, and tolerance was the vigilance he applied to the poetic form best suited to the dissemination of his thoughts and feelings. He chose the epic, for example, for *The Henriade,* convinced it was the aptest form to convey his admiration for Henry IV. The elegy, written in alexandrines and octosyllables, enabled him to express his sorrow over *The Death of Mademoiselle Lecouvreur (La Mort de Mademoiselle Lecouvreur).* Moving romantic stanzas, the 15th in particular, were addressed to his beloved Emilie Du Châtelet. Lilting and melodic rhythms garnished *The Man of the World (Le Mondain),* an apology to luxury and gracious living. A vitriolic satire, *Vanity,* was directed to the marquis de Pompignan for charging the philosophes with corrupting a nation's soul. A sidesplitting burlesque, *The Maid (La Pucelle),* reduced the French national heroine and future saint to less than human dimensions. Mention must also be made of Voltaire's translations of the Bible's Ecclesiastes and the Song of Songs.

Epistle to Urania (1722)

Epistle to Urania, subtitled *The For or Against,* is an overt declaration of Voltaire's Deist convictions. Mme de Rupelmonde, who had accompanied him on a brief trip to Belgium and to Holland, had asked him such provocative questions concerning his religious beliefs that he felt compelled to answer them in dangerously controversial terms. Wisdom fortunately prevailed: the *Epistle to Urania* was secreted for the following 10 years and was not even included in Voltaire's complete works until 1772 (Besterman, 88).

The opening lines of the *Epistle* are here rendered in prose:

> So, lovely Urania, you want me [to] become by your command a new
> Lucretius, to tear away with a bold hand, before you, the blindfold of
> superstition; to display before your eyes the dangerous image of the
> sacred lies with which the world is filled; and to learn from my philoso-
> phy to despise the horrors of the tomb and the terrors of the other life.
> (Besterman, 89)

Voltaire summarily rejected the tyrannical and antagonistic God of
the Judeo-Christians for having plagued and tyrannized humanity even
more overtly than had Oedipus's divinities. Equally noxious for him was
the biblical recounting of God's creation of the world, and his making of
man in his own image, his debasement of earthly beings, and his drown-
ing of them in the Flood. Dismissed as being "unworthy" of divinity was
the notion of God become man, that is, the incarnation of God as Jesus
Christ. Voltaire's conclusion: God used the pleasure principle he introduced into the world in order to chastise his creatures.

Deism, as understood by Voltaire, is devoid of a supernatural Christ
figure. Christ's very presence on Earth, as depicted in the New Testa-
ment, Voltaire maintained, encouraged superstitious fanatics and clerics
to gather to his banner and to accentuate hate, not love; sacrifice, not
virtue. Voltaire's distrust of metaphysics, coupled with his unending
search for God, encouraged him to admonish Urania to believe in a natural religion and in the Deist's god of justice. That god emphasizes neither fear nor death, but serenity and love in the awareness of righteousness and compassion.

> Consider that the eternal wisdom of the most high has with his hand
> engraved natural religion in the bottom of your heart; believe that the
> simple candour of your mind will not be the object of his immortal
> hatred; believe that before his throne, always, everywhere, the heart of the
> just man is precious; believe that a modest bonze, a charitable dervish,
> find grace in his eyes rather than a merciless Jansenist or an ambitious
> pontiff. Ah! what matter indeed by what name he be implored? Every
> homage is received, but none does him honour. A god has no need of our
> assiduous attention; if he can be offended, it is only by injustice; he judges
> by our virtues, and not by our sacrifices. (Besterman, 90)

Voltaire's attacks on the Bible, the Church, Judaism, Christianity,
and all organized religions were based on his contempt for their multiple
ceremonies, their conflictual dogmas, and the fanaticism and intolerance
that these bred. Bloodshed and torture, as evidenced in the Crusades

and the Inquisition in Spain, Portugal, and elsewhere, fostered not freedom of thought and dialogue, but a need to dominate and exterminate.
Since morality was uppermost in Voltaire's credo, Deism or natural religion, he reasoned, was the single faith upon which all people could
agree, and thus the only power capable of stilling massacres.

Scholars have made a distinction between Voltaire's constructive
Deism prior to his stay in England and his critical Deism upon his
return to France. As revealed in the *Epistle to Urania,* natural religion is
grounded in the concept of a universal morality and the worship of a
vague Supreme Being or Supreme Intelligence. Having become knowledgeable about Newtonian and Lockean concepts during his exile in
England, Voltaire broadened his views to the point of viewing God
within the framework of cosmic order, and thus as a power beyond
human understanding. Like Montaigne, he diminished the inflated position accorded to reason, perhaps fearing that were he to consider it all-
powerful, his readers would identify his beliefs with Descartes's erroneous notion of innate ideas. Increasing his critique of established
religions, he focused more intently on developing his thoughts on relativity between earthly and cosmic spheres.

Voltaire's belief in a nonsectarian God is conveyed most succinctly and
explicitly in the following line from the *Epistle to Urania*: "I am not a
Christian that I may love thee more." Not only does it reveal the breadth
and magnitude of his approach to Divinity, but it represents a whole libertine and epicurean tradition inculcated in him as a youth by his mentor,
the semipagan freethinking abbé de Chaulieu (Torrey 1938, 22).

The Henriade (1723–1728)

In 1715 M. de Caumartin, Intendant of Finances, had drawn Voltaire's
attention to Henry de Navarre, who, after his ascension to the throne of
France as Henry IV (1589–1610), became one of its most extraordinary
monarchs. Intent upon writing a national epic, Voltaire began its composition during his 11-month imprisonment in the Bastille (1717–1718).
Lord Bolingbroke's heartening words to Voltaire upon reading it encouraged its author in 1722 to have it published clandestinely.

Well versed in Homer's *Iliad,* Virgil's *Aenead,* Tasso's *Jerusalem Liberated,* and Milton's *Paradise Lost,* Voltaire bemoaned the fact that France
did not have its own national epic, the implication being that he alone
was capable of such an undertaking. In his *Essay on Epic Poetry* (1727),
Voltaire indicated the formula he considered appropriate to the epic

form: its theme should be majestic, even sublime; its action should be both unified and diversified so as to hold the reader's attention. The 10 dramatic and swiftly moving allegorical cantos of *The Henriade* are replete with panoramic tableaux. Patheticism, pomp, grace, gaudiness, and horror thread the description of events prior to and during the reign of Henry IV. Voltaire recounts with bravura the successful battles Henry de Navarre waged against the Catholic League, pointing out the political machinations involved in his forced conversion from Protestantism to Catholicism—the price required to gain the kingship of France.

Although Henry IV's efficiency, administrative competency, integrity, compassion for his subjects, and insistence on religious toleration were considered unique for the times, his crowning glory was his proclamation of the Edict of Nantes (1598), which, as has been mentioned, was later abrogated in 1685 by Louis XIV.

In highly visible and mobile sequences, Voltaire presents Henry IV, the "renowned" ruler of France, who "conquered" and "forgave," as a peacemaker intent upon ending the bloody clashes between Catholics and Protestants. As in rapidly unfolding filmstrips, the king is juxtaposed before the reader's eye with shifting framings featuring pillagings, love episodes, duels, and laudations. Scenes of pomp and splendor are apposed to those of pathos and poignancy, lending credence to a memorable story. Blending philosophy with wit, brilliance with compassion, Voltaire is intent upon revealing a society that had been.

Rather than bring Greek and Roman gods to life, as Homer and Virgil had accomplished, Voltaire has recourse, in his descent into hell episode, to allegorical figures such as Discord, Fanaticism, and Truth to concretize his ideas. Unforgettable in its hugolianism is Voltaire's gruesome account of the fanatic slaughter of Protestants by Catholics during the Saint Bartholomew's Day Massacre (1572)—ordered by Charles IX and instigated by his mother, Catherine de Medicis, and the aristocratic de Guise family. "Half of the nation butchered the other, with a dagger in one hand and a crucifix in the other," cries Voltaire, in a real and powerful burst of outrage against such carnage.[1]

> God does not punish them for having closed their eyes to the knowledge which he himself placed so far from them; he does not judge them like an unjust master because of the Christian laws they had no means of knowing, because of the insensate zeal of their sacred rage, but by the simple law which appeals to all hearts. (Besterman, 97)

Scenes of the Paris mob during a regicide were movingly rendered. In his prose sketch of the life of Henry IV, Voltaire had written:

> It is a very deplorable thing that the religion which enjoins the forgiveness of injuries should have occasioned so many murders to be committed, and this only in consequence of the maxim that all who think differently from us are in a state of reprobation, and that we are bound to hold such in abhorrence. (*Henriade*, 15.2:115)

Voltaire depicted not only some of the monarch's character traits, but abstract notions as well: "Power, love, and reason, / united and divided, form his essence." Astute, Henry IV was not one to be duped. Because of his ability to see "fraud and fury on both sides," he assessed the ravages of "ambitious chiefs of a too credulous people, hiding their interests behind the benefits of heaven" (Besterman, 97). Consistently seeking peace and reform, working hard to instill a sense of freedom in his people, he was a model king, a paragon of strength and courage, endowed with a sense of justice and benevolence. In many ways he represented Voltaire's ideal: an enlightened man of action imbued with greatness of soul and a spirit of clemency.

Because *The Henriade* was stylized and abounded in technical artifices, it did not gain the same acclamation as the epics of Virgil, Milton, or Ariosto. Condemned by the bigoted for its denunciation of Christianity's crimes against humanity, *The Henriade,* like so many of Voltaire's writings, suffered a predictable fate. Inasmuch as it had earned the disfavor of the censors, the first version of *The Henriade* was published secretly in Rouen in 1723 under the title *The League.* Once smuggled into Paris to enthusiastically expectant readers, it earned a succès de scandale. Printed in England in 1728 in a deluxe edition through public subscription, which included the participation of the royal family, *The Henriade* was extolled.

The Maid (1755)

Mme Du Châtelet, who watched over Voltaire's writings with an eagle eye, judged his burlesque *The Maid* (*La Pucelle*), begun in 1731 or thereabouts, too dangerous to publish. Its explicit language and satiric remarks aimed at the revered Joan of Arc could easily awaken the anger of the censors. Wisely, she ensconced it, but she could not prevent its author from reading it aloud to those who visited Cirey.

Voltaire's first reference to *The Maid* appeared in a letter to his friend Formont (1734):

> I have worked rather in the vein of Ariosto than in that of Tasso. I wanted to see what my imagination would produce when I gave it free rein, and when fear of that narrow critical spirit now reigning in France did not restrain me. I am ashamed of having progressed so far on such a frivolous work, which is not designed for publication; but after all, time might be employed to worse advantage. I want this work to give my friends amusement from time to time; but I do not want my enemies to know a thing about it. (Torrey 1938, 27)

According to Voltaire, 6,000 copies of *The Maid* were in circulation in Paris by 1755; some versions had been pirated, others excessively altered; the version authorized by him was printed only in 1762 (Besterman, 375). Publication meant the very real possibility of Voltaire's imprisonment, either in Switzerland or in France. Of most concern to him was the bawdy "Donkey Canto." To d'Argental he wrote with trepidation:

> You cannot imagine how afflicted I am. The work as I wrote it more than twenty years ago is today in very disagreeable contrast with my position and my age; and in its present current condition it is a horror for any age. The bits that have been sent me are full of folly and impudence; they are enough to give the tremors to good taste and decency; it is the height of opprobrium to see my name on the title page of such a work. (Torrey 1938, 29)

When a pirated version of *The Maid* appeared in Geneva in 1755, Voltaire not only disclaimed authorship but even asked the ruling executive and legislative body to repress such a villainous work. Ironically, *The Maid*, Joan of Arc, was again burned—this time not in the flesh, but in paper replica, on August 5, 1755, in Geneva.

A knavish, ultrasatiric travesty of Chapelain's epic glorifying the real Joan of Arc, Voltaire's *The Maid* was modeled on one of his favorite works, *Orlando Furioso* by Ariosto (1474–1533). Voltaire's 21 cantos, filled with the witticisms, sardonic humor, and lightly pornographic allusions so characteristic of his writings, were considered in his day high art "clothed . . . in raiment of flawless form—an embodiment of the impeccable precision and academic elegance marking a literary masterpiece" (Lanson, 81). His long decasyllabic stanzas with flexible rhyme schemes injected into his verses musical resonances that some critics believed were reminiscent of Chaucer's *The Canterbury Tales,* although no proof exists that Voltaire had ever read them.

Who was Joan of Arc (1412–1431), the adolescent who became one of France's national heroines? The tale opens as the Hundred Years' War (1337–1453) is raging and England occupies most of France north of the Loire. Joan of Arc claimed to have had visions of the Archangel Michael and others, ordering her to rally the French armies to fight for the defense of their land. Obedient in all ways, the historical Joan triggered French patriotism and escorted the pusillanimous future Charles VII to Rheims, thus ensuring his coronation there in 1429. Captured by the Burgundians a year later, she was sold to the English, who had her tried for heresy and witchcraft. Found guilty on both counts, she was burned at the stake in Rouen in 1431. The English were defeated in 1453. By 1456 a papal commission had reversed the verdict of guilt.

At the outset of *The Maid,* Voltaire's burlesque introduces his heroine in the most lofty and laudatory terms: "Joan of Arc had a lion's heart, as you will see if you read this work. You will tremble at her new feats; and the greatest of her wondrous works was to keep her maidenhead for a year" (Besterman, 376; see also Moland, 9:25). Candidly, facetiously, and most appropriately does Voltaire introduce one of his main themes: the absurdity of man's preoccupation with a woman's virginity; and as a historian, he writes explicitly and wittily about the sexuality involved in Charles VII's passion for Agnès Sorel, and hers for him.

To accent the dramatic unfoldings in *The Maid,* Voltaire cleverly shifts from one scene to another, usually from personal to collective events. The lascivious Narrator apostrophizes Agnès's "Charming tit, never at rest, you invite one's hands to press you" (Besterman, 377; Moland, 9:29). Shame vanishes and only love remains, as Charles VII and Agnès enjoy their togetherness.

The French leaders hold a crisis meeting at Orléans: their patron saint, Denis, auspiciously appears to them, his head surrounded by a halo of gold and silver. He announces his intent to look for a virgin who will free their land. The council snickers: "A maidenhead is a useless weapon when it comes to saving a city. Anyway, why seek it in this country? You have so many in paradise! . . . There is none left, alas, among the French" (Besterman, 376; Moland, 9:36).

Without uttering a word, Saint Denis mounts his horse. No sooner does he arrive at Domrémy (Joan's birthplace) than he finds the "honest . . . vigorous . . . adroit . . . proud . . . and appetizing" Joan working in a stable at an inn. Ribald and risqué, Voltaire depicts her fleshy assets: "Her brown tits, firm as rocks, tempt the robe and the helmet and the gown" of poor Saint Denis (Besterman, 377; Moland, 9:41). Aware that the destinies of both England and France lie beneath her short petticoat, he determines that the time is at hand to save France. Later, in the stable, Saint Denis becomes somewhat of a hero himself, saving Joan from the sensual delights of which the lustful monk Grisbourdin seeks to partake. Putting a temporary stop to all anticipated revelries, Saint Denis discloses Joan's brilliant future to her, furnishes her with armor and a donkey, and leaves with her to go to Tours to meet the future Charles VII. On their way, they stop at the tent of one of the great English captains, John Chandos. After promptly stealing his "fearsome" sword and the sleeping man's velvet breeches, Joan then takes some ink and draws three fleurs-de-lis on the buttocks of his 14-year-old page, Monrose (My Rose), who is sound asleep at his side.

No sooner do Joan and Saint Denis finally arrive at court than the latter announces that God has spirited "this august amazon" to the future king Charles VII. Saint Denis rouses the soon-to-be monarch from his lethargy, due certainly to his continuous lovemaking with Agnès, and stirs his sense of patriotism. "Be a man," he tells him, and if his destiny calls him to be led by a girl, let him at least flee the one who lost him and follow the one who will avenge him. Fired with enthusiasm, Charles suddenly wonders whether Joan is a devil or an envoy of the Lord. "Are you a virgin?" he asks. She answers with sincerity, going so far as to suggest that he might invite doctors, matrons, clerics, pedants, and apothecaries to "sound out these feminine mysteries" (Moland, 9:51). No sooner said than done. They undress her, examine her every nook and cranny, and declare her chaste. Satisfied, the king and Joan depart for Rheims. Denis blesses them. Agnès remains at home.

A long allegorical section in the Palace of Folly features Agnès who, having refused to be separated from the king, arrives and cleverly waits the appropriate moment—until everyone is asleep—to proceed to steal Joan's armor and Chandos's breeches and sword. On her way to accomplishing her mission, this would-be warrior prays that she will be able to entice the future king back to her bed. On her way to her beloved, she is taken by the English and brought to Chandos's camp. "I am Agnès," she cries out. "Long live France and Love." With that, the English hero not only retrieves his breeches and sword, but nabs her graceful self as well (Moland, 9:69).

Meanwhile Joan and the hero Dunois fight the enemy. Aware that France's future rests on the intactness of Joan's "hidden jewel," Dunois resists his sexual urges (Moland, 9:81). The two repair to the Castle of Hermaphrodix, where readers are made privy to multiple erotic and sadomasochistic scenes, one featuring Joan being undressed and whipped. In a kind of *walpurgisnacht* ritual, Joan is saved by the lascivious priest/sorcerer Grisbourdin, who arrives just in time to prevent her deflowering. Driven by passion himself, he attempts to violate Joan, but fails in the endeavor. For his sin, he is sent to hell, where he regales the devils with Joan's adventures and all laugh heartily (Moland, 9:105).

The interplay between ancients and moderns in hell gives Voltaire ample opportunity to satirize the Christian doctrines of perpetual condemnation for sinners and of perpetual punishment for those born prior to Christ's coming.

> Sepulchre in which languishes ancient wisdom, wit, love, knowledge, grace, beauty, and that immortal, innumerable crowd of the children of heaven all created for the devil. You know, dear reader, that the best kings are with the tyrants in these devouring fires. We send there Antonine, Marcus Aurelius, the good Trajan, the model prince; the gentle Titus, beloved by the universe; the two Catos, the scourge of the wicked; Scipio, master of his courage, he who vanquished both love and Carthage. You burn there, wise and learned Plato, divine Homer, eloquent Cicero, and you Socrates, child of wisdom, martyr of god in pagan Greece; just Aristides and virtuous Solon; all wretched dead unconfessed. (Besterman, 378; Moland, 9:99)

On Earth once again, Voltaire focuses on the peregrinations of Agnès, who indulges in a plethora of hilarious love episodes on her way to meet the king. On one occasion she finds herself in a convent bed with Sister Besogne, ostensibly there to protect her. As fate would have it, the English take the convent. An excruciatingly humorous battle is then fought between Saint Denis, the patron saint of the French, and Saint George, the patron saint of the English.

Hilarious and libidinous scenes follow in swift succession. Finally the king finds Agnès, who has been consoling herself with Chandos's young page, Monrose, in the Castle of Cutendre. In time Joan fights Chandos, who defeats her, and is saved from rape by a *miracle*. Her adventures take her to Orléans and to the king, whom she encourages to take up arms against the English. An uproarious scene in heaven features Saint Peter attempting to placate Saint George and Saint Denis by promising them a prize for the best ode, followed by an episode in which the king, Joan, and others go mad and are restored to sanity by the royal confessor's exorcisms.

The last two cantos, considered the most objectionable of Voltaire's entire burlesque, are devoted exclusively to Joan. Readers learn that Saint Denis, jealous of Joan's military successes, punishes her during her wanderings by having the devil enter her donkey. Attempting to seduce her, the animal squats at the foot of her bed and, in a most charming manner, compliments her on her invincibility. The mellifluous tonal modulations of his descriptions of her beauty reach new highs. He asks her to visualize him as Balaam's donkey, mentioned in the Bible, then as Denis's mount. Were she to mount him, it would bring him the greatest honor. Angered by his attempt to seduce her, Joan cries out indignantly that "to love a donkey, and give him her flower" would be to dishonor her. Nonetheless, she is attracted to him and extends her hand his way, only to withdraw it moments later, blushing ashamedly and blaming herself for her audacity. In confessional style, she tells the beautiful donkey that his desires cannot be realized—she and he are too different from each other. No, he retorts, bringing as examples the relationships of Leda and the swan, Pasiphae and the bull, Ganymede and the eagle. Suddenly Dunois, who is in the next room, overhears their voices; curious, he enters to see his rival in love. Saint Denis arrives not a moment too soon to save Joan in her moment "of extreme peril."

Back to battle, Joan and Dunois defeat the English, whereupon:

Denis on his horse applauded. . . ; on his horse, St. George shuddered; the ass intoned his grating octave, which redoubled the terror of the British. The king, who was ranked with the conquerors, supped with Agnès at Orléans. That same night the proud and tender Joan, having sent back her fine ass to heaven, faithful to her oath, kept her word to her friend Dunois. Lourdis, mingling with the faithful crowd, cried: "English! she is a virgin!" (Besterman, 380; Moland, 9:338)

To have written a burlesque on Joan of Arc in eighteenth-century France, even though she was not canonized until 1920, was considered an act of blasphemy. Indeed, some reverent critics went so far as to erroneously date the onset of Voltaire's ills with the publication of this "sacrilegious and unpatriotic" work.

The aim of burlesque, let us recall, is to ridicule by grotesque exaggeration or comic imitation. It serves to remove saints and heroes from their pedestals. Via burlesque, Voltaire fulfilled his goal of destabilizing collective opinions, cleansing the atmosphere of its cobwebs and detritus, and encouraging new scrutinies of longtime heroes and heroines.

Did Voltaire really ever regret having written *The Maid*? Did he, as he stated, consider it merely a youthful bagatelle? Probably not. On the contrary, he was delighted to learn that when it was read at the Prussian court, it amused Frederick the Great; Wilhelmina, the margrave of Beyrouth, Frederick's sister; and the pious duchess of Saxe-Gotha. That his Swiss friend, Pastor Bertrand, had not been shocked by it was equally pleasing to him. Indeed, *The Maid* brought laughter and mirth to many open-minded eighteenth-century readers. On the other hand, it once again revealed the important role played by society's fanatics and hypocrites—whose worlds were guided not by thirst for love, but by lust for hatred.

As a paradigm for Voltairean scabrous banter, *The Maid* is unique in its verve, levity, and satiric intent. Although vulgar and pornographic on occasion, as were *Zadig* and *Candide,* it nonetheless mirrored a type of writing popular in its day. A diversionary spoof for Voltaire, *The Maid* took him out of his more depressed moments (Pomeau 1969, 125).

The Temple of Taste (1733)

The Temple of Taste (*Temple du goût*), Voltaire's version of the French Academy, is a baroque work in which multiple portraits of creative individuals are interwoven into insightful and suggestive patternings. Those writers, painters, and artists whose skills did not meet Voltaire's standards were barred entry to his temple. His values and judgments not only disclosed his predisposition for classical techniques with regard to works of art, but also constituted paradigms of his highly developed esthetic and critical sense.

To fit Voltaire's guidelines, a work of art had to be divested of platitudes, adulterations, and idol worship—that is, unthinking adoration of fads, cults, and passing styles. It had to be animated with a spark of life, tastefully written, revelatory of discernment and judgment, and capable of pointing to the defects and perfections of the subject treated. Summarily dismissed from his Temple of Taste were, for example, "mediocre" writers such as Saint-Evremond and Voiture.[2]

Voltaire, like many of his contemporaries, felt nothing but contempt for Gothic architecture. His Temple of Taste was instead a model of elegance and beauty.

> The structure's of a simple taste,
> Each ornament is justly placed;
> The whole's arranged with so much care,
> Art seems to copy nature there;
> The beauteous structure fills the sight,
> Not with surprise, but with delight.[3]

Visiting the Temple of Taste, the Narrator/Voltaire is confronted with a group of dull attitudinarians striving to be admitted through its immortal portals. As authors of large tomes on subjects that inevitably surpass their meager understanding, they are looked upon by the Narrator/Voltaire as simplifiers, amassers of "scraps" of information. They are considered merely would-be writers. "Taste is nothing," they maintain; "we are accustomed to record at length and in detail what was thought; but we ourselves do not think" (Besterman, 169). Certain arbiters of perfection are also denied admittance to the Temple of Taste on aesthetic grounds: their works, pedestrian and imitative, lack clarity and simplicity. Overblown and prejudiced critics motivated by envy are similarly rejected. The gifted critic discriminates between good and bad taste, perceives beauty amid defects and defects amid beauty. Voltaire's captiousness heaps praise on Boileau for his discernment, as expressed in his *Art poétique*. Objects of satire in *The Temple of Taste* are found in the very real quarrel between French and Italian singers and composers, as well as in certain musical compositions and performances. The Narrator/Voltaire declares, for example, that "nothing can be as ridiculous as French scenes sung in the Italian taste, except Italian ones sung in the French taste" (*Taste*, 10.2:45).

Moral as well as aesthetic factors are also determinants in gaining entrance to the temple. Barred are writers, critics, composers, and performers lacking feeling, finesse, delicacy, and all-important good taste. Slanderers devoid of purity of purpose are also forbidden access. Not more acceptable are authors of untasteful genres such as metaphysical romances.

Because only works of genius—and not those manufactured simply via *reason*—were to be granted entry into the sacred portals of the Temple of Taste, Voltaire proscribed adjudicators who based their evaluations of literary, pictorial, and musical creations on preestablished concepts of taste. Welcomed, however, were those generated by fine minds sharing a community of principles and open to spontaneity, even to vulgarity if necessary to dislodge "geometric Reason" from its pedestal (Naves 1967, 192). Also admitted into the sacred halls were writers capable and humble enough not only to recognize their shortcomings but to rectify them.

In Voltaire's view, Fénelon, Bossuet, Corneille, La Fontaine, Boileau— of course Molière and Racine—earned supremacy. Other favorite writers were Fontenelle, Lucretius, and, surprisingly, Leibniz—the latter "because he had written tolerably good Latin verses, although he was a metaphysician and geometer" (*Taste*, 10.2:45). Whereas painters parroting the canvases of Antoine Watteau, or inflated artists who considered their talents superior to those of Sanzio Raphael are objects of scorn for Voltaire, Nicolas Poussin, Charles Le Brun, and Eustache Le Sueur were singled out for praise. So, too, were sculptors like Jean Goujon and Edme Bouchardon and architects such as Saint-Gervais and Desbrosses.

The comparatist Narrator/Voltaire, indicating that different cultures, customs, and instincts produce an array of variegated artistic creations, always singles out for praise those he considers geniuses. No matter the language in which they choose to communicate their unique visions, he welcomes them wholeheartedly into the Temple of Taste. Nor is art static, Voltaire implies. Creative types must evolve, along with readers and critics, broadening their fields of expertise, expanding, deepening, and beautifying their conceptualizations, even while adapting and transposing them to suit specific needs.

Looking back with nostalgia to the high aesthetics of seventeenth-century France, Voltaire was very much aware of the emphasis placed on rationalism in his century, perhaps to the detriment of artistic perfection. Nonetheless, he was grateful for the energy his era directed toward the growth of open-mindedness and the multivalence of knowledge. To Cideville he wrote:

All possible forms must be bestowed on the soul. It is a fire God has entrusted to us; we must nourish it with whatever we consider most precious. All imaginable modes must be made to penetrate our being; all doors to the soul must be opened to all the sciences and to all feelings.[4]

Like Boileau, Voltaire, as we have seen, was a great defender of classical rules and techniques, valuing these insofar as they compelled writers to convey their thoughts and judgments in lucid, simple, and graceful ways. Discernment, the use of direct rather than pretentious and flowery language, elegance, balance, and unity of purpose were also recommended. With these factors in mind, the artist was equipped to reach beyond, even transgress ephemeral modes by refusing to capitulate to the facile needs of mass laudations (Naves 1967, 195).[5]

Although admiring seventeenth-century classicism, some critics looked with disfavor on Voltaire's *Temple of Taste*. They accused Voltaire of claiming that purity of genre was a byword of classicism, while committing the cardinal sin of adulteration by his frequent blendings of poetry and prose in *The Temple of Taste* as well as in *The Man of the World* (*Le Mondain*).

The Man of the World (1736)

Voltaire, unlike Rousseau, disavowed neither luxury nor gracious living nor pleasures of the flesh. On the contrary, he enjoyed the comforts offered by civilization: fine dining, elegance, homes garnished with memorable sculptures and paintings, theatrical performances, concerts, and so forth. In full accord with Locke's belief in the inalienability of rights and property, he was not averse to Bernard de Mandeville's philosophy as enunciated in *The Fables of the Bees, or Private Vices, Public Benefits* (1714). Mandeville was a theorist who rejected Shaftesbury's optimistic view of a benevolent human nature. He argued that individual ambition was crucial to activating a nation's economy and adding to its wealth. Voltaire agreed. Luxury, commerce, business enterprises, the stock exchange, embellishments of all types encouraged gracious living. "I love luxury, and even indolence, / All the pleasures, arts of every kind, / Cleanliness, taste, and adornments," he wrote (*Man of the World*, 1.2:289).

Nature in the raw was, for Voltaire, barbaric and indecorous. Nor was Eden an attractive place: deprived of clothes, of a bed, of the comforts of the home, he would not choose to dwell there, for "earthly paradise is where I am" (Moland, 10:83–88).

A return to the state of nature ran counter to his philosophy of life. His very goal of alleviating human suffering rested on the slow development of enlightenment and economic progress, coupled with gradual legislative reform.

He opted for cleanliness, abundance, and even the superfluous, which he considered a necessity. As for his ancestors, Adam and Eve, they lived in ignorance and ran around naked; their long fingernails were dirty and their hair unkempt. Not only could they not enjoy a good French wine, silks, and gold, but after their meal they were without a bed, thus forced to sleep on the cold and hard ground. Deprived of any knowledge of the exquisite joys of lovemaking, they were reduced to the gratification of their instincts only.

> My dear Adam, my greedy eater, my father,
> What did you do for this foolish human species?
> Did you caress Madame Eve, my mother? . . .[6]

Direct expression—one of Voltaire's trademarks—and his humorously risqué comments about Adam and Eve aroused the ire of some of his readers. To protect himself from receiving the infamous lettre de cachet, he went into exile in Holland at the end of 1736, returning to Cirey in March of 1737.

Discourses in Verse on Man (1738–1739)

Voltaire's seven-sectioned *Discourses in Verse on Man* was inspired by Pope's philosophical optimism as voiced in his *Essay on Man* (1733–1734) and by Mme Du Châtelet's high regard for Leibniz's doctrine. It was she who strongly encouraged Voltaire to set forth his own relatively positive, perhaps even utopian, philosophy of life. He responded to Mme Du Châtelet's suggestion with *Discourses in Verse on Man*. Moving away from the overt optimism espoused in *The Man of the World*, Voltaire's thoughts had evolved. Notwithstanding people's social standing or their proclivities, or the inroads made by good and/or evil in their lives, he suggested that happiness exists alongside of misfortune as the basic component of worldly existence. That people have been armed with free will helps them to offset and/or overcome the obstacles—evils—that beset them at every juncture in life. The power to choose, which involves thought, also encourages individuals to carve out their own directions, thereby finding happiness as they understand it.

Free will ushers in the notion of responsibility as well, noted Voltaire in the second discourse. Thinking beings are no longer under the dominion of "Deities' despotic power"; they cannot be likened to the "powerless machines" or "thinking automatons" of the Calvinists and Jansenists. Nor may they erroneously claim: "I did nothing, God alone is the author," thereby refusing all accountability for their acts.[7] If the preceding were true, then one could reason that the "God of justice and peace" would have also authored the most heinous of horrors. Since no

mortal can fathom the nature of an infinite God, suffice it to say that
liberty in people depends on the health of the individual's soul. Liberty
may be lost to an uncontrollable lust for power, anger, pride, the seduc-
tions of love, and other deceptions and illusions.

Underscoring human values in the fourth discourse, Voltaire cau-
tioned philosophers, scientists, men of the cloth—people in general—to
follow the path of moderation.

> Take but a few more steps, but limit your course.
> At the edge of the infinite your trajectory must cease;
> There begins the abyss, it must be respected.
> *(Verse on Man, 1.2:289)*

"Use, don't abuse" the passions that have been awarded to mortals,
he suggested. They not only add to life's pleasures but may be called
upon to heal in time of sorrow. Society would be better served, he also
noted, if individuals focused on living wisely, lovingly, and happily in the
earthly realm, rather than shirking their responsibilities in their
attempts to divine "the subtle mechanisms, / of the Eternal Artisan."

Character traits such as envy negate the possibility of happiness;
they constrain individuals to become captive of their own behavioral
extremes. The true genius, Voltaire maintained, is devoid of envy. He
admires others, enjoys pleasurable events, but always within bounds and
never to excess. Extremes, Voltaire posited, are noxious.

Untenable to him as well, as affirmed in his *Philosophical Letters,* was
Pascal's excoriatingly pessimistic concept of sin, guilt, and redemption.
Rejecting organized religions that counsel asceticism and all types of
self-flagellation, Voltaire did not look upon the world as a vale of tears.
On the contrary, there was no need for human beings to suffer pain in
order to exculpate themselves from Original Sin; nor should they yearn
their entire lives for supernal salvation. Human beings were created to
enjoy the pleasures of this earth. Voltaire's approach to life encouraged
him, like the true Epicurean that he was at this time, to experience his
earthly sojourn without ever longing for the hereafter.

Mortals cannot possibly know their origin or their fate, nor can they
construe the reasons for their creation. To define God, his qualities or his
law, in human terms deprives him of his transcendence. In this connection, Voltaire expressed his concern about people's anthropocentrism and
the arrogance such an "I"-focused world breeds. Mice, fleas, impercepti-

ble insects, donkeys, or humans—each entity has the brazenness, he wrote, to consider him- or herself the center of the world. Let us listen in to the conversation of some mice in the sixth discourse:

> How charming is this world! what an empire is ours!
> So superb is this palace, elevated for us;
> For all eternity God has provided us with large holes.
> *(Verse on Man,* 1.2:89)

Voltaire sought to define "true virtue" in markedly different terms in the seventh discourse. Whereas he had ridiculed Jesus four years earlier, disbelieving his divinity, he now represented him in sympathetic terms, as a figure who preached love and good works in *this* world. "Love God ... but love mortals ... / The world is slanderous, vain, superficial, envious; / To flee it is well / to serve it is even better: / To one's family, to one's own, I want people to be useful" *(Mélanges,* 237).

Poem on Natural Law (1756)

Although addressed to Frederick the Great and his sister Wilhelmina during Voltaire's stay at Potsdam in 1752, the doctrinal *Poem on Natural Law* was published only in 1756. One of Voltaire's chief concerns at the time was his desire to counteract Julien Offroy de La Mettrie's (1701–1759) materialism, atheism, and denial of the moral value of remorse as adumbrated in his *Natural History of the Soul (Histoire naturelle de lâme,* 1745), and *Man Machine (L'homme machine,* 1747). Let us recall that La Mettrie, as well as Voltaire, found refuge from persecution by the French in the court of Frederick II of Prussia.

Poem on Natural Law mirrored the deepest concerns of Voltaire, the Deist: his belief in a universal morality, independent not only of all revealed religious ideologies, but of all systematized notions concerning the nature of the Supreme Being.

His idealism encouraged him to substitute Descartes's belief in *innate ideas,* which he rejected, with his own conviction that humankind was born with *innate instincts.* A moral sense, such as pity and remorse, evolves from the latter, which, like walking and reasoning, develop during the course of a person's life. Since God operates in people via conscience and sorrow, egoism should be offset by love for others, and hatred transformed into understanding.[8]

Natural religion, as understood by Voltaire, presupposed the existence of a beneficent deity who had furnished humankind with all that was necessary to his well-being.

> Whether a self-existent being laid
> The world's foundations, out of nothing made,
> If forming matter o'er it he presides,
> And having shaped the mass, directs and guides;
> Whether the soul, that bright ethereal spark
> Of heavenly fire, too oft obscure and dark,
> Makes of our senses or our acts alone;
> We all are subject to the Almighty's throne,
> But at His throne round which deep thunders roar
> What homage shall we pay, how God adore?[9]

Although guardedly optimistic—perhaps realistic would be the better term—*Poem on Natural Law* expressed Voltaire's unequivocal belief in the existence of God, as understood in Deism. Moral law engraved in the hearts of people by God is universal in scope and has not only made humans conscious of right and wrong, but has endowed them with a sense of justice as well. "Morality, unvaried and the same, / Proclaims to each God's holy name" (*Natural Law* 1988, 25). Morality comes from God; it is one and the same throughout the world. Because dogmas are human-made, they are diverse; they divide and disfigure. God's natural religion unites all peoples.

> Sons of one God, in these our days of woe
> Let's live like brothers whilst we dwell below.
> Let's strive to lend each other kind relief.
> (*Natural Law* 1988, 34)

God's creation, his purpose, and his design for people as well as for the rest of nature transcends human understanding. Voltaire neither believed that all was well in this world nor that humankind was enchained in a woefully pessimistic Pascalian universe. Pleading for mutual understanding, he asked that individuals not poison the pleasures of this earth and that religions not spread their credo of hate. Why should a good Catholic, after mass, run toward his neighbor and in good faith cry out to him: "Wretch, think like me, or else this moment die!" (*Natural Law* 1988, 32). Monstrous as well was Voltaire's image of the "kindly inquisitor" who, with cross in hand, having burned a human— or many—in an auto-da-fé, grabs his money and weeps over his fate. Nor is the fanatic of one creed any better than that of another. While Calvin was to blame for Servet's destiny, had Servet won his case, he in turn would have strangled Trinitarians. Armenians are no better: "In Flanders gained the martyr's glorious name, / In Holland executioners became" (*Natural Law* 1988, 32).

What is the meaning of this "pious rage" that has taken hold of some believers? Voltaire questioned.

> Religious wars did our forefathers wage?
> From nature's law allegiance they withdrew,
> Or added others dangerous as new;
> And man to his own sense an abject slave,
> To God his weakness and his passions gave.
>
> (*Natural Law* 1988, 32)

While the *Poem on Natural Law* is a prayer for humanitarianism and an attack on anthropocentrism and fanaticism, it also encourages governments to step in to quiet disputes, especially religious altercations that periodically trouble societies. Empirically oriented as always, Voltaire wrote in the fourth part of his poem:

> 'Tis the grand duty, doubtless, to be just
> And the first blessing is the heart's repose.
> How could you, where so many sects oppose,
> Amidst incessant wrangling and debate,
> Preserve a peace so lasting in the State?
>
> (*Natural Law* 1988, 35)

Although Voltaire was well aware that people could not live without religion, he felt atheism to be undesirable as well. All religions, he maintained, contain a basic truth. In his *Profession of Faith of the Theists*, addressed to Frederick the Great, Voltaire declared:

Our religion is without question divine, since it was engraved in our hearts by God himself, by that master of universal reason, who said to the Chinese, to the Hindus, to the Tartars, and to us: "Adore me and be just." (Torrey 1938, 235)

Arguing ceaselessly in favor of tolerance, he unwaveringly declared harmony and compassion to be the best means of developing a better society. Understandably Voltaire's heroes were philosophes: Henri IV, Cicero, Confucius, and Socrates were men of feeling, courage, and concerned with the welfare of humanity.[10] As conveyed in the *Poem on Natural Law* Voltaire's credo was, as it had been for some years now, "Adore God, be just, and love your country."

Poem on the Lisbon Earthquake (1756)

Rather than a didactic philosophical discussion, Voltaire's *Poem on the Lisbon Earthquake* is a horrified outcry against the suffering and death caused to 30,000 or 40,000 people by an earthquake that occurred on All Saints' Day, 1755, in Lisbon. His compassion for the terror and pain endured led him to reject not only what he understood to be Leibniz's and Pope's optimistic views on life, but, more importantly, the notion of divine benevolence. Although Voltaire believed that God "cares little about the individual," he did not reject the notion of Providence outright. Averse to the theological doctrine of Original Sin and Redemption, as previously noted, he nonetheless considered it more palatable than Leibniz's and Pope's cruel illusion-gilded ideas on the subject.

Voltaire had sidestepped the question of evil in his *Treatise on Metaphysics* (1734), believing the concept to be of human manufacture and thus gratuitous. Now, however, he targeted the very essence of Pope's statement "Whatever is, is right" and of Leibniz's optimism, as glorified by the utterances of Dr. Pangloss's (Wind-Bag) utterances that were to make history in *Candide*: "All is for the best, in this best of all possible worlds."

In his *Poem on the Lisbon Earthquake,* Voltaire referred to these optimists as "grim speculators on the woes of men. / Ye double, not assuage, my misery."[11] The problem of evil tormented him increasingly and poignantly. Nightmarish visions of utter distress flooded his scenes.

> Contemplate this ruin of a world.
> Behold these shreds and cinders of your race,

This child and mother heaped in common wreck,
These scattered limbs beneath the marble shafts—
A hundred thousand whom the earth devours,
Who, torn and bloody, palpitating yet,
Entombed beneath their hospitable roofs,
In racking torment and their stricken lives.

(Lisbon, 1)

As the earth opened up and flames leaped forth burning, torturing, and mutilating innocent beings, Voltaire again bore down on misguided philosophers such as Leibniz, who said "All is well." Let them contemplate Lisbon's hideous ruins, Voltaire retorted, and then utter "All is for the best."

He adamantly rejects the thought that the Lisbon catastrophe was, as some theologians believed, God's punishment for Original Sin: "God is avenged: the wage of sin is death" *(Lisbon,* 1). Decrying such faulty reasoning, Voltaire responded: "What crime, what sin had these young hearts conceived / That lie, bleeding and torn, on mother's breast?" *(Lisbon,* 1). A handful of rational philosophers attributed such catastrophes and threats of more to an attempt to keep humanity in check. Here, too, Voltaire questioned the validity of such reasoning.

Did fallen Lisbon deeper drink of vice
Than London, Paris, or sunlit Madrid?
In these men dance; at Lisbon yawns the abyss.

(Lisbon, 1)

Rather than try to fathom the reasons for such catastrophes, thinkers would do better to question the survivors of this and other bloody events and ask whether suffering had driven them to empathize with the pain and anguish of others.

Think ye this universe had been the worse
Without this hellish gulf in Portugal?
Are ye so sure the great eternal cause,
That knows all things, and for itself creates,
Could not have placed us in this dreary clime
Without volcanoes seething 'neath our feet?

> Set you this limit to the power supreme?
> Would you forbid it use its clemency?
>
> (*Lisbon*, 2)

How can smug philosophers claim that "all is good, all is necessary" after witnessing or even hearing of Lisbon's disaster? Dismantling other spurious arguments, Voltaire questioned the notion that evil works toward the general good of a population. To attempt to explain that which transcends human understanding is to limit the infinite power of the Eternal Artisan. Would self-important thinkers also forbid God to exercise clemency? Or deprive God of the means of carrying out his plans for the universe? To the irritation of many of Voltaire's readers, he again iterated that "God holds the chain: is not himself enchained" (*Lisbon*, 3).

Then how may evil be explained? If the Eternal Artisan is just, as the religious claim, why does suffering exist? The answer on Voltaire's part is cryptic. "There is the knot your thinkers should undo. / Think ye to cure our ills denying them?" (*Lisbon*, 3). Once again Voltaire examined the flaws and omissions in Leibniz's approach to human pain and suffering:

> From Leibniz learn we not by what unseen
> Bonds, in this best of all imagined worlds,
> Endless disorder, chaos of distress,
> Must mix our little pleasures thus with pain;
> Nor why the guiltless suffer all this woe
> In common with the most abhorrent guilt.
> 'Tis mockery to tell me all is well.
> Like learned doctors, nothing do I know.
>
> (*Lisbon*, 6)

Over and over again did Voltaire, the Deist, voice his respect for God, and most emphatically, *his love for the universe*. Too readily were philosophers and theologians given to rationalizations, certain that their solutions to insoluble metaphysical problems were the correct ones. If God was benevolent and omnipotent, Voltaire claimed, might evil then be part of his divine plan?

> Silence: the book of fate is closed to us.
> Man is a stranger to his own research;
> He knows not whence he comes, nor whither goes.

> Tormented atoms in a bed of mud,
> Devoured by death, a mockery of fate,
> But thinking atoms, whose far-seeing eyes,
> Guided by thought, have measured the faint stars,
> Our being mingles with the infinite;
> Ourselves we never see, or come to know.
>
> *(Lisbon*, 6)

Voltaire, who was to continue questioning and writing on the notion of evil in one form or another throughout his life, never offered any ready-made answers.

As a comparatist, Voltaire acquainted readers in his preface to *Poem on the Lisbon Earthquake* with the fact that in 1699 in China 400,000 people had been swallowed up by an earthquake. Lima, Collao, the kingdom of Fez, Portugal, and so many other areas of the globe had been struck by similar disasters. Although some might have been led to believe that these events had been ordained and ordered by Providence, one could believe with equal certitude just the opposite: that these catastrophes had not been arranged by Providence to enhance humanity's well-being—nor did they improve the quality of earthly existence. Whatever the answer, Voltaire simply noted:

> All will be well one day—so runs our hope.
> All *now* is well, is but an idle dream.
> The wise deceive me: God alone is right.
>
> *(Lisbon*, 7)

Older and wiser, Voltaire still reminisced about his continuously evolving philosophy:

> Once I did sing, in less lugubrious tone,
> The sunny ways of pleasure's genial rule;
> The times have changed, and, taught by growing age,
> And sharing of the frailty of mankind,
> Seeking a light amid the deepening gloom,
> I can but suffer, and will not repine.
>
> *(Lisbon*, 7)

Despite human suffering, the notion of *hope* still permeated his conclusion.

The poet's wrenching outcry against human agony, no matter its origin or form, was instrumental in bringing this latest example of excoriating suffering to the attention of the world. Detractors were in this instance in short supply—rarely the case with regard to Voltaire's writings. Mention must be made, however, of Jean-Jacques Rousseau's reply upon receipt of both of Voltaire's poems—*Poem on Natural Law* and *Poem on the Lisbon Earthquake*. Not only did he disagree with Voltaire, but defended his own optimistic concept, that is, his belief in a general (and benevolent) Providence. Voltaire's conclusion, as stated in his poem, was simple and clear-cut—*"I respect my God, but I love the universe."*

The most objectionable declaration for Voltaire and for modern readers as well was Rousseau's statement referring to the Lisbon earthquake: had humans still been living in a pastoral culture, there would have been no cities, therefore no lives would have been taken and no destruction and suffering would have ensued. Voltaire responded with *Candide*.

Condorcet's appraisal of Voltaire's poetic élan, and of his goal to please and to instruct people of all ages and of all classes, was summed up as follows:

> Poetry gave him the freedom to express himself in vaster fields; and showed him how it can bond with philosophy in such a way that, without losing any of its essential grace, it reaches out to ever-new beauties, while philosophy divested of aridity and bombast, conserves its exactitudes and its depth. (Moland, 1:284)

Chapter Four

An Innovative Theater Traditionalist

From the outset of his career as playwright (*Oedipus,* 1718), to his last stage piece (*Irene,* 1778), Voltaire was considered one of the finest dramatists of his era. Although his talents did not measure up to the genius of Corneille or Racine, the thrust, style, multiplicity of thematics, and, paradoxically, the innovations that this traditionalist brought to theater and to staging are noteworthy.

Voltaire's subtle circumvention of the sacrosanct unities of time, place, and action; his manipulation of the conventions of *bienséance* (or decorum) and verisimilitude; his attempts to change the longtime French practice of allowing spectators to sit on the stage during performances; and the importance he accorded to costume design and acting techniques—all these, though seemingly paltry in comparison with the advances in the performing arts today, were in his era considered acts of courage.

He militated to abolish the practice of allowing spectators onstage, begun in 1636 with Corneille's *Le Cid.* Not only did spectators' ongoing conversations throughout the performance prevent them from hearing the lines, but their unruliness impeded the actors' play, to the point of denying them the opportunity of creating realistic interpretations of their roles. By diminishing, almost obliterating, the possibility of audience identification with the characters and the grandiose actions portrayed, performances frequently fell, so to speak, on deaf ears. Among Voltaire's verbal onslaughts is his "Dissertation on Ancient and Modern Tragedy" (1748), in which he stated that "one of the greatest obstacles to the presentation of any grand and moving action in our [French] theaters is the crowd of spectators mingled pell-mell on the stage with the actors."[1] It was not, however, until 1759, when Count de Lauraguais paid 60,000 francs to the Comédie-Française to reimburse the company for excluding theatergoers from their high-priced onstage seats, that abstract notions were transformed into concrete terms. His magnanimous act finally cleared the French stage of spectators.

Voltaire was one of the first to base some of his tragedies on French national history, looked upon at the time as too sacred a subject for theater. To heighten a play's emotional appeal, he took great pains to emphasize the spectacle side of performance. To be sure, his heroic tragedies for the most part followed well-worn modes and facile stage techniques: coups de théâtre, recognition scenes, and surprises, as well as borrowings from the Greeks, Romans, Shakespeare, and, of course from his seventeenth-century predecessors. Nonetheless, his use of multiple melodramatic elements in his tragedies leads us to consider him an important transitional man of the theater, linking Racine's classical dramas to Hugo's romantic theater. Furthermore, he may be seen as a precursor of the writers of *pièces à thèse* (Henri Becque, Oscar Méténier), as well as of the adapters of novels by Edmond and Jules de Goncourt, Émile Zola, and others.

Though a remarkable craftsman, deftly inserting suspense, excitement, and visual stage activity to stir his dramatic unfoldings, Voltaire lacked the imagination and psychological depth to create full-blown characters. Rather than reach into the heart of his protagonists and to extract their uniqueness, he placed emphasis on external situations, attitudes, and objects. The creatures of his fancy were frequently unidimensional and stereotypic. His melodramatic plots were often predictable and derivative. Although vacillating between new trends in theater— the choice of prose for its naturalness, for example—he opted for the 12-syllable alexandrine that had ruled French tragedy as a medium of expression for a hundred years. Pitfalls frequently beset traditionalists, and Voltaire was no exception. Although he prided himself on the high quality of his verses, his poetics were divested of the stark, visceral, and searing images that characterize Corneille's and Racine's peerless dramas. Interlaced as Voltaire's were at times with heavy, redundant, and banal overtones, his tragedies more often than not drew tears from his audiences.

Voltaire, the polemicist and moralist, authored 52 plays. Of these, 27 were tragedies, the rest comedies.[2] The former, more or less thesis dramas, waxed in high-wrought sequences, each in its own way attempting to rectify the protagonists' duplicitous relationships, to spiritualize their base intents, to transform their fanaticism into tolerance, and their xenophobia to xenophilic attitudes.

A passionate devotee of drama, as attested to by the theaters he built wherever he lived for any length of time—Cirey, Les Délices, and Ferney—Voltaire not only wrote plays, but, as has been mentioned, directed and performed in them. He involved himself in the creation of their sets and costumes as well and worked closely with his performers, namely, Adrienne Lecouvreur (1692–1730); Marie-Françoise Marchand, called Dumesnil (1713–1802); Claire-Josèphe Leris de la Tude, spoken of as Clairon (1723–1803); and Henri-Louis Cain, referred to as Lekain (1729–1778). He knew exactly how to pry the best out of his artists, illustrating how to communicate emotions via gestures, facial expressions, and props and teaching them to distill the essence of their lines.

Voltaire was grateful to Lecouvreur for having substituted simplicity, naturalness, grace, and nobility for the traditional French custom of exaggerated and affected declamation and chanting. So impressed was he by the authenticity of her speech that after her death he wrote: she had "almost invented the art of speaking to the heart, and of showing feeling and truth where formerly had been shown little but artificiality and declamation."[3]

While training Dumesnil in her role for Mérope (*Mérope*), Voltaire was so insistent that she express greater passion that in desperation she cried out: "Really, one ought to have *le diable au corps* to strike the note you want." He responded: "Just so, mademoiselle, *le diable au corps* in all art, if you want to attain perfection" (Cole and Chinoy, 173).

Always meticulous and conscientious in the preparation of her roles, Clairon was praised by Voltaire for her arresting acting—its polish, its finesse, and the nobility needed to achieve the grandeur required for her portrayals. In Clairon's "Reflections on Dramatic Art," she wrote of the special emphasis she placed on voice training: "In order that she [the actress] may be enabled to give the necessary shade to the picture she means to represent, her voice must be clear, harmonious, flexible, and susceptible of every possible intonation" (Cole and Chinoy, 170). Arduous work was required in the preparation of such roles as Mérope in the play of the same name, or Aménaïde in *Tancred*. Clairon referred to the naiveté of some actors who believed

> that the author had done all that was necessary; that to learn the parts, and to leave the rest to nature was all the actor had to do. Nature! How many use this word without knowing its meaning. The difference of sex, of age, of situation, of time, of countries, of manners and of customs demand different modes of expression. What infinite pains and study must it not require to make an actor forget his own character; to identify himself with every personage he represents; to acquire the faculty of representing love, hatred, ambition, and every passion of which human nature is susceptible,—every shade, every gradation by which these sen-

timents are depicted with their full extent of coloring and expression. (Cole and Chinoy, 171)

A great admirer of Clairon's "natural" acting style, Voltaire was not loath to convey his feelings on the subject:

> Who, before Miss Clairon, would have dared to play the scene of the urn in *Orestes* as she had? Who would have imagined nature portrayed in this manner; of falling in a faint holding the urn in one hand, while letting the other fall down immobile and lifeless? (Ridgway, 173)

Nor did Lekain, who used his vocal skills and silences to convey the conflictual nature of his characters, deliver the traditional turgid and exaggerated declamatory tirades. Having trained him since youth, Voltaire may have been instrumental in teaching him the art of infusing his lines with tragic power, and of instilling in him the willpower and discipline needed to become a great performer. Commenting on the superb acting techniques of Lekain and Clairon, he compared their stage tableaux to a Michelangelo painting. Voltaire also underscored Lekain's "audacity" as he emerged from Ninus's tomb in *Sémiramis* with bloodied arms, and he lauded the acting techniques of the "admirable" Clairon as the dying Sémiramis, dragging herself onto the steps of the very same tomb (Ridgway, 173). Had Voltaire not benefited from the genius of the preceding performers, he perhaps might not have enjoyed a lifetime of great theatrical successes.

Voltaire and the French Classical Theatrical Tradition

Voltaire was not only a skilled playwright but a true man of the theater, expert in every branch of this art, be it directing, acting, lighting, decors, or costume design. Judging from his many writings on the theater—prefaces, articles, essays, correspondence—his cardinal rule was to invest each of his tragedies with powerful emotional appeal. Fire, not ice, was the sine qua non of his tragedies. Instinctively he knew that he would reach his audiences through feeling, not didacticism. "Tragedy must speak to the heart," he stated over and over again. "Whether tragic or comic, theater is a living depiction of human passions."[4]

Voltaire's stay in England had opened him up to a remarkable period in the creative arts, sciences, and philosophy. The Restoration (the return of the Stuart dynasty to England in 1660) was marked not only by an overt reaction to Puritan austerity, but also by the introduction of broad-mindedness in matters of religion and mores. The closing of the theaters in 1642 by an act of Parliament, and their reopening 18 years later, had created a void in the arts. Two forms of Restoration drama filled this vacuum: the heroic play, which owed a great deal to Corneille; and the comedy of manners, with its ultraromantic moments and exceedingly complex plots. Some of the best-known playwrights of the period—Dryden, Congreve, Wycherley, Cibber, Farquhar—were instrumental in the development of prose drama.

Voltaire's energy and sense of commitment to the arts, as well as his exposure to Shakespeare and the dramatists already mentioned, served to broaden his understanding and vision of theater. Although lacking Shakespeare's genius, he was stirred by the breadth of the English bard's emotionally explosive stage personalities, and by the loftiness of their epic grandeur. "Shakespeare's brilliant monsters," he wrote in the 18th of his *Philosophical Letters,* "are a thousand times more pleasing than modern-day wisdom" (*Mélanges,* 84). Unable to experience or to understand the profound psychological depths of a Hamlet, a Macbeth, or an Othello, Voltaire wrongly attributed their haunting power to external factors, such as the rapidity with which Shakespeare's scenes unfolded, the shock value of violence and gore in the stage spectacle, the frenzy of supernatural encounters, and so forth. That English national history had been considered food for dramatization, as opposed to the traditional interdict on staging moments in the lives of "sacred" French heroes and heroines, added yet another allure for Voltaire.

Shakespeare remained a source of inspiration for him throughout his life, despite the fact that French taste, taken with manners, courtly ways, and repression of instinct, was frequently jarred by Shakespearean creatures. Voltaire himself referred to Shakespeare as "barbaric," but he explained his genius as he saw it to the uninformed in France, who had rejected Shakespeare outright for what they considered to be his crudities:[5]

> It is Shakespeare, barbaric as he was, who injected this power and this energy into English; something no one else has been able to heighten since that time, without exaggerating, and consequently weakening, its thrust. What is the origin of this great poetic effect that forms and finally fixes the genius and language of peoples? (*Mélanges,* 244)

Voltaire conveyed his admiration for English theater in the following metaphor:

The poetic genius of the English until now has resembled a thick-spreading tree planted by nature, lifting its thousand branches as it pleases, and growing irregularly and with vigor. Prune it against its nature to the shape of a tree in the gardens of Marly,[6] and it will die. (*PL*, 89)

Upon his return to France, Voltaire, the polemicist with a smattering of hubris, even suggested ways, simplistic to be sure, of enhancing English theater:

In England, tragedy is really an action; and if the authors of this country joined to the activity which enlivens their plays a natural style combining decency and regularity, they would soon surpass both the Greeks and the French.[7]

Although remaining under the spell of Shakespeare—and herein lies the dichotomy—Voltaire nonetheless saw himself as the continuator of French classical theater. As the protector of Corneille and Racine, he struggled to uphold the alexandrine, considered by him as representing the highest artistic form.

Numerous playwrights, and especially Houdar de La Motte, favored prose over verse for tragedy; Voltaire vacillated, but opted always for verse, convinced that it was crucial to the maintenance of artistic interest. The alexandrine alone had the power to convey the nobility, refinement, and elegance of aristocratic passions.

Voltaire upheld the sacrosanct rule of the three unities (time: the play's plot is to be spun out in 24 hours; place: the play is to be performed in a single location; and action: the play is to have only one central plot). Staunchly chauvinistic in this regard, he refused to allow French classical tragedy to become polluted by anarchical and audacious theater, Elizabethan or otherwise.

Despite his fine resolutions, however, Voltaire was conflicted on the subject of theatrical rules. Although imprisoned in traditional modes, he dreamt of staging spectacular tragedies that would rouse the audience's visual, aural, and emotional universe. When he felt his story line required the circumvention of the strict regulations imposed on French tragedy, he disregarded the unities of time, place, and action—and even those of verisimilitude and decorum.

His misreadings of Shakespeare, certainly not uncommon in the eighteenth or even the nineteenth century in France, led him to believe that he could both broaden and modernize the scope of French theater by simply injecting it with certain Shakespearean techniques. He saw these,

as has been mentioned, in terms of shortening the habitually lengthy
tirades of French theater and of speeding up its scenic action by having
recourse to patheticism and coherency in plot and ideology.

Needless to say, the French classical tradition in eighteenth-century
France was in a state of flux. Many playwrights sought a different type
of theater to fulfill a changing society's vision of the world. With
Corneillian and Racinian tragedy on the decline, the artifices of a refined
court reacted favorably to Philippe Quinault's polished but insipid
Romanesque tragedies. The paltry theatrical pieces of Jean-Galbert de
Campistron, Joseph Lagrange-Chancel, and Longpierre flooded the
market. Although attempting to break new ground, these imitators,
devoid of psychological depth and imagination, had to resort to clever
repartee, surprises, and other minor titillations to foment interest.

Mediocre playwrights filled the rosters. Having grown lax, many disregarded the once stringent seventeenth-century theatrical code.
Whether or not a tragedy had five acts, as tradition dictated, depended
on the whim of the dramatist. Many considered reality better served by
blending genres, such as tragedy and comedy, rather than by rigorously
separating them, as during the classical era. Some dramatists even went
so far as to disregard the once-sacred rules of verisimilitude and of decorum, not to mention the unities of time, place, and action. Whimsically
treated as well was the requirement concerning the subject matter of
tragedy: that it must be drawn from antiquity, either classical or biblical. Also dismissed by the derivative dramatists of the period was the
classical code regarding characterization: emphasis must not be placed
on a protagonist's specific traits, but rather on his or her archetypal
nature. To universalize and thereby eternalize human characteristics
would enable audiences the world over to better identify with them.

Was Voltaire's advocacy of classical form due perhaps to a love for
and dependency on tradition? Or did he unconsciously feel insecure as a
playwright, resulting in a fearfulness to venture too far in new directions? Could his writings on the preservation of the unities have been
motivated by a need to denigrate the doctrines put forth by such rivals
as Houdar de La Motte? Yet he had been touched by the sentiments
expressed in La Motte's tragedy *Inès de Castro* (1723). Perhaps he was
jealous of its success. *Inès de Castro* had been one of the earliest examples
of the *drame larmoyant* (tearful drama), a genre Voltaire was to emulate
not in name but in content. La Motte, pointing up the glorious senti-

ments of conjugal tenderness in his play, championed the cause of modern drama freed from classical restrictive and fixed traditions, including those of the three unities and the conventional alexandrine. But the breaking of rules advocated by La Motte did not add a sense of inexorability and tragedy to his drama, although it did indicate a change in the direction of French tragedy. Voltaire realized that despite La Motte's successes, his rival's talents were far from great.

The abbé Dubos had advocated (*Discours*, 1730) that tragedy draw tears from its audiences. A dramatist could achieve this, he noted, by increasing the realism of his staged tableaux, thus adding to the intrinsic pathos of the extravaganzas. The underscoring of sentiment and feeling, rather than the emphasizing of self-analysis, heroic grandeur, and character building, as evidenced in Corneille's strong-willed hero types, was to make inroads in Voltaire's theatrical agenda.

Nivelle de La Chaussée's *comédies larmoyantes* (tearful comedies) brought a new genre of theater to public attention. By combining tragedy with stage pieces in which preeminence was given to tears, pathos, and sentimentality, the playwright had divined the perfect recipe to elicit the audience's sympathy for the misfortunes of others.

Denis Diderot's *The Illegitimate Son* (1757) and *Father of a Family* (1758) constituted an even newer vintage: the *drame bourgeois,* which set aspects of "tearful comedy" in situations mirroring contemporary life in its sorrows and its joys. Recognition of their own problems not only would help viewers cope with their needs in the real world but also would pave the way for social reform, as in the late-nineteenth-century naturalist dramas of Zola, the Goncourts, and Becque.

Despite the rush toward theatrical modernity in eighteenth-century France, Voltaire stood firm in his position against the prose dramas advocated by La Motte, the oversentimental works of La Chaussée, and the bourgeois banalities of Diderot's plays. Adamant in retaining the tried and true forms of "our great masters," he defended the unities, despite his own frequent nonobservance of them. Although justifying his desire to maintain tradition as a means of instilling into audiences rightful philosophical, moral, and psychological notions, he may also have chosen to adhere to its dicta because it had proven to be an effective way to catalyze their emotions. Voltaire's ground rule for theater reads as follows: "I consulted my heart alone; it alone directs me; it has always inspired my actions and my words" (Moland, 5:295).

Voltaire's Tragedies

The Modern Hero: *Oedipus* (1718)

Even before his exposure to English drama, Voltaire had injected his *Oedipus* with a new identity. It deviated markedly in its psychological approach not only from Corneille's ego-centered protagonist but also from the "inexorable brutalities" interwoven in the tragedies of Sophocles.

Although he was an admirer of Corneille's *Oedipus,* Voltaire maintained that the liberties Corneille had taken with the plot of the Greek myth, coupled with the aridity of his poetry, had depleted the play of its intrinsic energy.[8] Nor did Voltaire concur with Corneille's character-building approach to Oedipus, nor with his introduction of the question of free will. Corneille underscored Oedipus's growing awareness of his inability to transcend his destiny, which simply encouraged him to rise up in indignation against the gods—a ploy, Voltaire reasoned, that gave him the possibility of earning both his punishment and the means by which he could test his mettle. Accordingly, an individual would need only to discipline his or her will in order to rise above a sense of excoriating guilt.

Although cognizant of the "contradictions, absurdities, and useless declamations" in Sophocles' *Oedipus,* Voltaire confessed that without this work he could never have begun to really understand the protagonist's searing hurt, nor would he have undertaken the writing of a play on the same subject. He admired Greek tragedy for its powerful passions and for the starkness of its poetry but criticized some of its technical aspects: its stasis, its lack of suspense, and the raw and coarse situations it dramatized (Pomeau 1969, 87). He also took great umbrage with Sophocles' emphasis on the crimes of incest meted out to both Jocasta and Oedipus, and the latter's additional one of parricide. These, he maintained, predestined them to suffer and sacrifice in order to earn redemption.

Oedipus's deep-seated self-abhorrence in Voltaire's play neither stemmed from an innate sense of culpability nor resulted from punishment of the gods. Since he had disobeyed their dicta unwittingly and in all innocence, he viewed himself as guiltless of any criminal act, and, therefore, disculpated:

> O no! I am not; this destructive hand
> Hath broke the sacred tie, and deep involved
> Thy kingdom in my ruin. O! avoid me,
> Fear the vindictive God who still pursues

> The wretched Oedipus; I fear myself,
> My timid virtue serves but to confound me.[9]

Voltaire's very human Jocasta even more overtly believed in her son's innocence:

> Do not accuse, do not condemn thyself;
> Thou art unhappy, but thou art not guilty;
> Thou didst not know whose blood thy hand had shed.
> *(Oedipus,* 4.3.195)

About to die, she rejected any burden of guilt: "I have lived virtuous, and shall die with pleasure" (5.6.209). And in her last utterance, she again cast out all culpability for her sinful acts: "for heaven alone / Was guilty of the crime, and not Jocasta" (5.6.209).

While according to Jansenist credo mother and son had been predestined to commit crimes of incest and murder, Jesuit doctrine saw them as sinless, their acts having been perpetrated unconsciously and involuntarily. Their faultlessness absolved them of all accountability for their acts (Pomeau 1969, 87).

Voltaire's interpretation of the Oedipus myth was both modern in concept and in keeping with his own Deistic views of God. Not only was Oedipus stainless, but he had never, as in the case of Corneille's hero, suffered from hubris. Voltaire's Oedipus could never conceive that he—or anyone else—might ever triumph over, and thus alter, his destiny:

> Heaven led me on to guilt, and sunk a pit
> Beneath my sliding feet: I was a slave
> Of some unknown, some unrelenting power,
> That used me for its instrument of vengeance:
> There are my crimes, remorseless cruel gods!
> Yours was the guilt, and ye have punished me.
> Where am I? what dark shade thus from my eyes
> Covers the light of heaven?
> *(Oedipus,* 5.4.205)

In keeping with Voltaire's strong anticlerical stand and his own natural forthrightness, his Jocasta mocked the gods and oracles—all those

who claimed to discern the wishes of what was beyond human understanding:

> These priests are not what the vile rabble think them,
> Their knowledge springs from our credulity.
>
> (4.1.187)

Mortals entertaining the idea of dominating their fate, or trying to read
into the Book of Destiny, would be a theme Voltaire would later probe
in such works as *Zadig* and *Candide*.

Although *Oedipus* had brought the 24-year-old Voltaire his first great
success, a minority of spectators were understandably scandalized by
what they believed to be his outrageous attacks on organized religion.

The Love Motif in a Historical Context

Voltaire believed that *amour galant* love motifs were more appropriate to
comedy than to tragedy. To avoid simplistic and effete "gallantry"
sequences on stage, amorous motifs were to be omitted, or to be melded
directly into the inner workings of the drama, or developed into full-
fledged passions capable of fomenting jealousies, crimes, or other
extremes. Nor was love to be used to hyperemotionalize audiences.

In such tragedies as *Zaïre* and *Alzire*, Voltaire claimed to have deleted
all traces of sentimental, flaccid, and Romanesque relationships, only
retaining great passions, reminiscent of Corneille's *Polyeucte* and Racine's
Phaedra. As theatrical celebrations of blind love, the visceral appetites
dramatized in *Zaïre* and *Alzire* not only impacted on the protagonists'
psyches but were indelibly linked to the situations as well. Nor was love
used as an excuse for long analytical discussions on the subject, nor to
firm up a plot, which would have detracted from the poetic, philosophical, and psychological vigor and nobility of the tragic form per se. Had
Voltaire not respected these principles, critics would have likened his
works to the trivia served to audiences by Thomas Corneille, Philippe
Quinault, Prosper J. Crébillon, and Alexis Piron.

Zaïre *(1732)*

Zaïre, identified as a *tragédie tendre,* was, Voltaire noted, "the first play
which I wrote in which I dared yield to my heart's great sensibility"
(Besterman, 517). In the throes of experiencing his own deep love relationship with Mme Du Châtelet, Voltaire knew well how to inject a very

special brand of tenderness into his stage relationships. That he wrote *Zaïre* in 22 days seems to confirm the thought that he had been moved by a flood tide of emotions.

Adhering to the traditional five acts and to the unities as well, Voltaire equipped his Racinian protagonists not with specific character traits, so popular in the theater of his day, but with the required collective qualities demanded by classical drama. That he borrowed neither his subject matter nor his characters from legendary material or from past dramatists was an innovative step on his part. He had not set out to demonstrate, in the manner of a Corneille, the superhuman willpower or emotional strength of the creatures of his fantasy; uppermost in his mind was the depiction of his heroine's tragic universe in a way that would elicit tears from his spectators.

The subject of *Zaïre* lies in the period of Saint Louis (1214–1270) and the Crusades. While many in Voltaire's day erroneously considered the Crusades to have been great and noble endeavors, he, the historian, emphasized the brutalities, pillagings, persecutions, killings, and violations of human rights that marked these Christian military expeditions. Understandably his foray into national history was deemed a transgression of sacred material.

Historical references in *Zaïre,* such as the sailing of Saint Louis's fleet on May 30, 1249, for the Holy Land, were few and far between, the bulk of the material being pure invention on Voltaire's part. As in most of his theatrical works, Voltaire had an agenda and a mission. To this end, he highlighted the issue of religious toleration. Making audiences aware of the crimes that had been committed against humanity in the name of religion was to educate believers and bigots as to the deviously persuasive methods used by established religions to indoctrinate their followers. It also served to increase their understanding and compassion for those of other faiths.

Zaïre's complex and tragic plot revolves around the mutual love of Orosman, the sultan of Jerusalem, and Zaïre, a Christian. Much to her joy, Orosman has agreed to give up the custom of polygamy by making her his only wife. Although converted to Islam after having been taken captive as a child by Orosman's followers, Zaïre had, unbeknown to her, been born a Christian. In time she discovers that she is the daughter of the imprisoned Crusader Lusignan and the sister of Nérestan, a Christian zealot, who is aghast to learn that Zaïre has embraced Islam. So great is Lusignan's joy upon learning that his children are alive that his heart gives out and he dies, but not before Zaïre, although hesitant, promises to be again baptized as a Christian. Unaware of Zaïre's secret and unable to fathom her reasons for delaying the marriage ceremony, Orosman wrongly believes Nérestan to be in love with her. Like Shakespeare's *Othello*, he suffers such jealousy that when he learns that Zaïre and Nérestan are to meet, he stabs his beloved offstage. Once informed of Nérestan's true identity, Orosman not only releases all the Christian prisoners, but suffers such extreme guilt that he commits suicide onstage.

Voltaire's stage techniques are evident. The role of his Orosman is in keeping with Racinian passion as it culminated in the murder of Bajazet, in the play of the same name. Voltaire inserted melodramatic highs and lows, borrowing from Shakespeare's *Othello,* among other sources. What was strictly Voltairean, however, was his emphasis on religious intolerance. Lusignan and Nérestan, having rejected all conciliatory steps toward understanding Zaïre's terrible dilemma, were to blame for her death and for Orosman's suicide. The latter's genuine love for Zaïre, the guilt experienced after his crime, and his act of clemency at the play's conclusion were reminiscent in their depth and power of Corneille's *Polyeucte.* In keeping with Voltaire's philosophy as well is the larger picture that comes through in *Zaïre.* By opposing the Muslim's virtues and the Christian's ignominies, he once again proved his two fundamental truths: morality is both natural and universal, whereas dogma is inculcated in the child via education, as Zaïre iterates.

> Our thoughts, our manners, our religion, all
> Are formed by custom, and the powerful bent
> Of early years: born on the banks of Ganges
> Zaïre had worshipped Pagan deities;
> At Paris I had been a Christian; here
> I am a happy Musulman: we know
> But what we learn; the instructing parent's hand
> Graves in our feeble hearts those characters
> Which time retouches, and examples fix
> So deeply in the mind, that naught but God
> Can e'er efface: but thou were hither brought
> A captive at an age when reason joined
> To sage experience had informed thy soul.[10]

Not as all-consuming as the passion of Racine's Hermione, Zaïre's somewhat reasoned and controlled emotions caused critics to liken her to an "Oriental Frenchwoman." Nonetheless, she touched her audiences by arousing their pity rather than simply exciting their admiration. Because she was weak, submissive, and naive, some considered Zaïre to be the paradigm of the born victim—ready to sacrifice herself for a superior cause. Her idealism and purity of purpose transformed her into a paragon of virtue.

Orosman, a complex stage character, proudly aristocratic yet sensitive, punctilious, broad-minded, and endowed with the authoritative ways of a Saladin, was a fusion of Romanesque passion and the moral elegance of "the gallant man." His mood swings, ranging through fear, rage, love, and pain, and concluding in his act of self-violence, combined a roster of melodramatic traits. Having decided to adhere to the rules of decorum, Voltaire had Zaïre stabbed in the wings and not onstage.

To diminish the very real possibility of offending his audiences, Voltaire created his own recipe for success: he served them a great passion garnished with all types of artificial seasonings—rapid scenic changes, recognition scenes, coups de théâtre, less talk and more action, and a dialogue filled with exclamations designed to arouse feeling and tears. Most important, Voltaire explained:

> I owe it not so much to the merit of the performance, as to the tenderness of the love scenes, which I was wise enough to execute as well as I possibly could: in this I flattered the taste of my audience; and he is generally sure to succeed, who talks more to the passions of men than to their reason.[11]

He did not, however, stoop to violence. Although his characterizations were shallow and his situations mainly contrived, with pathos/bathos reigning, Zaïre's conflict between love and religion was believable, stirring, and in some ways unforgettable. La Harpe, one of the century's best-known critics, considered Zaïre "the most touching of all existing tragedies."[12] It may also be claimed that Voltaire's Zaïre finely integrated French national history and the stage. Immensely successful, it was performed in France, England, Germany, and Italy. Voltaire's own production and direction of the play at Cirey, and his performance in the role of Orosman, must have been memorable.

Alzire (1736)

By transforming passion into a weapon for tolerance and understanding, Alzire's love motif was considered to have ennobled passion. Its Rousseauesque implication was that the simplicity, purity, and integrity of the so-called uncivilized Peruvians made them superior to the hypocrisy, lies, and murderous intents of their patently "civilized" Spanish conquerors.

The action takes place in Lima, Peru, following the Spanish conquest of this land. Alzire, truth and integrity incarnate, is the youngest daughter of an Inca king referred to as an "infidel" by the so-called righteous and God-fearing Christians, one of whom, Guzman, loves the native princess. Alzire's concept of honor, so deeply inculcated in her since birth, keeps her from joining her fiancé, Zamor, a Peruvian chieftain, who has been fighting the Spaniards for the past three years and whom she now believes has been killed. Her passion for Zamor reinforces her inborn sense of righteousness and aversion to deception, betrayal, and duplicity—the former characteristics, Voltaire inferred, virtually unknown to Spanish conquerors. Aware that Guzman has been responsible for her beloved's torture, Alzire resists his advances. Finally, and for reasons of state, she reluctantly agrees to marry him. Her conflict, however, is so acute that she confesses to him her still-passionate love for her Incan chieftain.

Guzman, the odious, intolerant, and brutal colonizer, is placed in opposition to Alvarez, his tolerant and charitable father, who has chosen his son to succeed him as governor of Peru. Whereas Alvarez is a spokesman for idealistic Christianity, Guzman distorts its meaning, as is demonstrated by his following words:

> For so our laws require, they must be Christian;
> To quit their idols, and embrace our faith,
> Alone can save them; we must bend by force
> Their stubborn hearts, and drag them to the altar;
> One king must be obeyed, one God adored.[13]

Zamor suddenly reappears on the scene and, although imprisoned and sentenced to die, succeeds in mortally wounding Guzman. Believing Alzire to have been guilty of encouraging Zamor's act, Guzman has her sentenced to death. Only after he fathoms the loyalty and love she bears for Zamor does his hatred and fanaticism transform itself into kindness and charity. Before dying, he forgives the lovers, urges them to marry, and asks Zamor to convert to Christianity.

Despite *Alzire*'s great success, the so-called Incas on the French stage gave the impression of being transplanted Europeans. Alzire's ultra-noble character, deep-seated conflict, and plentiful tears were effectively used to sustain emotional highs. As for the stereotypic "noble savage," Zamor, although diverted from goodness by his obsession for vengeance, turns into a loving individual at the play's conclusion. For some, however, he came across as absurd. That the melodramatic monster of a Guzman, in his predeath conversion to idealistic Christianity, is suddenly transformed into a compassionate and loving being adds yet another artificial note to the drama.

> Yes Zamor,
> I will do more, thou shalt admire and love me:
> Guzman too long hath made Alzire wretched,
> I'll make her happy; with my dying hand
> I give her to thee, live and hate me not,
> Restore your country's ruined walls, and bless
> My memory.
>
> (*Alzire*, 5.7.61)

Finally, Voltaire's use of hackneyed theatrical devices, coup de théâtre, recognition, and other scenes, to increase suspense, as well as his paucity of psychological depth, are ever evident.

Olympia *(1763)*

Written in six days but reworked several times, as was Voltaire's habit with regard to most of his writings, *Olympia* dramatizes the shocking manner in which the female lead settles her love dilemma. Daughter of Alexander and Statira, Olympia had been asked by her dying mother to marry Antigonus, rather than Cassander, the king of Macedonia, whom she loves but who has murdered her father. Unable to muster sufficient strength to counter her mother's desire, the love-torn Olympia stabs herself, then throws herself onto her mother's burning pyre as an aghast audience looks on.[14]

Banishing the Love Motif

Voltaire sought to instill notions of morality and virtue in his protagonists without having recourse to agonizing scenes of unrequited or

impossible love. Rather than relying on pity and terror as the sine qua
non of tragedy according to Aristotle's *Poetics,* he affirmed that terror,
compassion, and tears should be aroused for loftier purposes.

In his "Discourse on Tragedy," published with his *Brutus* (1730),
Voltaire declared:

> For love to be worthy of the tragic theater, it must not be used to simply
> fill a void in English or French tragedies most of which are too long any-
> way, but rather made the very crux of the drama itself. Passion must be
> truly tragic, considered a weakness, and struggled against via remorse.
> Such a love must either lead directly to the misfortunes and crimes of the
> heroes and heroines, thereby demonstrating how dangerous it truly is, or
> that virtue be triumphant, thereby dispeling all notion of its invincibility.
> Otherwise its power is reduced to the love levels implicit in eclogues and
> comedies.[15]

The techniques advanced by Voltaire to arouse audience anticipation
and participation during polemical thrusts in *Brutus, The Death of Caesar,
Adelaïde Du Guesclin,* and *Mérope* were relatively straightforward. Tirades
were slimmed down so that the situation revolving around the play's
politically idealistic arguments would become sufficiently abrasive to
further irritate and bloody the spectators' already raw nerves.

Brutus *(1730)*

French audiences were stunned by the power of Brutus's patriotic *passion*
for both the city of Rome and the liberty with which it was associated.
Equally invincible was Brutus's profound hatred for the kingship,
which, if it had been restored in Rome, would have put an end to the
republic.

> Rome already knows
> How much I prize her safety and her freedom;
> The same my spirit, and the same my purpose. . . .[16]

> Stop, and learn with more respect
> To treat the citizens of Rome; for know,
> It is the senate's glory and her praise
> To represent that brave and virtuous people
> Whom thou hast thus reviled: for ourselves,

> Let us not hear the voice of flattery,
> It is the poison of Etrurian courts,
> But ne'er has tainted yet a Roman senate.
>
> *(Brutus,* 1.2.242)

Brutus was Voltaire's "republican" play, imbued with the power and energy that inspires noble freedom of thought, and the ring of authenticity sounded loud and clear each time the hero condemned the kingship in order to defend freedom of speech and a popular government. The very thought of possible repression not only energized Voltaire's moralistic credo but also replicated his own all-too-well-founded fears. Addressing the Senate at the play's outset, Brutus declaims:

> At length, my noble friends, Rome's honored senate,
> The scourge of tyrants, you who own no kings
> But Numa's gods, your virtues, and your laws.
>
> (1.1.239)

Nor did Voltaire cease his attacks on political despots and the priesthood, guilty of developing and maintaining a slave mentality in the people:

> Etruria born to serve,
> Hath ever been the slave of kings or priests;
> Love to obey, and, happy in her chains,
> Would bind them on the necks of all mankind.
>
> (1.2.245)

Memorable is the concluding scene, spotlighting Brutus standing proudly defiant, embracing his son, Titus, whom he then sends with infinite but controlled sorrow to be executed for having conspired against republican Rome in a moment of weakness. Maintaining the beauty of his noble cause, Brutus speaks out yet again:

> Ye know not Brutus who condole with him
> At such a time: Rome only is my care;
> I feel but for my country: we must guard
> Against more danger: they're in arms again:

> Away: let Rome in this disastrous hour
> Supply the place of him whom I have lost
> For her, and let me finish my sad days,
> As Titus should have done, in Rome's defence.
> (5.8.307)

Until the early part of the eighteenth century, little attention had been paid to sets, props, costumes, and accessories. With *Brutus* Voltaire opened up French taste to stage issues, choosing apparel befitting the characters and their times. The brilliance of the full-toned red togas worn by the senators standing starkly outlined against the semicircular altar of Mars was electrifying. Equally memorable was the austere but magnificently proportioned house of the Roman consuls on the Tarpeian cliff, with the temple of the Capitol in the background. Because its doors opened onto an apartment upstage, Voltaire was accused—and rightly so—of violating the classical unity of place.

Brutus's powerful idealism may explain why this play was briefly revived in 1789, at the outset of the French Revolution. The renowned actor Talma performed in the role of Proculus in a costume considered revolutionary for the time: he appeared onstage without powdered hair, with bare arms and legs, a red toga covering his torso.

The least performed of Voltaire's plays, *Brutus* was nonetheless translated into more languages than all of his other stage dramas. It had been begun as a prose piece during his stay in England, but the traditionalist Voltaire opted for poetry and transformed the play to suit his inclinations. To abandon the alexandrine, he affirmed, would diminish the spectators' pleasure. Nonetheless, his innovative side drove him to begin seeking ways of clearing the stage of spectators, for how, he admonished, could Brutus's genius be effectively experienced amid talkative, and even rowdy, spectators seated right next to him?

The Death of Caesar *(1735)*

Voltaire's *The Death of Caesar* (*La Mort de César*), although treating *grosso modo* the same thematics as *Brutus,* is unusual for its psychological twist. Unlike Shakespeare's *Julius Caesar,* Voltaire's play focuses on additions by Suetonius and Plutarch, to the effect that Brutus was Caesar's son by Servilia. The heart of the drama, then, no longer revolved around the conflict between the ideal and the real, but between the ideal and the filial. Voltaire reasoned that the affixation of a subjective conflict to the political crisis increased the poignancy of the situation. Caesar's revelation to Brutus that he was his son, born from a secret marriage, broadened the play's motif: parricide was added to the assassination. The more agonizing Brutus's conflict, the more determined he was not to allow his republicanism to be swayed, nor his duty toward his country to be impeded. The pursuit of *his* cause in no way diminished his efforts to persuade Caesar not to seek the throne, but rather to content himself with the honor of being the first citizen of the Republic. Following Caesar's refusal, Brutus unabashedly revealed his filiation to the senators, declaring his obligation toward Rome unchanged:

> O Rome,
> My eyes are ever open still for thee;
> Reproach me not for chains which I abhor.
> Another paper! *No: thou art not Brutus*:
> I am, I will be Brutus; I will perish,
> Or set my country free: Rome still, I see,
> Has virtuous hearts: she calls for an avenger,
> And has her eyes on Brutus; she awakens
> My sleeping soul, and shakes my tardy hand:
> She calls for blood, and shall be satisfied.[17]

Stoic to the extreme, Brutus placed his country above his family, thereby remaining a man of ideals—in many ways a Voltairean hero.

Attending a performance of Shakespeare's *Julius Caesar* during his stay in England, Voltaire, it was reported, had gasped at the gory scenes unfolding before him. The sight of Brutus standing on the tribune explaining his act, holding his dagger still dripping with blood in front of his friends, remained indelibly engraved in his mind's eye. Not surprisingly, Voltaire attempted to avail himself of similar shock effects. Following Caesar's murder, while a teary-eyed Antony mounts the tribune to discourse on this great leader's virtue and his will, a curtain is drawn upstage to reveal Caesar's body covered with a bloodied robe. Unlike Shakespeare, however, Voltaire, incapable of digging deeply into a personality, failed to penetrate beyond surfaces; thus he fell short of understanding the profundity and universality of creatures in turmoil. Tragic situations, he erroneously believed, could be evoked onstage by a mere sleight of hand—by accelerating the speed and the horror of the staged scenes. He was sensitive to Shakespeare's shattering visualizations but was unable to imitate the power and energy implicit in the works of this "tasteless genius . . . this English Barbarian," as he had referred to him in his "Discourse to the Academy" (*Mélanges*, 244).

Adelaïde Du Guesclin *(1734)*

Voltaire's *Adelaïde Du Guesclin* (1734) not only featured highly prized French historical figures—Guesclin, Vendôme, and Nemours—but violated the sacrosanct rule of decorum as well. Taking his cue from Shakespeare, or perhaps from Crébillon's *Atreus and Thyestes* (1707) or *Rhadamiste and Zenobia* (1711)—dramas replete with horrific scenes— Voltaire allowed full sway to the shock factor in *Adelaïde Du Guesclin,* which focused on war, passion, and jealousy.[18] When, for example, Nemours entered the proscenium with bloodied face and a blood-soaked arm in a sling, audiences were aghast. Even more provocatively, instead of beautifully turned phrases to bear evil tidings, a cannon shot resounding offstage announced the death of Nemours's brother, Vendôme. It earned jeers from the spectators, who were equally disgusted by Voltaire's attributions, without support, of criminal acts to Du Guesclin (c. 1315–1380), a prince of the blood and one of the great heroes of the Hundred Years' War. Voltaire yielded to public taste on those issues and offered a new version of *Adelaïde Du Guesclin* in 1752, entitled *Duc de Foix*. With Lekain playing Vendôme, Du Guesclin's role clarified, and the blood scenes and cannon shots deleted, his play was well received. By 1765 taste had so altered that another version of *Adelaïde Du Guesclin* was again performed, this time successfully.

Mérope *(1743)*

Voltaire's highly prized *Mérope,* although not the first play featuring this heroine to reach the French stage (Maffei, Gilbert, La Chapelle, Lagrange-Chancel, etc.), was divested of a traditional love plot. Focusing instead on the heroic love and devotion of a mother, Mérope, for her son, Aegisthus, Voltaire affirmed that the theme of maternal affection in all of its purity was both the core of the drama and the motivation of his protagonist.

Mérope, the widow of Cresphontes, the slain king of Messenia in southern Greece, senses that her son, Aegisthus, who had been reported dead, is still alive. She lives for the day that he will become Messenia's crowned head. Although the faithful Narbas, who had fled with the child following the king's assassination, had written to Mérope during their years of separation, his letters had been intercepted. When Mérope

learns that Polyphontes, the present tyrant of Messenia, hopes to win
the kingship by marrying her, she is overcome by feelings of revulsion
for him. Unknown to her, he has posted soldiers at Messenia's borders
with orders to kill any young man attempting to enter the land.
Although ignorant of his lineage, Aegisthus is wise for his years. Upon
setting foot in Messenia, he confronts the border guards who attack
him, kills one, and routs another. But then he is arrested for "murder,"
and Polyphontes announces falsely that he has died at the hands of a
nameless and now-incarcerated stranger. He promises Mérope that if
she marries him, he will allow her to avenge Aegisthus's death by killing
the mysterious prisoner. Although Mérope agrees, she plans to kill herself immediately afterward. A memorable moment in French theater
now occurs. Just as Mérope raises her hand to carry out her act, Aegisthus's
old guardian, Narbas, comes forth and stays it, secretly informing her of
the young man's identity and of the fact that Polyphontes had murdered
her husband and two of their sons.

Lavish praise was heaped on Dumesnil for her portrayal of Mérope.
Most striking was the scene in which she advances toward her son,
whom she is about to ax; "her eyes and voice broken with tears, [she]
raises her trembling hand," which, when she learns his identity, remains
fixed in midair. Moments later, just as a soldier is about to kill
Aegisthus, she cries out "Stay, barbarian, / He is—my son," crossing the
stage to embrace him:

> "Thou art:
> And heaven, that snatched thee from this wretched bosom,
> Which now too late hath opened my longing eyes,
> Restores thee to a weeping mother's arms
> But to destroy us both."[19]

Polyphontes, master of the situation, gives her a final choice: marry him
or witness her son's death. Falling to her knees, she agrees to the former.
In time, however, we learn from Mérope's confidante, Ismenia, how
Aegisthus took hold of a sacred ax and killed the tyrant, after which he
was proclaimed king.

The beauty, lyricism, and poetry of the stage sets used in the 1763
production of *Mérope* were particularly impressive. Act II, for example,
featured "a wooded grove outside the city, consecrated as a royal burial
ground. It is filled with a number of ancient tombs and different forms,

cypress trees, obelisks, pyramids, everything that characterized the pious veneration of the ancients for the dead. Among these tombs can be seen that of Cresphontes, adorned with everything precious that Mérope could provide" (Quoted in Lanson, 90).

The influence of Antony's "Friends, Romans, and countrymen" in Shakespeare's *Julius Caesar* was all too obvious in Mérope's final words to her people:

> Priests, warriors, friends, my fellow citizens,
> Attend, and hear me in the name of heaven.
> Once more I swear, Aegisthus is your king,
> The scourge of guilt, the avenger of his father,
> And yonder bleeding corpse, a hated monster,
> The foe of gods and men, who slew my husband,
> My dear Cresphontes, and his helpless children.
>
> (*Mérope*, 5.7.97)

As the curtain installed downstage opened, Mérope pointed to Polyphontes's bleeding corpse covered with a bloodied robe. Shocked, the audiences looked on, aware that they had once again been exposed to another of Voltaire's transgressions.

Voltaire's Taste for the Macabre: Shakespeare's Ghost

Melodramatic to the extreme, although not always artistically felicitous, Voltaire's *Eriphyle* (1732) featured one of the first ghosts on the French stage. Watered down, but nevertheless reminiscent of the ghost of Hamlet's father, it stunned the protagonist, Eriphyle, by the reality of its presence:

> I saw him . . . I see him . . . He is coming. . . . cruel one, stop!
> What is this bloodied knife you hold over my head?[20]

Although Eriphyle bears the same name as Racine's protagonist in *Iphigenia* (1674), she in no way resembles her predecessor. Queen of

Argos in Voltaire's tragedy, Eriphyle, although instrumental in the murder of her first husband, exudes virtue in scenes of excoriating remorse for a crime she helped commit in her impulsive youth:

> This fatal young youth; without experience.
> Open to passions, weak, filled with imprudence;
> This indiscreet young age is to blame for all my sorrows.
>
> (2:466)

Eriphyle receives her due after being mistakenly killed in the wings by her son. By focusing on maternal love once again, Voltaire had hoped to fuse tragedy's "modern elegance" with its "ancient power." ("Discourse," 2:459).[23]

Sémiramis (1748)

Although replicating Eriphyle's supernatural, terrifying, violent, and macabre elements, the thematics of Sémiramis were so felicitous that the play was staged and restaged during Voltaire's lifetime and throughout the Romantic nineteenth century.

Sémiramis, the Assyrian queen, had not only been mentioned by ancient historians, especially by Herodotus in his Histories, but during the course of time had taken on the allure of a legendary figure, inspiring composers such as Gluck and Rossini, and writers such as Calderon and Valéry as well.

Powerful and ambitious, Sémiramis assumed the queenship after having approved Prince Assur's plan to poison her husband Ninus. Although her 15-year rule thereafter has been exemplary and her virtue has earned admiration the world over, remorse has taken hold of her. Increasingly she focuses on her son, who disappeared when he was a child and whom she now fears is dead. Intent upon preserving her dynasty, she marries Arzace, a young and proven hero. When she comes to discover that he is her son, Ninias, the maternal feelings that she has repressed for so long well up within her. She confesses her crime to him, and to protect him from Assur's plot to kill him, as he had killed his father—a plot that she learns is to take place in the eerie corridors of the mausoleum where her husband is entombed—she enters these darkened inner spaces. Meanwhile Ninias, having been informed by the high priest, Oroès, of his origins and of Assur's murder of his father, also enters the vaulted precincts intending to kill the assassin. Rather than slaying his enemy, however, Ninias mistakenly and fatally wounds his mother.

Voltaire's bent for the macabre called for all types of stage machinery during the catacomb interlude. The sight of the dead king rising up from his tomb as it began trembling with incredible force to the accompaniment of deafening thunderclaps created shock waves throughout the audience. Moments later, when sounds of stabbings and screams emanated from the terrifying darkness that enclosed a section of the stage space, the atmosphere grew increasingly horrifying. Aware of his tragic error, the aghast, bloodied, and guilt-ridden Arzace emerged from the dimly lit side of the stage to look at his mother, portrayed by Dumesnil, as she mustered her rapidly waning strength to make her way out of the catacombs.

Of particular interest in *Sémiramis* was the depiction of a mother's guilt:

> Sunk in grief,
> Sémiramis hath spread o'er every heart
> The sorrows which she feels; sometimes she raves,
> Filling the air with her distressful cries,
> As if some vengeful God pursued her; sits
> Silent and sad within these lonely vaults,
> Sacred to night, to sorrow, and to death,
> Which mortals dare not enter; where the ashes
> Of Ninus, our late honored sovereign, lie:
> There will she oft fall on her knees and weep:
> With slow and fearful steps she glides along,
> And beats her breast besprinkled with her tears:
> Oft as she treads her solitary round,
> Will she repeat the names of son and husband,
> And call on heaven, which in its anger seems
> To thwart her in the zenith of her glory.[21]

Also fascinating was the high priest's admonition at the play's conclusion that one learns from past experiences, and that one develops a deep-rooted sense of responsibility for one's acts:

> Learn from her [Sémiramis's] example,
> That heaven is witness to our secret crimes:
> The higher is the criminal, remember,
> The gods inflict the greater punishment:
> Kings, tremble on your thrones, and fear their justice.
>
> (5.8.225)

Although Voltaire claimed that *Sémiramis* was a new and bold type of tragedy, the play holds little psychological interest for today's reader or theatergoer ("Tragedy," 4:501). Indulging increasingly in coups de théâtre, in scenic effects designed to heighten shock and anguish, Voltaire also managed three changes of decors. All told, he succeeded in triggering sufficient fright and terror in the hearts of his spectators—in times that were very different from our own—to fill the play's vacuity.

The Polemicist

Mohammed, or Fanaticism (1741)

The polemicist, although visible in most of Voltaire's plays, takes center stage in *Mohammed, or Fanaticism*. Our author's growing hostility toward prejudice and superstition inspired him to use Islam's Mohammed as a buffer to condemn Christianity's uncompromising and intolerant attitude toward those of other faiths. Voltaire's veiled attacks were based on the contention that because both Christianity and Islam had spread their doctrines by the sword, they had also encouraged persecutions and killings in many areas of the globe. So outraged were spectators by Voltaire's revelations that *Mohammed* was withdrawn after only three performances. The dramatist compared his treatment with that meted out to Molière following his production of *Tartuffe*.

A stunning protest against fanaticism, *Mohammed* is, nonetheless, even more melodramatic than *Zaïre*. Its pathos, even bathos, to some extent places it in the category of *drame larmoyant*. Significant as well is its evocation onstage of a celebrated religious figure, the founder of one of the world's great religions. Voltaire's personage, however, is only loosely based on fact. His thesis in *Mohammed,* as well as in all of his writings, is that individuals must be encouraged to *think* for themselves, rather than relying blindly on pat answers offered by so-called spokespeople of God. People must do their utmost to solve their own problems and regulate their own destinies.

The very real dangers of fanaticism come to the fore in the person of the prophet Mohammed, who, as transformed by Voltaire, becomes a diabolical figure. Self-indulgent, arrogant, and cruel, he knows how to play on the weaknesses of his followers. The plot unfolds as follows: because the governor of Mecca, Zopire, refuses to change his religious convictions to placate Mohammed, the latter resorts to Machiavellian devices to have him assassinated. Audiences learn that Zopire's son, Seid, and his sister, Palmyra, kidnapped as children by Mohammed's henchmen, have been brought up as Muslims and are unaware of their origins. Much to the dismay of Mohammed, who seeks Palmyra's favors, affection deepens between Seid and Palmyra. To rid himself in one fell swoop of a foe and a rival in love, Mohammed persuades Seid, a religious fanatic, to assassinate his political adversary, Zopire. Convinced he is carrying out God's will, Seid agrees, all the more willingly since he is also promised Palmyra as a bounty. He mortally stabs his father in prayer at the altar. A bleeding Zopire drags himself across the stage in full view of the audience. Just prior to dying, he recognizes Seid and Palmyra as his children. The guileful Mohammed, lest he be named as instigator of the crime, has Seid arrested and poisoned. In despair, Palmyra stabs herself, falling on both her father's and her brother's bodies. Mohammed orders his followers to repress all knowledge of his designs on Palmyra. He must, in the eyes of his people, remain inaccessible to vulgar passions:

> She's gone; she's lost; the only dear reward
> I wished to keep of all my crimes: in vain
> I fought, and conquered; Mahomet is wretched
> Without Palmira: Conscience, now I feel thee. . . .
>   Omar, we must strive
> To hide this shameful weakness, save my glory,
> And let me reign o'er a deluded world:
> For Mahomet depends on fraud alone,
> And to be worshipped never must be known.[22]

Seid and Palmyra were instruments and victims of a religious impostor and fanatic. Despite Voltaire's portrayal of a despicably perverse Mohammed, he was, nonetheless, a man of genius whose ignominy lay, according to Voltaire, in his condemnation of freedom of thought.

> But to deliberate: far from Mahomet
> Be all who for themselves shall dare to judge
> Audacious; those who reason are not oft
> Prone to believe; thy part is to obey.
> Have I not told thee what the will of heaven
> Determines? if it be decreed that Mecca,
> Spite of her crimes and base idolatry,
> Shall be the promised temple, the chosen seat
> Of empire, where I am appointed king,
> And pontiff, knowest thou why our Mecca boasts.
>   (*Mohammed*, 3.6.55)

Although some critics affirmed that Voltaire used *Mohammed* to attack
Jesus Christ, it may be said that "he was attacking any religion that
claimed a monopoly of virtue and sought by inhuman or untruthful methods to gain its ends" (Lancaster, 1:208.[23] It is interesting to note in this
regard that Voltaire dedicated *Mohammed* to Pope Benedict XIV, "the head
of the true religion . . . written in opposition to the founder of a false and
barbarous sect." Upon receipt of the pope's flattering answer of acceptance, the author conveyed his gratitude: "I cannot help considering this
verse as a happy presage of the favors conferred on me by your excellency.
Thus might Rome cry out when Benedict XIV was raised to the papacy:
with the utmost respect and gratitude I kiss your sacred feet."[24]

Tancred (1760)

Voltaire's use of the full stage, cleared of spectators for the first time for
Tancred, enabled him to fill the proscenium with an unforgettable array
of 66 medieval knights. An eye-dazzling spectacle was created by their
shields, weapons, coats of arms, and trophies, suspended on columns or
displayed on a wall, depending on the production, as crowds of warriors
carried their flags in triumph around the newly acquired stage space. To
underscore the rhythmic interplay of the variegated colors displayed on
stage, Voltaire had the flamboyant costumes worn by the Norman
knights of Sicily toned down (Lancaster, 2:416).

Complementing the pageantlike vision on the proscenium was the
play's tragic tone. The hero, Tancred, along with his knights and the
father of his beloved Aménaïde, has committed the fatal error of believ-

ing the accusations leveled at her. In his eyes, Aménaïde is guilty of having betrayed not only France to the Moors, but his love by yielding her favors to his rival, Solamir. Although Tancred fights on her behalf, he refuses to see her, thus disregarding the medieval code of honor requiring a knight to have complete trust in his beloved. Victimized and pathetic, Aménaïde is nonetheless stalwart in her love and devotion to the hero Tancred, even unto his death and hers.

Mlle Clairon, as the wrongly accused Aménaïde, crossed the stage in the last act "leaning from exhaustion on the executioners around her, her knees collapsing, her arms dangling as lifeless." Gasping, she threw herself on the dying Tancred, performed by Lekain (Lanson, 87):

> He is dying, and you are weeping . . .
> Let hell swallow you both, and you, and my country. . . .
> You, cruel tyrants, who cost him his life![25]

Moments later, Aménaïde rose, only to expire in the arms of her beloved.

It was in *Tancred,* acted on an audience-free stage, that Voltaire took another innovative step: he circumvented classical verse by opting for alternating rhyming alexandrines. In so doing, he encouraged the more conversational and natural style advocated all along by Clairon and Lekain. Revolutionary in many ways, Voltaire had, as previously mentioned, always vacillated on the subject of grandiloquent classical declamation as opposed to a less mannered and more natural style of speech. In his "Discourse on Tragedy" (1730), he had complained of the "severity" of French poetry, its "enslavement to rhyme," and dreamed of freedom for writers to choose the style best suited to their talents ("Discourse," 2:312). In his "Dissertation on Ancient and Modern Tragedy" (1748), he reminded his readers of the grandeur of declamation and complained of performers whose proselike speech diminished the subtle poetry of the lines, thus detracting from tragedy's awe-inspiring magnificence ("Tragedy," 4:488). In his preface to *The Scythians* (1760), Voltaire again reiterated his fear that to give up declamation was to divest drama of its inner harmonies, rhythms, and tonal qualities.[26]

Voltaire and Costume Reform

Because performers, generally speaking, were obliged to pay for their costumes—and these were frequently expensive—they usually bought gowns they liked. If a play took place in Greek or Roman times and the actress wore the latest French fashions, the effect was incongruous. *Zaïre* and *Alzire* are two cases in point, the former taking place in Jerusalem during the Crusades, the latter after the Spanish conquest of Peru. Lusignan, Guzman, and Alvarez in the latter play were adorned in the latest Parisian styles. Alzire's gown was equally anachronistic: although she played an Indian princess, she wore a copy of one of the unforgettable dresses at the court of Versailles.

Clairon and Lekain, adamantly in favor of costume reform, influenced the Comédie-Française and Voltaire in this regard. Nonetheless, despite the pressure they exerted on the company, Mme Vestris, playing *Mérope* in 1790, appeared onstage in the role of the widow of ancient Messenia in a black silk dress and a belt decorated with diamonds.[27]

Immense headway was made in costume reform in Voltaire's *The Orphan of China* (*L'Orphelin de La Chine,* 1755). During his research for his *Essay on Mores,* a French translation of a fourteenth-century Chinese drama, *The Orphan of Tchao,* was brought to his attention. Reworking this play and changing its name, Voltaire set a peace-loving China against the machinations of Genghis Khan, a ruthless Tartar warrior who had fallen passionately in love with the wife of a Chinese mandarin.

For the sake of accuracy, Voltaire, at his own expense, created an onstage palace decorated in keeping with Chinese taste (Lancaster, 2:410). Because eye-arresting attire was required to heighten the reality of the events, Mlle Clairon, as the mandarin's wife, wore a Chinese dress, "a double skirt of white cloth, a corset with green embroidery and a network of gold tassels," with "a robe or polonaise of gauze, flame-colored and lined with blue taffeta . . . without hoop-skirts or sleeves and with bare arms." Her Chinese-like gestures included the placing of "one or both hands on her hips, and sometimes a clenched fist to her forehead." In sharp contrast was Lekain's Genghis Khan, whose costume consisted of a "striped gold and crimson tunic, his hefty butcher's arms emerging from wide, short sleeves; on his back a lion skin and a quiver full of arrows; a Turkish saber at his side; and an immense bow in his hand. On his head he [wore] a huge helmet made from a lion's head adorned with eleven large plumes and a red aigrette" (Lanson, 86).

Although he was following a trend set by such playwrights as Florent Carton Dancourt (*The Stylish Knight*: *Le Chevalier à la mode,* 1687) and Philippe Néricault Destouches (*The Glorious*: *Le Glorieux,* 1732), Voltaire's vigorous intent to moralize by accentuating righteousness and the spirit of enlightenment went further than that of his contemporaries. Taking very much to heart human suffering caused mainly by religious fanaticism, intolerance, unfit living standards, and war, Voltaire aimed for social, political, and religious reform in *The Scythians* (1767), *The Guebrians* (The Persian Parsees, 1769), *The Laws of Minos* (1773), and other plays. Thus did he pave the way for the future *pièce à thèse*.

Magnetized by the vigorous and electrifying characterizations and poetics of Racine and Shakespeare, as well as of Greek and Roman dramatists, he was nevertheless, as previously mentioned, incapable of fleshing out the archetypal creations of his mentors. His lack of psychological insight accounted to a great extent for the stereotypes that crowded his stage. As a master technician of the theater, however, he knew exactly how to work his thoughts and feelings into tightly structured patterns, thereby creating recipes for success. His blendings of cerebral and emotional ingredients enabled him to generate excitement: terror, pity, compassion, and love. If interest flagged or aporias prevented evident solutions, Voltaire had, as we know, recourse to infallible melodramatic devices—coups de théâtre, disguises, surprises, and recognition scenes—to galvanize affectivity, suspense, and emotional involvement.

Innovative for having disregarded an unwritten law of French classical tragedy—that ancient historical sources not be drawn on for dramatization—he courageously deviated from its dictates in such plays as *Adelaïde Du Guesclin* and *Zaïre* by basing them on French history. So, too, was the venerated rule of decorum set aside in *Adelaïde Du Guesclin* and *Zaïre,* as well as the equally sacred rule of unity of place, in *Mohammed, Caesar, Eriphyle, Brutus,* and *Alzire.* In some cases, he disregarded the single-set unity by cleverly enclosing space upstage behind curtains, which, when drawn at the appropriate moment, highlighted an entirely different set.

Although Voltaire resorted to complicated plots and technical ploys, thereby compensating unconsciously for his inability to explore the complexities of human nature, these very deficiencies may have inspired him to make headway in other theatrical directions. To relieve the monotony of the traditional overly long tirade, he patterned a style based on an economy of words, used in *Brutus, Eriphyle, Zaïre,* and even more stunningly in *The Orphan of China.* The resulting deletions accentuated both the action and the visual elements of performance. Rather than a series of bland stage tableaux, he offered his spectators a feast for the eyes and for the ears as well.

Nonetheless, instead of revitalizing theater, Voltaire, like the bulk of eighteenth-century dramatists—except for Marivaux and Beaumarchais—imitated past creations. They adhered to tried but now well-worn molds of production, and in so doing, incarcerated themselves in the conventional doctrines of their models. Yet unlike Crébillon, Campistron, Lagrange-Chancel, Piron, and Thomas Corneille, who spoon-fed their watered-down theater pieces to approving audiences, Voltaire offered a global vision that expanded his own audiences' understanding of the world. Rather than limit the locales of his plays to Greece, Rome, the Holy Land, and the Middle East, Voltaire, the historian and philosopher, universalized his scope to include England, the Americas, and China, thereby encouraging humanity to reach out to people the world over—in an embrace of understanding and mutual respect.

Chapter Five

The Deist/Pyrrhonist/ Empiricist Historian

Voltaire's Deism, Pyrrhonism, and empiricism in matters of organized religion, history, and intellectual inquiry in general may have stemmed not only from an early yearning for learning but also from a desire to free thought and speech from constriction. Just as one of his intents as essayist, poet, dramatist, and storyteller was to rectify social ills by setting a clear line of demarcation between right and wrong, as historian he tried to instill high moral standards in his readers. Like rulers and those who occupy important posts in a land or institution, historians should, he maintained, guide the uninformed and/or those deviating from what he considered to be the ethical path. The historian's texts, therefore, must distinguish between moral and immoral codes of behavior in the conduct of political, social, and religious affairs. Equally crucial is the attention historians should pay to documentation: they should use archival materials, personal interviews with notables involved, and books on and relating to the thematics broached in the study undertaken.

Voltaire's *History of Charles XII* (1731), *The Age of Louis XIV* (1751), *Essay on the Customs and the Spirit of Nations* (1756), *Annals of the Empire* (1756), *History of Russia Under Peter the Great* (1759), *Handbook of the Century of Louis XV* (1768), and *The History of the Parliament of Paris* (1769) stand out as remarkable examples of this Deist/Pyrrhonist/empiricist historian. For a better appreciation of Voltaire's immense contribution to the field of history, and for the sake of comparison between his method and that of past historians, there follows a very brief excursus on the treatment and evolution of this discipline.

Have People Always Felt Compelled to Record History?

In one way or another, societies have always felt a deep-seated need to record their past, in an effort to fix their beginnings and trace their course through the ages. To do so must have filled—and still does—an urgent psychological need to give structure, continuity, purpose, and order to people's lives, along with the belief, erroneous or not, that such documentation instills a sense of hope in some distant future. To this end, religious/historical tracts such as the Bible, the Rig Veda, the Kojiki, the Koran, the Book of the Dead, the Annals of Lu, and the Shu Ching, and epics such as Gilgamesh, the Odyssey, the Mahabharata, and the Song of Roland provided ancients and moderns with both a memory and an identity. The story of how each nation or race came into being and the manner in which individual and collective societies developed the rudiments of their cultures and their complex natures assumed and conveyed value and importance.

The epithet "Father of History" was awarded to Herodotus (480–425 B.C.E.), who recorded in detail the struggles between Persia and Greece. Rather than rely exclusively on myth and legends for answers to the mysteries of the past, he documented his work rationally as far as possible, applying logic and empirical knowledge to underscore significant events and research their causes and motivations, applying logic and empirical knowledge. Although centuries separated Herodotus from Voltaire, both men relied on written records and on interviews with alleged witnesses to the specific happenings under scrutiny, and, at times, they even based their arguments on hearsay.

Thucydides (460–400 B.C.E.) limited himself to notions of state and military conflict in his *Peloponnesian Wars,* endeavoring, like Voltaire, to structure his work in as factual and chronological a manner as possible, even while trying to draw sober lessons from the dramatic series of events he was relating.

Parallels are also in order between Voltaire's historical writings and those of Xenophon (430–355 B.C.E.). Moving, but also didactic, the latter's *Anabasis* is the account of his command of 10,000 Greeks who made their way under pain, suffering, and duress through Persian territory to the Black Sea. An intensely dramatic moment is described by Xenophon when his men cry out *"Thalassa! Thalassa!* (Water! Water!)" upon first seeing their beloved Greek sea. Similarly, Voltaire emphasized emotionally charged situations, drawing moral lessons from them in his historical narratives.

Subsequent historians, historiographers, and chroniclers are innumerable. Some subverted facts to fit their inclinations and religious zeal; others—such as Caesar, Tacitus, Josephus, St. Augustine, Saxo Grammaticus, Gregory of Tours, "The Venerable Beede," Procopius, Ibn

Khaldun, Villehardouin, Froissart, Joinville, and Commynes—based their accounts of events on relatively solid documentation.

With the revival of classical learning during the Renaissance and the onset of humanism, greater emphasis was placed on textual judgments and judicial methods of documentation, as evidenced in the works of Machiavelli, Marsilius of Padua, and others. Critical techniques were also applied by such theorists as Bodin (*Six Books of the Republic*, 1576), a major contributor to the notion of the modern nation-state. The Benedictine monk Mabillon also made a name for himself. Author of *De Re Diplomatica* (1681), he was looked upon not only as the creator of the science of diplomatics, but as the one who had almost single-handedly developed a critical method of determining the authenticity of documents, thereby placing historiography on a scientific level. Others, like the French archbishop Bossuet, began with the biblical Creation in his recording of facts in his monumental *Discourse on Universal History* (1681). Thus he determined the course of history not as the outcome of human acts, but as the outcome of Providence—based on literal readings of the Scriptures.

Examples of religious bias, distortions of fact, or simply overenergetic imaginations may be seen in the works of other seventeenth-century historians. Father Vichard de Saint-Réal, for example, was either unaware of facts or frequently altered them for the sake of psychological and dramatic effect. Even François Eudes de Mézeray and Father Gabriel Daniel, considered by some to have furthered the cause of humanist historiography, accorded too much trust to myths, miracles, and fabrication in their endeavor to entertain their readers.[1] It has been reported that historians such as Father Daniel, who had always encouraged historical research and accuracy in others, swerved sharply from his intended goal the day he was presented with "eleven or twelve hundred volumes of original documents and manuscripts at the King's Library." After glancing at them for "an hour," he left, informing Father Tournemine "that all those documents were just so much useless paper, of no value to him in writing his history" (Lanson, 95).

Pierre Bayle's *Critical and Historical Dictionary* (1697) proved instead to be a monumental compendium of facts designed to appeal to skeptics and to forward religious liberty. Attacking dogma by resorting to logic, revealing contradictions in the Scriptures themselves, and exploring the validity of sources, Bayle went far in achieving his goal. Although Voltaire was critical of his style and his extensive use of anecdotes, he owed much of his historical Pyrrhonism and critical understanding of the Bible to him (Brumfitt, 33).

Fénelon's *Adventures of Telemachus, Son of Ulysses* (1699), although not history in the true sense of the word, both explored and criticized social and educational institutions in a type of presocial primitivistic Golden Age. Fontenelle, the author of *The Origin of Fables* (1724) and *History of Oracles* (1686), applied historical data in his very modern approach to the study of comparative religion. Attacking belief in oracular pronouncements and superstition, he suggested that historians would do well to study the "history of the human mind." With Montesquieu's *Considerations on the Grandeur and Decadence of the Romans* (1734), which focuses on explaining the rise and fall of the Roman Empire in terms of human motivations rather than of divine intervention, "Enlightenment historiography becomes a reality" (Brumfitt, 4).

Voltaire's Historical Thrust

Ironically, Voltaire's godfather, the abbé Châteauneuf, a disparager of miracles despite his adherence to a religious order, had been responsible for the young man's introduction into the debaucheries of the libertine (freethinker) Société du Temple (Brumfitt, 6). Regent Philippe d'Orléans, and other frequenters of this group, made it possible for the young Voltaire not only to meet people of note, but to experience history in the making as well.

Voltaire's epic poem *The Henriade* (see chapter 3) marked his entry into the field of history. An enemy of all wars, Voltaire pointed up the bloody massacres that had taken place between Catholics and Protestants throughout the sixteenth century, and the subtle persecution of the latter that continued thereafter.

The research required to write *The Henriade* not only broadened Voltaire's knowledge of the subject but also catalyzed his interest in what was to become for him the science and art of social history. Although the primary sources for his histories were books, correspondence, and archival material, whenever possible these were supplemented by firsthand interviews. In 1722, for example, Voltaire visited the distinguished politician Lord Bolingbroke, who was living in exile in France at the time. The sweep of this Englishman's understanding of ancient and modern events so deeply impressed Voltaire that he may have sought (perhaps) unconsciously to emulate him in the field of history.

Although facts and figures concerning specific events were crucially important to Voltaire, what motivated him most profoundly in the writing of history was his need to discover the mysterious factor or factors that compelled certain people to violence and cruelty, or to their opposites, kindness and compassion. To search out the *human* element, as previously noted, remained of primordial interest to Voltaire, the *moralist*.

To this end, he pointed out the errors and/or accomplishments of heads of state, philosophers, religious leaders, creative people in general, and other luminaries. Prompt to praise achievers who remedied certain noxious empirical situations, he was equally denigrating of diminishers and destroyers of society. In this sense, Voltaire was an optimist, at least as a young man. Although he became increasingly pessimistic with the passing of years, he never ceased believing that if the wise occupied positions of power, human suffering would be mitigated.

According to Voltaire, the historian (albeit not a ruler) occupied a position of power, and, as previously mentioned, had a moral obligation to his readers. By presenting the facts of a monarch's reign as objectively as possible, by revealing the salient personality traits of important contiguous figures, detailing their actions and the events in which they participated, to find their causes and effects, the historian could be instrumental in curbing humankind's propensity for evil—playing a significant role in teaching future generations how to avoid war.

As Gustave Lanson pointed out, Voltaire was the "first historian of civilization." To this end, he was determined to understand what lay behind an act—a monarch's intent to make war or to subsidize creative endeavors, for example—to ferret out the values leading to the flourishing or declining of the cultures under scrutiny (Lanson, 100).

Let us note that the life of a historian in eighteenth-century France was not without its dangers. The fear of imprisonment by government officials, of excommunication by the Catholic Church, or of the inability to sustain oneself economically was an ever-present reality. All three possibilities always loomed during Voltaire's life, as author of, inter alia, *The History of Charles XII* (1731), *The Age of Louis XIV* (1751), and *Essay on the Customs and the Spirit of Nations* (1756).

The History of Charles XII (1731)

Voltaire's fascination with Charles XII, king of Sweden, had been kindled in part by his meeting with the Swedish foreign minister, Baron Goertz, in 1717. Ten years later he was introduced to Baron Fabrice, former Holstein envoy to Charles XII during the monarch's captivity in Turkey—a meeting that allegedly sparked his undertaking of *The History of Charles XII* (1731) (Brumfitt, 8).

Voltaire's empirical and moralistic approach as recorder of past events stressed the folly of war. What factors, for example, had driven an intelligent, handsome, winsome, but wild young man such as Charles XII (1682–1718) to spend his short life indulging in hostilities just to satisfy his passion for the glories of battle?

Since history was a learning vehicle for the young historian, Voltaire sought to determine a line of conduct that leads with few exceptions to devastation, drawing on the example of Charles XII. "No king, surely, can be so incorrigible as, when he reads the *History of Charles XII,* not be cured of the vain ambition of making conquests."[2] To this end, rather than focus on the distant past, Voltaire's first historical work dealt with the life of a contemporary monarch. Kings and potentates, he contended, must be taught not to yield to "the folly of conquest," but rather to encourage the spirit of enlightenment to prevail over that of heroic glory. "The princes who have the best claim to immortality are such as have benefited mankind" (*Charles XII,* 20:5).

Voltaire's *History of Charles XII* also proved to the world that history did not have to be dull, arid, and soporific, as was H. P. Limiers's *History of Sweden Under the Reign of Charles XII* (1720). It could be dramatic, exciting, and adventurous, involving readers in the facts at stake, while also educating and encouraging them to create for themselves virtuous rules of conduct. Voltaire's *History of Charles XII,* which reads as historical biography, continues even today to yield thrilling accounts of what could have been a fruitful and pleasurable existence but turned tragic instead.

Comparative in intent and humanistic in approach, the plot of *Charles XII* revolves around an exceptional young man who, like many heroes of old, suffered from hubris that led to his undoing. Constructed in the manner of a classical French tragedy, this lucidly drawn work has an exposition, an agon, and a conclusion. Because Voltaire's concept of historical writing was that it should be entertaining and exciting, he highlighted the suspense factor in its interaction with topography, geography, climate, and the political makeup of the lands—Finland, Poland, Russia, and Turkey—that his protagonist traversed during the course of his battles.

Setting the Stage

Voltaire's incursions into Charles's character traits, as well as his country's climate, demography, and government, provided the necessary background for the powerful events to come.

What were the strengths and weaknesses of Charles XII? His positive
outlook, his industrious temperament, his certainty of his own judgments, in addition to his physical and moral strength, enabled him to
withstand the rigors of Sweden's nine-month-long winter. Mind over
matter was his guide. He forced himself to learn to face and then to
challenge and finally to overcome the severities of the Swedish climate.
The sun, Voltaire intimated, played a significant role in helping him
accomplish his goals. The reflections of its blind radiance, Voltaire
asserted, like so many prismatic crystals covering the seemingly endless
whiteness of an ice-covered landscape, compensated for what may have
impacted on Charles as the eerie grimness of life, and served to energize
his being. However, Voltaire may have wondered, did such blind radiance ironically obscure the dangers implicit in his behavioral extremes?
(*Charles XII*, 20:11.)

Demography and governmental institutions were also important factors in building the king's temperament. The former, as Voltaire noted,
reflected Swedish desire to deal overtly with reality: in keeping with the
land's sterility, and by implication the population's poverty, births were
wisely limited. With regard to governmental institutions, Voltaire suggested, the Swedes, as people of a "republic," were by nature relatively
optimistic. In this respect they resembled the English, who lived under
an enlightened monarchy. Unlike the French and the Spanish, who lived
in fear under the rule of absolute monarchs, the Swedes had been granted
basic freedoms that inspired them with a sense of their own worth and
responsibility to others and to the state. No laws could be promulgated
in Sweden without the permission of the Senate, which was dependent on
the Estates Generals, a representative political body that met frequently.
Nonetheless, noted Voltaire, such a modus vivendi had not been achieved
without civil strife and external wars against Denmark and Poland. Having succeeded in shedding foreign political domination, the Swedes were
left free to embrace Lutheranism, but their survival necessitated continuous vigilance and constant readiness to overcome the endless difficulties
posed by daily life and the rigidity of their climate.

Testing the Hero

Upon Charles XII's accession to the throne, Voltaire assessed him as follows: "the most extraordinary man, perhaps, that ever appeared in the
world. In him were united all the great qualities of his ancestors; nor
had he any other fault or failing, but that he possessed all these virtues

in too high a degree" (*Charles XII*, 20:19). Strength, discipline, vigor—all fine character traits when tempered by moderation—were transformed by the Swedish ruler into agents of destruction.

Intelligent, quick to learn, and endowed with an iron will, as evidenced in his studies in Latin and German, Charles mastered whatever skill he undertook to acquire. Demonstrating courage and determination in the physical domain, he became an excellent horseman at the age of seven and an outstanding athlete in his teens. His arduous, self-imposed daily exercise routine, consisting of lengthy violent exercises, made him a proficient practitioner of martial arts.

Just as his powerful mind-set filled him with stamina, so he fixated on an imagined ideal—that of fame and conquest. His goal was to become a second Alexander the Great. When a court dignitary informed him that the Macedonian hero had lived only 32 years, Charles responded, "Ah! is not that enough, when one has conquered kingdoms?" He was resolute in his desire to be indomitable, "his unconquerable spirit would frequently discover some traces of those heroic qualities which characterize great souls," Voltaire noted, pointing out that the unrelenting fire that had blazed within him since his earliest years would continue to blaze throughout his life (*Charles XII*, 20:31).

Charles's independence of mind and spirit became all the more overt following his mother's death in his 11th year. Allegedly her health had waned as a result of her husband's cruel treatment of both her and the Swedish people, with whom she had always felt great affinity and toward whom she showed great compassion. For example, not long before her death, she begged her husband to relieve his subjects of the exorbitant and cruelly burdensome taxes he had levied on them. He replied: "Madam, we took you to bear children, and not to give advice" (*Charles XII*, 20:21). Charles's despotic father died in 1697, four years after his mother's demise. Judging the 15-year-old lad too young to rule Sweden, government officials appointed his grandmother regent. Charles, however, determined otherwise. Feeling confidence in his own talents and declaring himself physically and intellectually equipped, he assumed the kingship of his land with the approval of the Swedish people. During the coronation ceremony, just after the archbishop of Uppsala had anointed the prince and was about to place the crown on his head, Charles snatched it from him and crowned himself (*Charles XII*, 20:25). This overtly aggressive act, revealing the young king's inner strength and self-assurance, would be replicated nearly a century later by another military hero, Napoléon Bonaparte.

The first years of Charles's reign were neither eventful nor revelatory of any "dangerous passion" on his part. (*Charles XII*, 20:25). Three unexpected political events, however, forced out some of the Swedish monarch's "hidden talents." In conspiration, Frederick IV, king of Denmark; Augustus, king of Poland; and Czar Peter the Great of Russia— intent upon taking advantage of Charles's youth and his lack of experience—joined against him militarily. Detailing the reasons for the outbreak of the wars that followed, Voltaire concentrated especially upon Peter the Great, whose reputation loomed formidable after his stunning victory over the Turks in 1697.

To acquaint the reader with Peter's genius—his vision of what Russia could be—and his powerful drive to alter the status quo, Voltaire sketched in the facts underlying the regressive, ignorant, superstitious, and barbaric conditions existing in eighteenth-century Russia. To equip himself to rule such a vast empire, which included not only an extensive land mass but a variety of ethnic groups, Peter decided to spend two years abroad educating himself. In Holland he worked incognito as a carpenter and learned mathematics, navigation, and the art of planning and building fortifications, as well as other disciplines. His priority during a stay in England was to familiarize himself with the science of shipbuilding. His achievements bore fruit upon his return to Russia. He began building not only what was to become the city of Petersburg, but ports and a fleet, thus encouraging international trade. He transformed his medieval army into a fine fighting force and established colleges, academies, printing presses, libraries, engineering schools, and other institutions. Because the Russian Orthodox Church was so firmly ensconced in his land, he found it virtually impossible to wipe out superstition. But by declaring himself head of state as well as of this religious body, he did make some slight headway in diminishing its stranglehold on the people.

Voltaire the empiricist intruded into his narrative, as he was wont to do, noting that despite all of Peter's reforms, he had flagrantly omitted the installation of "virtue and humanity." The czar's brutal, ferocious, and barbaric revenge tactics reached new highs on those occasions when he executed his own sentences by killing the criminals with his bare hands. On one of these occasions, Voltaire added, Peter allegedly went so far as to display his talents by cutting heads at the table.

Voltaire's detailed excurses into Peter's and Charles's backgrounds set the stage for his descriptions of the rise of the former's great nation and the demise of the latter's.

The Tragic Hero: The Fatal Flaw

In keeping with Aristotle's definition of the tragic hero, so Charles XII suffered from a fatal flaw: his lust for war—"his vain ambition to make conquests" (*Charles XII*, 20:8). He envisaged himself as triumphant, advancing no other possibility. He was unable to assess his acts and penchants objectively. His so-called integrity, courage, and purpose, although remarkable on one level, were tinged with uncontrollability, impulsivity, and even ruthlessness.

Heads of state and people in power, as previously mentioned, have a responsibility to their contemporaries as well as to future generations. Their rulership must instill the highest virtues and ideals in their citizens, namely, tolerance, compassion, and understanding.

True to his archetypal nature, Charles frequently made spur-of-the-moment decisions that were not always to his or his country's best interests. On one occasion, he discarded as valueless the concerns voiced by his government officials over their ruler's lack of experience in matters of war. How could he, they questioned, fill the giant maw in the kingdom following the recent demise of the great Swedish generals? Rising to the occasion, Charles noted with gusto: "Gentlemen, I am resolved never to begin an unjust war, nor ever to finish a just one but by the destruction of my enemies. My resolution is fixed. I will attack the first that shall declare war against me; and, after having conquered him, I hope I shall be able to strike terror into the rest" (*Charles XII*, 20:45).

Voltaire noted that within the space of only a few months after Charles had claimed the kingship for himself, the monarch underwent a severe personality change. Or was this seeming alteration of some of his behavioral patterns merely an exteriorization of a latent idée fixe—that burning ardor nascent within him that had suddenly gotten out of hand? Ready to overcome all obstacles, physical, emotional, or governmental, Charles focused his energies for the months to come exclusively on soldiering. Determined to lead the life of a religious ascetic, he banished all pleasures and all luxuries from his daily routine. Endurance tests of every type, including the most taxing of physical exercises, were practiced by him not only to strengthen himself to the extreme, but—like the *sol invictus*—to inspire his soldiers to do likewise. As a role model to the foot soldier, he was looked upon as an ideal, a kind of divinity figure, to be emulated in every way.

Voltaire's step-by-step depiction of Charles's political maneuverings, his military preparations and tactics on land and on sea, is highly impressive. Readers are informed, for example, prior to the Swedish king's departure for war, how he methodically put government matters in order. Then Voltaire, with his usual flair for the dramatic, introduces an ominous note into the narrative, indicating prophetically that when Charles set out on his first military campaign on May 8, 1700, *he left Stockholm never to return* (*Charles XII*, 20:48).

Today's military tacticians might find Voltaire's discussions of the Swedish monarch's military strategies interesting and even useful. But in Voltaire's day, the author's expatiations in such swift succession read like a popular thriller. After concluding a war against the Danes in six weeks and mastering Poland shortly thereafter, Charles was offered the latter's kingship. Although tempted to accept at first, he declined the honor, for "glory was his idol" and not politics (*Charles XII*, 20:101). Charles's military skill and his deployment of troops as adumbrated panoramically and colorfully by Voltaire, was visually exciting and suspenseful. The young king met the greatest of all challenges—the czar's army of 80,000 soldiers at the Battle of Narva—by defeating his enemy, thanks to his judicious maneuverings and the stoutheartedness of his 20,000 men.

Hubris

Not only did Charles prove himself to be a magnificent hero, emulating his model, Alexander the Great, to the letter; he also demonstrated his statesmanship, or so he rationalized, claiming that he made war only to work for peace. If this were so, Voltaire intimated, than why did he pursue further battles against Peter?

As a military visionary, Charles not only measured up to Peter, but surpassed him. Weighing heavily in the Swedish king's favor was his great humanity, at least with regard to his soldiers, and his consideration for people in general. To these qualities, Voltaire opposed the czar's misguided brutality, adding, however, that Peter's plans for the future of his country were far more inclusive and positive than the Swedish king's single-mindedness could possibly be.

In September 1707, Charles's army of 43,000 men, in addition to 10,000 en route from Poland and 15,000 from Finland, with new recruits and the best of generals, was ready for immediate attack. The king's humanity toward each man encouraged him to provide the group with extra food and equipment during the arduous winter. As a superb military strategist, he supplied them with the tools necessary to cut down large sections of the thickly forested areas through which they had to pass. Voltaire, unequaled as a storyteller, peppers his narrative with deceptive interjections, such as the following, designed to keep the reader in a state of suspense: "With all these forces it was not doubted but that he would easily dethrone the czar" (*Charles XII*, 20:149). Nor do Voltaire's continuous warnings about the monarch's strong-headedness diminish the reader's anticipation of the outcome of the hostilities. Having won so many battles, Voltaire suggests, Charles XII had grown overly confident. Even more dangerously, he had left unheeded the advice of his most trusted generals: to retrench until reinforcements arrived.

The battle began. Months dragged on. Resources ran low. Charles's army was reduced to eating small chunks of moldy bread, and what had once been a mighty fighting force was now depleted to 18,000. Nevertheless, Charles persisted, reaching Poltava (the eastern part of Ukraine), where his men laid siege. Despite the excruciating pain he suffered from an enemy's carbine shot, "which pierced his boot and shattered the bone of his heel," his determination to transcend his pain was such that no one could have guessed from his countenance that he had been wounded. One of his servants, noting blood on the sole of his boot, called a surgeon, whose opinion was that amputation was the only remedy. Another surgeon, however, with greater skill and courage, stated that "by making deep incisions he would save the king's leg." The king ordered him to do so: "cut boldly, and fear nothing." Charles held his own leg "with both hands, and beheld the incisions that were made in it, as if the operation had been performed upon another" so great was his control over pain (*Charles XII*, 20:170).

In the days to follow, not only did inordinate pain plague him, but infection and high fever also set in. Nonetheless, Charles ordered the assault on the czar's army at Poltava on July 8, 1709. Voltaire noted succinctly that Charles, who had battled victoriously for glory and for peace for the preceding nine years, now could be alluded to as a combination of Alexander the Great and Don Quixote.

Having lost the battle at Poltava, Charles XII fled to Bender in Turkey, where the Ottomans gave him permission to reside. One might have thought that Charles had learned from experience, Voltaire inferred. On the contrary, once his wounds had healed, he again returned to his routine of violent exercise. Instead of assessing the long-range effects of his great loss at Poltava and the growing power of Peter the Great, Charles remained adamant in pursuing his cause. Nor did he return to Sweden. Plotting and planning ways of arming some Ottoman troops to fight a war with the goal of dethroning Peter, he became a persona non grata and was asked to leave Turkey. Had he foreseen the possibility of his own expulsion, Voltaire questioned? Probably so, since he had had a special house, designed to withstand attacks from the outside, constructed on the property where he lived. He must have known, however, that it was only a matter of time before the Turks would attack him in his so-called impregnable stronghold. How could he and his 40 domestics ever hope to battle an army? Charles and his enclave were taken on February 12, 1713, and treated henceforth like prisoners. Still unaware of the impact of his rash—or illogical—acts, Charles was transferred to Démirtash, where he further indulged in intrigues, among these fostering harem revolts. After more upheavals, the monarch was allowed—indeed, encouraged—to return to his homeland.

Instead of trying to alleviate the plight of his economically distressed people and accepting the reconciliation attempts offered by the czar, Charles crossed the Baltic Sea and besieged Frederikshall in Norway. During this skirmish he was accidentally hit in the right temple by a cannonball weighing half a pound. He died instantly.

To underscore his own antiwar attitude, Voltaire added that Charles's favorite French tragedy was, understandably, Racine's *Mithridates*. Like the Swedish king, its hero declared vengeance on his enemies, the Romans; fought valiantly his whole life—and maybe virtuously, depending upon the reader's point of view; and died in the process. The affinity between the two monarchs could not have been clearer or better stated.

Voltaire's fate following the publication of his *History of Charles XII* was not altogether happy. Although he had underscored the insanity that drove an intelligent, fearless, and sincere king to the killing fields, he had also emphasized the importance of holding monarchs accountable for their acts—an idea that French government officials did not take to kindly. Finding excuses for their negative response to Voltaire's volume, they claimed that its publication would harm their foreign relations with Sweden. The aftermath? Voltaire's *History of Charles XII* was seized almost immediately, explaining perhaps, at least in part, its instant success!

Never one to rest on his laurels, and always eager to add to his knowledge, Voltaire increased the scope of each forthcoming edition of *The History of Charles XII,* attempting to address and rectify some of the negative but at times judicious criticisms received. Some reviewers, for example, accused him of not having fleshed out the personalities of his protagonists in depth, of having relied too heavily on anecdotal material to spawn excitement, and of having passed supererogatory judgments on the hero's actions.

The dramatist in Voltaire had done his utmost in this, his earliest excursion into a relatively new discipline, to flesh out the warrior-hero type by contrasting him with his invincible enemy, Peter the Great. He also utilized scenically descriptive and poetic passages, which lend his work a distinctly Romanesque quality that perhaps belies the rigor of his research.[3]

Voltaire's approach to history henceforth became more and more socially oriented. Always on the alert for new information, but ever more wary of tall stories—miraculous or fantastic events narrated by dubious informants—Voltaire, under Bayle's influence, attempted even more forcefully than his predecessor to establish new scientific criteria by which to verify the accuracy of any material offered him (Brumfitt, 34).

Contention, disagreement, and opposing views with regard to historical narration had taught Voltaire never to abandon his Pyrrhonistic, empirical, and critical outlook. His growing awareness of the multisidedness and relative nature of questions relating to history and its social, political, religious, and other institutions increased with each successive volume.

The Age of Louis XIV (1751, 1768)

Voltaire's appointment as royal historiographer in 1745, giving him access to stores of invaluable documents, incited him to complete during his stay in Prussia his monumental *The Age of Louis XIV* (1751), which he had first begun in 1732. Unlike *Charles XII,* Voltaire's new work did not simply depict the life of a seventeenth-century monarch; it encompassed an age. It did not merely render an account of the rule of the Sun King at Versailles; it portrayed his active participation in bringing forth "the spirit of men in the most enlightened age the world has ever seen."[4]

The seventeenth century, or age of Louis XIV, was regarded by Voltaire—and "the thinking man" in general—as one of the four great periods of history. The others were the Golden Age of Pericles, Demosthenes, Aristotle, Plato, Phidias, Praxiteles, Philip of Macedon, and Alexander; that of Caesar and Augustus; and that of the Italian Renaissance. The age of Louis XIV very nearly spelled perfection because, "enriched by the discoveries of the other three, it accomplished in certain departments more than the three together," inasmuch as "human reason was brought to perfection" (*Louis XIV,* 2).

The Age of Louis XIV, with its resurrection and synthesis of both the achievements and the weaknesses of seventeenth-century France, has been alluded to as "a great historical work, one that still has considerable significance in our day since its views and interpretations continue to be discussed and debated by present-day historians" (Lanson, 97). With *The Age of Louis XIV,* Voltaire the philosopher, the reasoner, the doubter, the analyst, and the moralist had grown into the historian of the human spirit. To A. M. Thieriot he wrote around July 15, 1735:

> Of those who have commanded battalions and squadrons, only the names remain. The human race has nothing to show for a hundred battles that have been waged. But the great men I speak to you about have prepared pure and lasting *pleasures* for men yet to be born. A canal lock uniting two seas, a painting by Poussin, a beautiful tragedy, a newly discovered truth—these are things a thousand times more precious than all the annals of the court or all the accounts of military campaigns. You know that, with me, great men come first and heroes last.
>
>   *I call great men all those who have excelled in creating what is useful or agreeable.* The plunderers of the provinces are merely heroes. (Lanson, 101; see also *Correspondence,* 575)

The Age of Louis XIV went beyond the dramatic and scenic dimensions of *Charles XII.* The quantity and quality as well as the methodicalness of Voltaire's research of archival material revealed a giant step forward in his meditations as historian. His information was drawn from the usual impersonal sources—books, documents, correspondence—but also from direct and personal references, which gave another twist to events. He drew a variety of insights from survivors of the great reign, and among these were the libertines who had frequented the Société du Temple, as well as those who had been involved in the War of the Spanish Succession, the Revocation of the Edict of Nantes, the Thirty Years' War, the two Frondes, and the Cévennes revolt. From his informants he not only collected anecdotal material and memoirs that could cast light on political and religious personalities, but he gained access as well to certain significant papers. Nonetheless, he lacked the modern tools necessary to carry out extensive research work and therefore could not cull a great deal of new information. The selections he did introduce to his readers, however, were marked by a variety of perceptions into his panoramic vision of the period and pointed up his main thesis: the uniqueness of seventeenth-century France.

Ironically Voltaire, who despised war, often depicted military confrontations with such fervor that readers, rather than assessing them negatively, were caught up in their excitement. He underscored injustices perpetrated by fanatics and bigots, no matter the religious denomination. When appropriate in *The Age of Louis XIV,* as polemicist, propagandist, social historian, and promulgator of justice as he saw it, he overtly questioned, doubted, and thought through difficult, frequently imponderable, situations. Innovative as well were the associations he made between political events and specific French social and economic contingencies.

Perhaps the finest assessment of Voltaire's *The Age of Louis XIV* was proffered by Gustave Lanson.

> The work unfolded on successive theatrical levels. After the grandiose proscenium depicting victories and conquests, there appeared the person of the king, the life and manners of the court, the refinement of the nobility, and the inner workings of the government, its useful institutions, and its ecclesiastical affairs. Finally, like a magnificent stage backdrop, there was the marvelous decor of arts, letters, and science, representing the outstanding achievement and superiority of seventeenth-century French civilization. The *Siècle* was planned and arranged as an apotheosis of the human spirit. (Lanson, 100)

The International Flavor of *The Age of Louis XIV*

Voltaire injects an international flavor into his historical incursions by guiding his readers through Germany, Spain, Portugal, the Low Countries, Italy, England, Denmark, Poland, Russia, Turkey, and other countries with which France was involved prior to and during the Sun King's rule. By delving into the character traits of the monarch as well as those of his ministers, Voltaire shed light on the reasons behind some of his artistic appointments and diplomatic, political, and economic ventures.

Voltaire played up the problematics of Louis XIV's minority years, when his mother, Anne of Austria, was regent (1643–1661) and Cardinal Mazarin her closest adviser. Describing those times as riddled with melodramatic intrigue and dangerous military ventures—the Thirty Years' War and two civil wars known as the Fronde—Voltaire made it clear why France was left exhausted and economically drained. Only after the death of Mazarin, in 1661, did Louis XIV assume the kingship and masterfully govern his kingdom.

A gallery of Voltairean verbal portraits injected a livingness into his work: Jean-Baptiste Colbert, Mme Françoise d'Aubigné de Maintenon, Louise de La Vallière, Nicolas Fouquet, Mme Françoise Athenaïs de Montespan, Henri de La Tour d'Auvergne Turenne, Catherine Deshayes La Voisin, to mention but a few that highlight the roster, marked their presences as instrumental in bringing about this rich and complex age.

Voltaire's Understanding of Louis XIV's Temperament

When Louis XIV came into his majority, his increasing confidence in his talents for rulership was seemingly evident. He gave the impression not only of being intelligent, perceptive, charming, and majestic in gait and appearance, but of being an aficionado of etiquette and endowed as well with a solid understanding of human nature.

One of the Sun King's earliest acts—the creation of specialized ministries with limited powers, answerable to him alone, revealed his insights into both people and rulership. Michel Le Tellier Louvois, who was appointed minister of war, for example, laid the foundations of France's military greatness. The monarch's nomination of Colbert, who favored protectionism, led to the growth of France's industry, commerce, and manufacturing. An indefatigable worker, Colbert, whom Voltaire admired, was also responsible for the reorganization of France's finances, for its judiciary, and for its navy. Colbert's encouragement of the arts—structural, pictorial, dramatic, philosophic, or landscape architecture—was crucial, Voltaire maintained, for the spread of culture and the spirit of enlightenment in France.

Nor did Voltaire omit the king's downside: his fascination with war, despite Colbert's tightfistedness. Louis XIV's military incursions into the Franche-Comté, his conquest of Flanders and Holland, the War of the Spanish Succession, and other battles left his treasury depleted. The monarch's inability to stem religious quarrels led to rampant acts of cruelty, but the worst was the "disgraceful" revocation of the Edict of Nantes (1685). The rise in persecution of Protestants accounted for the unfortunate departure from France of many merchants, traders, businesspeople, and skilled artisans, which left the nation economically distressed with famines, particularly the great one occurring in 1709. Tragic as well was the persecution of the Jansenists by the Jesuits, and the king's favoring of Gallicanism, which activated controversies with the various popes (1673–1693) until the monarch finally abandoned his position on the subject.

Devastating to France's finances as well was the king's love of luxury. Nevertheless, although many blamed the king for his extravagance not only in war but with regard to his building projects, Voltaire maintained that "luxury" itself serves a purpose in the long run: by motivating industry, it activates prosperity.

Louis XIV:
A Commanding Presence in the Arts and Sciences

There is no doubt in this reader's mind that the most fascinating and informative sections of Voltaire's *Age of Louis XIV* are devoted to his assessments of and reactions to the arts. While failing to give the Middle Ages and the Renaissance their due—both periods having made "little progress" in "the arts which do not solely depend upon the intellect"— Voltaire's approach to the seventeenth century was dithyrambic (*Louis XIV*, 372).

Governmental funds were spent on the erection of architectural wonders and the lavish gardens surrounding some of these: the Trianon, the Louvre, the Invalides, the Observatory, and the academies of sciences, of painting, and of architecture. As protector of multiple academies, including the famed French Academy still in existence today, Louis XIV was instrumental in French virtually becoming the universal language (see the following for the arts in general). Voltaire vaunted France's composers, musicians, painters, sculptors, and architects: Lulli, Rameau, Quinault, Poussin, Lebrun, Perrault, Mansart, and others too numerous to mention.

Regarding the theater, Voltaire pointed to Corneille as the originator of modern drama and of classical language, and to his *Le Cid,* which Cardinal Richelieu attempted to defame. Nonetheless, Voltaire gave preference to Racine's dramas for the passion, intelligence, and poetics he injected into his protagonists, but mainly for the playwright's understanding of the human heart. He considered *Athalie* Racine's masterpiece, despite the opinion of Mme de Sévigné, who, he added ironically, "had no rival in the sprightly recounting of trifles, [and] always thought that Racine *would not go far*" (*Louis XIV,* 366). But then, he further noted, her judgments of Racine were as significant as her pronouncements on coffee, which she deemed to be a mere passing fancy. As for Molière, he was not only master of the comic vein, but one of the greats in pointing up the "affectations of the *précieuses,*" and "the pedantry of the *femmes savantes,* and the robe and Latin jargon of the doctors" who sought to impress their listeners by injecting sequences of Latin words throughout their deadly discourses (*Louis XIV,* 366).

In the literary, historical, and philosophical fields, Voltaire pointed to Fénelon's *Telemachus,* praising this part novel, part poem for its morally positive point of view. The brilliant eloquence of Bossuet's *Funeral Orations* and the linguistic power of his *Discourse on Universal History* were accorded praise. Boileau was well thought of as a didactic poet; while La Fontaine, strangely enough, was denigrated for his archaic language. Although no mention was made of Pascal's *Thoughts,* his *Provincial Letters* received high praise as a work of art. Mitigated accolades went to La Bruyère's short, pithy characterizations and his new use of language. Encomiums were given to Fontenelle's *Plurality of Worlds* for its forays into outer space. Bayle's *Dictionary,* so admired by Voltaire, was "the first work of its kind which [teaches] one how to think" (*Louis XIV,* 363).

Whereas in his *Philosophical Letters* he detailed the concepts of Locke, Newton, Bacon, and Galileo, among others, Voltaire offered a general paucity of scientific explanations in *The Age of Louis XIV.* The achievements of such pathfinders as Torricelli, Huyghens, Roemer, and Cassini, for example, were skimmed over. He proved to be more broad-minded when it came to exploring his disagreements with Descartes's beliefs. Although lauding him as a geometrician, he added that "geometry leaves the mind where it finds it. Descartes's geometry was too much given to flights of fancy. He who was the foremost among mathematicians wrote scarcely anything else but philosophic romances." Voltaire denigrated him not only for "disdaining" the experimental method, but for failing to mention Galileo in his writings. Descartes, "who thought to build without materials, could erect but an imaginary structure" (*Louis XIV,* 353).

Nor did Voltaire spare his readers juicy gossip about Louis XIV's mistresses. Although he did gloss over the lavish feasts, parties, and dances of the era, he saw fit to mention La Voisin, the poisoner, who, together with her brother, a priest, and others, sold a special poison—*poudre à succession*—to those who sought to rid themselves of rivals standing in the way of their rise to fame and fortune (*Louis XIV,* 288).

Religious Matters

Disenchanted by the continuous battles between religious sects, and seeking "to crush the infamous" [the church] at every occasion, Voltaire added several chapters on infamous clerical cases to his 1768 edition of

The Age of Louis XIV. Rather than disparage the Roman Catholic Church for instigating antagonisms between religious sects, he avoided discussing theological questions, preferring to focus on the material acquisitiveness of the Church per se and the resultant evils. Substantiating every statement with appropriate facts, Voltaire criticized the clerics for docilely carrying out the Church hierarchy's orders, accusing those in charge of abusing their power by using it as a social vehicle to promote injustice, partisanship, and bigotry.

Sections devoted to Jansenism, Gallicanism, Protestantism Quietism, Calvinism, and their disputations and controversies, were all noteworthy for the light they shed on questions of faith, persecution, intolerance, and the manner in which minority sects were treated during the "great age" of the Sun King.

The Proscription of Missionaries in China

The last section of *The Age of Louis XIV,* entitled "Disputes on Chinese Ceremonies," introduced a spirit of levity and irony into the description of the frequently cruel and fanatical behavioral patterns of missionaries whose purpose was to convert the Chinese "heathen."

Stylistically reminiscent at times of Voltaire's dramatically oriented philosophical tales (see chapter 6), the "Disputes" section makes readers privy to the thoughts of sage Chinese emperors, Kanghi (d. 1724), a lover of European arts, and Youngtching, a monarch who seemed open to new ideas—that is, to reason tempered with humanity. After granting audiences to the Dominican and Jesuit missionaries (who themselves were in the midst of heated disputes over whether the Chinese were religious "idolators" or not), the emperor listened patiently to their ideas. So filled with venom, guile, and hostility were the missionaries toward each other as well as toward the Chinese people that the emperor finally grew disenchanted. Upon learning that his people had been accused of being "atheists" and "idol worshipers," thus bringing chaos to his heretofore harmonious empire, the emperor not only had the clerics driven out of China, but forbade their reentry. The Chinese emperor *naively* asked how Christians can, while preaching love, spread such hate. The question has yet to be answered!

"This mania for proselytizing," remarked Voltaire, "is a disorder confined exclusively to our climes, and has always been unknown in Asia proper" (*Louis XIV*, 460). How can one explain the actions of the missionaries? "Must they not be accounted the most wretched of men to have come from one end of the world to the other in order to sow the seeds of discord in the imperial family and cause two princes to meet death on the scaffold!" (*Louis XIV*, 460).

Although Voltaire did not explore the meaning of the word *idolater* or *idol worshiper* in *The Age of Louis XIV,* he had done so in his *Philosophical Dictionary* (see chapter 2). For reasons of clarity, we may simply say that an idol is an image of a false god that is worshiped as a deity by religious groups other than Christians, who consider only their representations of divine figures to be true. In keeping with the preceding definition, the Chinese, Voltaire maintained, may be said to be idol worshipers. He thus disculpates—with tongue in cheek—Christians who worship their Holy Family and other sanctified beings in sculptures, paintings, icons, and other types of effigies.

Although Voltaire was critical of many of the Sun King's acts, he considered his accomplishments, particularly in the domain of the arts, to have far outweighed his misdeeds or failures. Thus he felt free to accentuate his hypothesis that the seventeenth century—the Classical Age—was unique.

To maintain the dynamics of his ever-unfolding panoramas, and to guard against lagging interest in the narrative, Voltaire, unlike some other French historians such as H. P. Limiers, intentionally cut insignificant details from his history. Despite the universality of his views on economic, social, military, political, religious, scientific, and artistic matters, his text remained fragmented. Splintering, of which he was guilty, somewhat obliterated his volume's continuity and diffused the chronology of events.

Despite these shortcomings, however, *The Age of Louis XIV* is a monumental work, rich in detail and insights into the arts of the period, as well as in behind-the-scenes perceptions of the personalities involved. Voltaire applied a balanced and reflective approach to history, but this freedom fighter and staunch believer in progress had as yet to focus on how to rectify notable social problems. Nonetheless, he brought these to the attention of his readers by explaining and highlighting some of the knottiest questions plaguing *The Age of Louis XIV.*

Essay on the Customs and the Spirit of Nations (1745, 1756, 1769)

Voltaire's approach in writing his prodigious *Essay on the Customs and the Spirit of Nations* (1756) was global. Undertaken with even greater ardor than his previous historical works, it extended over the span of centuries from ancient times to the outset of the reign of Louis XIV. Eastern and Western nations are focused on in its panoramic vision, which imparts to this massive work a sense of universality and continuity. Voltaire included in his study information not only on the varieties of customs, dress, foods, commerce, and trade of many lands but also on their arts and letters, which lent the work a sophisticated and urbane quality. While such polyvalent thematics enhanced the reader's interest, it also made the riches of distant lands more accessible and thrilling to future travelers.

Voltaire's *Essay* was undertaken in 1740, ostensibly to convince Mme Du Châtelet that history was not only as important as mathematics and the natural sciences but also as fascinating. He also asserted that the universality of humankind's existence within an extended time frame took on meaning and reality only via the memory of past events—that is, historical records. By probing and comparing the achievements of societies in various disciplines such as mathematics, astronomy, economics, and the sciences, he could underscore their progress or regression. Nor did history have to be dull, he responded in answer to another of Mme Du Châtelet's complaints. On the contrary, it should be dramatic, informative, and relevant to the world of the day. Finally, the multicultural and multiracial aspect of Voltaire's study also served to arouse the reader's imagination.

Universal in scope and philosophical in approach, Voltaire's *Essay* did not, like Bossuet's *Discourse on Universal History,* rest on divine intervention—Creation, Fall, and Redemption—to explain human actions. Unlike Bossuet's work, it separated history from fiction, and above all rejected Providence, as well as any other religious doctrine based on the notion of finalism, to explain earthly happenings. "A wise reader," Voltaire wrote, "will readily perceive that he should believe only the great events that present some probability, and contemplate with pity all the fables with which fanaticism, the romantic spirit and credulity have at all times peopled the theatre of the world" (Besterman, 407).

Whatever the drawbacks of a universal history—its superficiality, for some; its emphasis on generalizations and omissions of specifics, for others—Voltaire achieved his goal: "I would like to discover what human society was like, how people lived in the intimacy of the family, and what arts were cultivated, rather than repeat the story of so many misfortunes and military combats—the dreary subject matter of history and the common currency of perversity" (Lanson, 108).

The title of the volume itself, *Essay on the Customs and the Spirit of Nations,* was an indication of Voltaire's new direction and innovative concepts. Words such as *mores* and *spirit of nations* suggested his intent of embracing distant civilizations—China, Japan, Africa, India, America—and of exploring cultural riches and paucities from a global perspective. Readers were introduced to combinations of disciplines alluded to in contemporary terms as comparative history, comparative literature, art, sociology, economics, anthropology, psychology, philosophy, religion, the sciences, multiculturalism, and so forth. Because of the multiplicity of frames of reference in the *Essay,* from Confucius's China (c. 551–479 B.C.E) to the coronation of Louis XIV, Voltaire succeeded in encapsulating a variegation of facts as well as lifestyles. The resulting correlations, juxtapositions, similarities, and antitheses among civilizations firmed up their uniqueness and, above all, emphasized their interdependency.

Down with the Anthropocentric, Up with the Cosmic/ Down with the Universe, Up with the Pluriverse

The sweep and intent of the long, detailed, and philosophically oriented introduction to Voltaire's *Essay,* as well as the succeeding chapters, indicate a veering away on his part from the Westerner's outdated and limited anthropocentric and geocentric approach to the world and its history. He gave a bird's-eye view of global happenings, thereby lending preeminence to world cultures rather than simply underscoring the uniqueness of the Westerner's contribution to world civilization.

His Copernican/Galilean relativistic and cosmic perspective was the very one he accented in his philosophical tale *Micromégas* (see chapter 6). De-emphasizing the concept of the universe, Voltaire underscored the notion of a pluriverse, thus opening his readers to the hypothesis of infinity. Ironically, he and Pascal shared the same feelings of awe for the untold vastness and mystery of the heavens. In Voltaire's case, however, dogma and terror were banished, while in Pascal's, the opposite was true.

The philosophical introduction to Voltaire's *Essay* consisted of brief sections devoted to reviews of global alterations, to explorations of seemingly boundless varieties of customs, races, governments, religions, cuisines, clothing, styles, architectural wonders, and so forth. That he related these to the rise and fall of ancient cultures—Chaldean, Babylonian, Persian, Syrian, Phoenecian, Arabian, Indian, Chinese, Egyptian, Greek, Cretan, Hebrew, and Roman—gave his foray into cosmic and pluriversal history solid frames of reference.

The Comparative Method and Its Structured, Circular Trajectory

Readers may be both impressed and baffled by the formidable number of facts, concepts, and philosophical assessments interspersed in the 197 chapters of Voltaire's *Essay*. The comparative method he applied in his enormous undertaking required a tightly knit organizational plan for the assessment of similarities and divergencies among cultures. The consistency and compactness marking each sequence of his volume revealed a bone-hard inner structure based on a deep sense of concision and continuity in his mind.

The structure of Voltaire's work, evident in the very first chapter (devoted to Chinese civilization), required the detailing of the prodigious philosophical, scientific, mathethematical, astronomical, and artistic achievements of a culture unfamiliar to the Westerner, and, admittedly, unfamiliar to Voltaire. Such wonderment and admiration on his part also served his purpose of destabilizing the reader accustomed to believing that the West, namely Europe, was the focus of all great culture. Nonetheless, generalizations based on relatively sparse documentation made for gross errors and contradictions. A case in point: Voltaire's eulogy of Confucius's moral doctrine, which he considered to be a paradigm of pure and essentially Deistic religion. That Voltaire erroneously considered the Chinese government to be of the highest quality was in contradiction with Montesquieu's reference to it as despotic in his *The Spirit of the Laws* (Brumfitt, 79). Why Voltaire had allowed his vision at times to grow clouded by yielding to impulsive subjective generalizations in order to prove a point may be marked up to the ambiguities involved in the makeup of genius.

Whereas relatively little space was devoted to the arts in the *Essay* as compared with *The Age of Louis XIV,* commerce and industry were fleshed out. Discoursing on the highly sophisticated achievements of the Chinese, Voltaire focused on such architectural wonders as the Great Wall, such inventions as the compass, and such commercial enterprises as the silkworm and the porcelain industries. The list was long.

The comparison of the orient to the West during Voltaire's global trajectories invited contrasts to be made on all levels, usually to the detriment of the latter. His demarcation of the lifestyles of the highly evolved Chinese (from Confucius, 551–479 B.C.E., to the Han dynasty, 202 B.C.E.–220 C.E.), set against that of the barbaric Gauls, enabled him to make his point. How, for example, had the undeveloped Gauls (Vercingétorix, 72 B.C.E.–46 C.E.) and the Frankish kings (from Clovis, 465–511, to Dagobert, Childebert, Clotaire, Chilpéric, and the despot Charlemagne, 768–814) comported themselves during a parallel period of time? Readers could not help but be startled by the scientific and artistic achievements of the Chinese, and the utter ignorance of the barbarian Gauls. Not only did the facts serve temporarily to dislodge the hubris of the seemingly cultivated Westerner, but Voltaire's ironically humorous asides accomplished this task as well. One can visualize his broad smile as he cast aspersions on the great Frankish emperor Charlemagne, a man idolized and sanctified by the French and the Church. How could he have accomplished all the things attributed to him, and ruled so remarkably as well, without the benefit of an "observatory"? Unlike so many historians in awe of Charlemagne's so-called great deeds and religious piety, Voltaire attacked this first emperor of France with all the facts at his disposal. As the founder of the Holy Roman Empire, he had waged wars of conquest that caused enormous bloodshed. That he had been sanctified for his high moral standards and taken his place among venerable saintly figures was, for Voltaire, a travesty of ethics. Not only had this canonizer of injustice robbed his nephews of their birthright; but his greatest achievement in sordidness was recognized in the accusation of incest leveled against him.

Denigrating Charlemagne on the one hand, Voltaire praised Saint Louis (1214–1270) on the other hand for having Paris policed and for promulgating laws favoring commerce. But when it came to his comportment during the "folly" of the Crusades, he was awarded a verbal trouncing by Voltaire, since lucre, power, and material gain, rather than idealism, prompted the departure of the great bulk of the Crusaders for exotic lands. That Voltaire pointed to the depletion of France's treasury by the Crusades was a reiteration of his unchanging belief that wars in general caused not only death and destruction but a nation's penury.

On a positive note, Voltaire asserted that since the Parliament of Paris, created by Philippe IV, le Bel (1268–1314), had been instrumental in the dismantling of feudalism, this monarch deserved praise. Similarly, his admission of the Third Estate to the National Assembly also had to be considered a step forward.

Chapters of the *Essay* were devoted to the gradual birth of the nobility and hereditary monarchy in the West, the emergence of the bourgeois class, and the development of a variety of governmental and social institutions. Voltaire held the reader's attention by his usual personal comments, asides, charges, and countercharges, and frequent interjection of levity in the right places. But his distaste for certain forms of medieval "justice"—judicial combat and trial by water—was blatantly expressed. From specifics, Voltaire swung into generalizations, mentioning the political machinations of England, Germany, the Scandinavian lands, Russia, the Near and Far East, and other areas, but returning to France as his base, and thereby lending balance and continuity to his gigantic opus.

Not to be omitted from Voltaire's comparative course through history were the pages devoted to the decline of the Roman Empire and the rise of the papal state, which, as we know, he did not hold in high esteem. Citing the example of England's king, William the Conqueror (1027–1087), dividing the booty he had acquired after killing Harold, king of the Angles and the Saxons, at the Battle of Hastings, Voltaire noted with his usual irony:

> Thus a barbarian, the son of a prostitute, the murderer of a rightful king, shares this king's remains with another barbarian, for take away the names of Duke of Normandy, the king of England, and of pope, and the whole thing becomes nothing more than the exploit of a Norman thief and a Lombard receiver: and that in fact is what all usurpation boils down to. (Besterman, 410)

Nor were the perpetrators of England's Wars of the Roses—namely, Henry VI (1421–1471) and Henry VII (1457–1509)—spared some lancinating remarks. Their sphere of action was depicted "as a vast theater of carnage, in which scaffolds were everywhere erected on the battlefields" (Besterman, 411).

Engrossing are Voltaire's chapters devoted to India's extraordinary civilization. Readers are apprised, for example, that the Indians, not Pythagoras, invented the properties of the "triangle rectangle" (Moland, 11:182). Voltaire openly conveyed his dismay at the infamous ritual of suttee: the prevalent Indian custom of the self-immolation of widows. That Buddha's name was seemingly unknown to Voltaire did not prevent him from including sequences on meditation in Brahmanism, Vedism, Lamaism, and other beliefs in which the transpersonal experience was so valued. Comparisons with Persian Zoroastrianism, Mithraism, and of course, Christianity, Judaism, and Islam were also included in the *Essay.*

All types of religious rituals, symbols, monuments, and mysteries characteristic of a variety of cultures were likewise highlighted by Voltaire for their similarities and differences. Comparisons and analogies, although drawn to generate excitement in the reader's mind, were a Voltairean technique to further denigrate some of the Judeo-Christian practices and the fanaticism to which they gave rise. Nonetheless, he did concede that Christianity became a powerful world religion *despite* the religious premises it upheld:

> The false legends of the first Christians did not harm the establishment of the Christian religion. . . . Jesus Christ permitted the false gospels to mingle with the true ones from the beginning of Christianity; and, in order the better to test the faith of the devout, the gospels today called apocryphal even preceded the four sacred writings, which now form the basis of our faith. (Besterman, 409; Moland, 11:230)

With regard to Mohammed—the eponym for the early play *Mohammed or Fanaticism,* which condemned the cruelties identified with intolerance—Voltaire approached the Prophet far more objectively in the *Essay.* Impressed on the whole by the Koran, Voltaire was favorably disposed toward the practice of polygamy as defined in this religious text. And why not? It was certainly attractive from a male's point of view. Moreover, the custom of polygamy had been practiced by Middle Eastern cultures for centuries. Never, however, did Voltaire omit mocking superstition, fanaticism, hero worship, and their destructive aftermaths in all religious cults. His description of Islam's Prophet may be understood as a paradigm of all organized religions:

> We must suppose that Mohammed, like all enthusiasts, violently impressed by his own ideas, retailed them in good faith, fortified them with fancies, deceived himself in deceiving others, and finally sustained with deceit a doctrine he believed to be good. (Besterman, 409; Moland, 11:205)

Voltaire, unlike Bossuet, did not resort to divine intervention to explain calamities, as already noted. Discussing natural disasters such as floods, tornadoes, or, for example, the earthquake of 1182 occurring during Saladin's reign, he wrote: "The Turks were told by their priests that God was punishing the Christians; the Christians were told that God was punishing the Turks; and the fighting continued amidst the ruins of Syria" (Besterman, 410; Moland, 12:454).

On the global questions of poverty, disease, rapacity, mendacity, mutilation, rape, incest, poisonings, religious wars, and national hatreds, Voltaire did not spare his readers the horrors of the Inquisition in Spain and Portugal, and some of its repercussions in France and Italy, a case in point being the burning at the stake in Florence of the fifteenth-century Dominican priest, Savonarola (1452–1498):

> One contemplates with pity all these scenes of absurdity and horror; nothing of the sort is to be found among the Romans and the Greeks, nor among the barbarians. It is the fruit of the most infamous superstition that has ever bestialized humanity, and of the worst of governments. But you know that it is not long since we left this darkness behind us, and that all is not yet light. (Besterman, 411; Moland, 12:180)

Voltaire, who rarely concluded a point he was trying to make on a note of despondency, informed his readers that although great and once-flourishing states had declined, some fading into oblivion, many had resurfaced anew, underscoring thereby the repetitive and frequently evolving nature of civilizations.

A Cast of Fascinating Characters

Since no specific hero was being highlighted, as in his *History of Charles XII* and *The Age of Louis XIV,* Voltaire's global assessment of great figures and the events with which they were associated passed in review as if on a cinematic screen. The rapidity with which they were imaged emphasized the all-important and original comparative note in his social history.

Signaled out for praise among Voltaire's enormous cast of characters was the Anglo-Saxon king Alfred the Great (878–899). Following his conquest of England, he revealed his talents as legislator and administrator, and Voltaire also admired him for his relatively pacific ways and interest in learning. Favorable comments were applied to Pope Alexander III (1159–1181) for having liberated Christians from serfdom. Accolades were bestowed most lavishly to be sure, on Henry IV of France for the promulgation of his Edict of Nantes, which helped, if not to end, at least to diminish the ferocity of the wars between French Protestants and Catholics. Nonetheless, whenever the question of religious antagonisms emerged in Christian times, including the Reformation and the Counter-Reformation, Voltaire blamed the fanatics, principally, "the See of Rome [which] has always sided with that doctrine which tended the most to degrade human understanding, and obscure the light of reason."[5]

The Benefits of Commercial Enterprises

Included as well, and more extensively described than in Voltaire's preceding works, were the benefits, and sometimes the shortcomings, of commerce and industry. Newly chartered trade routes had enabled nations and individuals to communicate with one another and had introduced heretofore unknown products to Eastern and Western lands, helping in many cases to elevate the standards of living of their people. The opening up of one land to another through commerce created a kind of interdependency as well, linking the various areas of the globe. Such community of spirit also required standardized monetary exchanges— ways of weighing silver coins, for example—to determine the purchasing power of a nation, a group, or an individual. Broaching economic problems associated with the revival of industry and commerce, particularly the English woolen industry, Voltaire tried to sort out the impediments brought on by money-oriented, free-spending princes. The construction of the Spanish Armada, with its enormous fleet, revealed the great quantities of wood available to inject life into this industry. Voltaire's sound business judgments and acerbic humor led him to conclude that France's economic growth was due more to the work of financiers such as Jacques Coeur than to the hallucinations of the Maid of Orléans, Joan of Arc (Brumfitt, 69). Nonetheless, although he satirized Joan of Arc in his play *The Maid,* he redressed some of his ironies in his *Essay* by referring to her with respect, even while speaking of the superstitious and chaotic times that gave birth to such a personage.

Social Customs

Because many readers in Voltaire's day were unfamiliar with the social customs of times past, as well as with those of foreign lands, he included and evaluated the distinguishing characteristics of food, dress, home heating, etiquette, and labor conditions in such trades as pottery and metalworking. Inventions of spectacles, clocks, the compass, paper, printing, and windmills also came under scrutiny for the important role they played in society, as did the introduction of chivalry and the art of dueling. But, alas, as Voltaire remarked, the paucity of scientific learning in the West during the Middle Ages was frightening (Brumfitt, 62, 67).

Leanness in the Arts

Voltaire's failure to detail the greatness of medieval and Renaissance art and literature in his *Essay* may be partly attributed to his lack of knowledge on the subject, coupled with his century's prejudices against these periods. Let us note that research work in eighteenth-century Europe was still relatively archaic, thereby handicapping Voltaire to the extent that he was obliged to rely almost exclusively on secondhand sources for his treatment of the Middle Ages.

The paucity of original sources and the rapidity with which he worked may also have accounted for certain errors in Voltaire's exploration of such cultures as the Chinese, Indian, African, and American. The dearth of original texts may nonetheless have given him a freer hand in choosing the specific facts that substantiated his point of view, and scanty information may also have prevented him from erring too gravely in these matters. What facts were extant to prove the contrary? In his comparison of Persian and Gothic architectures, for example, he wrote with regard to the former that "the figures are all as heavy and as dry as those which unfortunately ornament our Gothic churches" (Moland, 11:197). He was equally bereft of knowledge of Dante's *Divine Comedy,* which he described as "bizarre" (Brumfitt, 63).

Envious Deprecators

Critics, envious of Voltaire's fame, angered by his forthrightness, or in disagreement with his interpretations, deprecated the *Essay*—notably the Jesuit Nonnotte, in his *The Errors of Voltaire* (1770). But as René Pomeau has asserted, "Voltaire is sometimes wrong; but it is just as wrong to maintain that his text is replete with flagrant errors. It is equally false to contend that because of his haste, he felt gratified by accumulating easily accessible works."[6]

Was Voltaire's omission of discussions concerning the origin of the Franks and their conquest of Gaul intended? Severe and dangerous polemics were raging at the time as to whether the Franks were of Trojan, Gaulish, or Germanic descent. To theorize on such questions, however, had proven to be highly dangerous. Nicolas Fréret, among others, was sent to the Bastille for venturing to express his ideas on the subject (Brumfitt, 63). Refraining from battling the issue, Voltaire wisely thought that he would be better served relinquishing a minor skirmish to win a mightier victory.

As is the case of historians in general, and particularly of Voltaire, the Deist, empiricist, and Pyrrhonist, few could remain completely impartial when appraising the horrible cruelties perpetrated by humans against one another throughout history. The humanitarian Voltaire, forever threatened with imprisonment, exile, and perhaps even worse,

awarded religious fanatics full responsibility for the bloodthirstiness of
the Crusades, the Inquisition, and most visibly, the religious wars
between Catholics and Protestants. His conclusions, in part true and in
part false, led to further generalizations, such as the following, which
was blatantly erroneous: because the Chinese never sacrificed their children to pacify their gods, they were more civilized than Westerners.
Such a facile contention omitted to mention the Chinese practices of
female infanticide and poisoning, as well as the less than pleasurable
variety of tortures implicit in their mores.

Judging from the following pronouncement, one might suggest that
Voltaire's view of history was negative:

> All history is little else than a long succession of useless cruelties . . . a
> collection of crimes, follies, and misfortunes, among which we have now
> and then met with a few virtues, and some happy times, as we see some-
> times a few scattered huts in a barren desert. (*Customs*, 16.2:144)

If Voltaire really had believed this, would he have pursued his historical writings? Probably not, since they would then have been pointless.
Nor would he have reacted with such pleasure to the praise accorded
him by Empress Catherine the Great of Russia, when in a letter to him
(c. September 1763) she informed Voltaire that she would have liked to
commit every page of his work to memory, so great was the knowledge
she had gained (Besterman, 430).

The History of Charles XII was memorable for the drama Voltaire injected
into his study of the Swedish monarch, for his analysis of a personality
dominated by the folly of war. In *The Age of Louis XIV,* a compendium of
spiritual, philosophical, artistic, and governmental achievements, Voltaire
highlighted a period he deemed to radiate the ultimate in French culture. The *Essay,* a monumental trajectory into time and space, reached
even new heights, to become a precursor in many ways of H. G. Wells's
Outline of History and the works of later historians. The comparatist
stance Voltaire used in evaluating the achievements as well as the downside of civilizations around the globe was virtually unique in its spanning of more than 2,000 years of history and culture. It may, in this
regard, be placed to some extent on a par with Diderot's *Encyclopedia.*
That Voltaire succeeded in fleshing out and in collating as yet untried
modes and disciplines of study—namely, anthropology, psychology,
geology, philosophy, economics, religion, and others—allowed him to

draw sustenance from the world, better to give of the riches he had gar-
nered. To future generations he gave his learning and living experience.

One of the greatest historians of his age, Voltaire may be considered
on a par with Montesquieu, although the latter's *Considerations on the
Greatness and Decadence of the Romans* (1734) was more sociologically oriented; with David Hume (*History of Great Britain,* 1757, 1759, 1762);
with William Robertson (*History of Scotland During the Reign of Queen
Mary and of King James VII,* 1759); and with Edward Gibbon (*History of
the Decline and Fall of the Roman Empire,* 1776).

The giant tapestries woven by Voltaire, the historian—with their net-
works of lines, colorations, and shadows—invite readers to make connections and comparisons with past eras, thereby encouraging them to
further their analyses as well as activate their imaginations or propensi-
ties for innovation. Voltaire's own words in his *Essay* might be considered as a conclusion to his thoughts on history: "The true conquerors are
those who know how to make laws. Their power is stable; the others are
torrents which pass" (Besterman, 407).

Chapter Six
Art and Inquiry in the Philosophical Tale

Although he was not the creator of the philosophical tale, Voltaire "revealed himself [in this genre] as a great, powerful, and original artist" (Lanson, 127). Having firmed and popularized this type of narrative, he found it admirably suited to the fleshing out of human suffering, which he believed resulted in large part from the moral, religious, philosophical, political, and economic evils of society. In a tightly knit plot, Voltaire presented buffoonish characters who verbalized their author's yearnings to edify the rejected and degraded, and to point them toward a solid, balanced, and productive existence.

What makes Voltaire's tales unique is his ingenious wit and humor, and his uncommon faculty for entertaining his readers. Whether he emphasizes the ironic, satiric, parodic, or fantastic side of human nature and lifestyles, his expertise in drawing out the absurdity of an event or relationship is remarkable. The richness of his images—in *Zadig, Candide, Micromégas, The Ingénu,* and other tales—underscores his philosophical intent and engraves mental pictures in the reader's mind's eye, which serve as mnemonic devices. To enhance the excitement of his tales, he doses them with exaggerated or piquant details as well as with scatological and even pornographic scenes. So well placed and so artfully introduced are these off-color passages that they give the impression of utter spontaneity and naturalness, and though they shock some readers, they draw guffaws from others. Although the tales appear to be simplistic and transparent at first glance, Voltaire's protagonists—Babouc, Zadig, Candide, and others—as we shall see, remain memorable for their naiveté, the finesse of their judgments, and the rhythmic vivacity of their philosophical reasonings. Moreover, the absence of individuality and psychological analyses endows the creatures of Voltaire's fantasy with a certain endearing automatism or puppetlike quality as well.

Tales and legends had been popular in France long before Voltaire's time. With the advent of the Crusades and the discovery of the Byzantine world, fabulous oriental legends such as Charlemagne's pilgrimage to Jerusalem were being heard by Europeans. Celtic, Welsh, and Cornish tales, namely the *Novel of Brut* (1155) by the Anglo-Norman Wace, spread to France after the Battle of Hastings. So, too, did Latin and Greek writings—Virgil's *Aeneid,* Stace's *Thebaïde,* and Ovid's *Pyramus and Thisbe*—make inroads into French aristocratic circles.

A whole literary tradition was born with the *roman courtois*: *Tristan and Isolde, King Arthur and the Round Table, The Holy Grail.* Nor may we omit the wonderfully humorous/didactic fabliaux. Star-studded names appearing in the following centuries—Boccaccio, Fail, Marguerite de Navarre, Perrault, La Fontaine, Galland, Fénelon, Montesquieu, and more—regaled readers with a plethora of historico-fantastic events designed to educate by entertaining.

For Voltaire, the philosophical tale acted as a vehicle allowing him to speak out against his pet peeves: war, intolerance, fanaticism, miscarriages of justice, among other flagrant abuses. Although each of Voltaire's tales differs one from the other, there are, nevertheless, certain techniques that mark them all. The dichotomy, for example, between the absurdity of the events and the seemingly reasonable, rational, and objective manner in which they are narrated, divests readers of logical space/time limitations, leaving them in a quandary as to what or what not to believe. Creatures of Voltaire's fantasy continuously tergiversated, arousing feelings of frenzy or intense joy; or they moved in and out of heteroclite episodes that destabilized the readers and plunged them into the author's proverbial *doubt.*

Seemingly naive protagonists journey throughout the world—Europe, Middle East, Africa, Asia, and/or the Americas—experiencing either drastically cruel and tawdry or momentarily joyful and satisfying events. Voltaire's penchant for aberrant antics or behavioral revelations invited him to counter pathos with irony, humor with satiric asides, as his protagonists veered in their continuous mood swings. Voltaire's experience as a dramatist had taught him how to build suspense and create a spirit of wonderment, terror, and panic, while also triggering discernment and skepticism in viewers. Long separations, exiles, abductions, disappearances, enslavements, and torture, among other devices, peppered Voltaire's scenarios. The surviving protagonists generally *learned* to cope with, or at least face, heartbreak and suffering.

Usually basing himself on concrete events, specific people, and à la mode philosophies, Voltaire rarely strayed from the situation at issue. Unexpected stylization and distortion served him, however, to camouflage the reality of the event, circumstance, philosophical notion, or individual to be ironized. In most of the tales, the reader is veritably carried along by the rapidity of the action, the sweep of the dialogue, and the power of Voltaire's subtle derision.

The World as It Is (Le Monde Comme Il Va) (1748)

In his earthly paradise at Cirey, Voltaire reaped a learning experience, as already mentioned, deepening his knowledge of mathematics, science, and philosophy. Under Mme Du Châtelet's tutelage, he had ample time to compose such works as *Elements of the Philosophy of Newton* (1738); comparing the Englishman's beliefs with Leibniz's—which Mme Du Châtelet favored—he concluded on most counts in favor of the ideational superiority of the former. A believer neither in the latter's concept of immaterial monads as being the ultimate constituents of the universe, nor in their arrangement in an infinitely ascending scale, nor in their interaction with each other according to a "preestablished harmony," Voltaire gave credence to Newton's views. Only with regard to the concept of natural law, and the notion that the universe was the outgrowth of a divine plan, did Voltaire accept some of Leibniz's concepts.[1]

Anthony Shaftesbury's *Inquiry Concerning Virtue, or Merit* (1699) had become food for discussions between Voltaire and Mme Du Châtelet. Shaftesbury, rejecting rationalism as an ethical basis for community living, believed that morality could be enhanced by balancing egoism and altruism in terms of the individual and of society, general welfare being identical with personal happiness. Discussions between Voltaire and Mme Du Châtelet revolved as well around Bernard Mandeville (1670–1733), whose *Fable of the Bees* she translated in 1735. Mandeville, rejecting Shaftesbury's optimistic and benevolent view of human nature, maintained that industrial society, like a colony of bees, prospers and evolves thanks to individual acquisitiveness, love of luxury, and a drive to meet set goals. Only violation of laws of the land in the pursuit of individual or collective goals would be assessed as evil.

No longer the optimist he was when composing his *Man of the World* (*Le Mondain*) in 1736, Voltaire had become increasingly preoccupied with questions of good and evil, free will, determinism, and the notion of Providence. His partial misconception of Leibniz's approach to the complex and insoluble question of good and evil, which he had bandied about in *The World as It Is* led him to highlight and ridicule—nonetheless, to accept in part—certain philosophical reasonings. Is it true, for example, that what appears at first glance to be an evil may in the long run be beneficial to the individual? (Wade 1969, 656). Other factors also influenced Voltaire's decision to write *The World as It Is*. Among the painful events besetting the outspoken writer was the publication in 1738 of the "infamous" *Voltairomania* by Father P.-F. Guyot Desfontaines. To redress the volume's slanderous statements about him, Voltaire and Mme Du Châtelet decided to go to Paris. Although Voltaire was at first wary of the many people he met in the capital, he was soon caught up by its thrilling social and artistic activities. As in the case of Babouc, his protagonist in *The World as It Is*, the wrong perpetrated against him in *Voltairomania* was offset by the elation he experienced in the big city. He summed up his experience in philosophical terms in a letter to his friend Count Caylus: "Paris is like Nebuchadnezzar's statue, part gold, part mire."[2]

Babouc's Mission

Voltaire's conflictual and ambiguous reactions to the positive and negative sides of human nature were made evident in *The World as It Is*. What at first seemed to be a series of gratuitous misfortunes—imprisonments, exiles, persecutions, and threats—afflicting his protagonist, Babouc, the Scythian, proved on the contrary, to be beneficial to him. Artfully conceived, the fabricated situations designed to prove Voltaire's hypotheses were tightly knit into fanciful but meaningful episodes.

It may come as a surprise to learn that the angel Ithuriel, who descended to earth near the banks of the Oxus River sets the stage for *The World as It Is*.[3] Readers may have been unaware that Voltaire, always in search of philosophical explanations for life's vagaries and inequities, and Mme Du Châtelet, also fascinated by so-called miraculous events, had spent long hours steeped in biblical studies exploring most thoroughly and *en philosophe* such books as Genesis, Ezra, Job, and Proverbs.

The angel Ithuriel informs Babouc that not only his own anger but that of the entire population of genii of Upper Asia has been aroused by "the follies and excesses of the Persians." He orders Babouc to go to Persepolis, the ancient Persian capital founded by Darius, and, like a spy, to investigate the goings-on of its inhabitants.[4] Depending on Babouc's report, Ithuriel continues, either the Persians' deviant behavior will be corrected or they will be exterminated. Despite Babouc's protestations—he has never been to Persia and knows no one there—Ithuriel insists that since Babouc is devoid of preconceived ideas, the better he can render an impartial judgment. The angel admonishes him to "go, look, listen, observe, and fear nothing; you shall be well received everywhere" (*World*, 192).

Human Nature: Its Dual Proclivities

Babouc arrives in Persepolis just as the Persians and the Indians are preparing for battle. Intent upon obeying Ithuriel's commands, he walks up to a soldier to ask him why he is fighting this war. "By all the gods!" the soldier answers, "I know nothing about it. It is none of my business; my trade is to kill and be killed to earn my living; it makes no difference whom I serve" (*World*, 192). Dissatisfied with his answer, Babouc walks on, repeating the same query to the captain, who tells him that he not only does not know why he is fighting, but even if he did, it would make no difference to him. "I live two hundred leagues from Persepolis; I hear that war is declared; I immediately abandon my family and go, according to our custom, to seek fortune or death, seeing that I have nothing to do" (*World*, 193). Still in search of some sensible answer, Babouc walks up to a group of generals to ask them their reasons for fighting a war that has been decimating Asia for the past 20 years. He learns that its origin lies in a quarrel between a eunuch belonging to one of the wives of the Great King of Persia and a clerk in the office of the Great King of India, which led to a commitment to war. Up to 400,000 recruits have been enlisted yearly. "Massacres, fires, ruins, devastations multiply; the universe suffers, and the fury continues" (*World,* 193). The prime ministers of both lands protest that "they are acting solely for the happiness of the human race; and at each protestation a few towns are always destroyed and a few princes ravaged" (*World,* 193). Based on the information he has thus far received, Babouc underscores the stupidity of fighting men and hastily concludes that soldiers and generals rarely know why they are fighting.

Upon further questioning, Babouc is apprised by Persians and Indians alike of the generosity and humanitarian acts effected by individual soldiers during the bloodbaths. Stunned by the realization that murder has always been legitimized by war, he cries out, in the name of Voltaire, "Inexplicable humans . . . how can you combine so much baseness and so much greatness, so many virtues and so many crimes?" (*World*, 194).

After peace has been declared, Babouc enters Persepolis. He observes the ugliest and filthiest people of both sexes rushing in and out of a large, dark enclosure. Through the din of the deafening noise of pick-axes and shovels, he observes money being given in exchange for a seat or chair, and women kneeling, ostensibly in prayer, though in reality they are looking surreptitiously askance better to ogle the menfolk. He finally realizes that these people are, ironically, burying their dead in the same place they worship their God. The practice, he reasons, must spread disease like wildfire. But then, "Providence may have its reasons; let us leave it up to Providence" (*World*, 195).

No sooner does the sun reach its zenith than Babouc glimpses another part of the city. Not only do beautiful and well-ordered houses and places of worship exist in this quarter, but gorgeous, harmonious musical sounds are also audible. Whereupon he muses that "the angel Ithuriel is jesting about wanting to destroy so charming a city" (*World*, 196).

Upon further scrutiny, however, he soon learns of infidelities of wives; of rewards given to incompetent, lazy, greedy lawyers; and of bought judgeships, while subordinate jobs are filled by hardworking, honest, intelligent, and underpaid men of the law. While Babouc attempts to assess the extent of the corruption of the legal system, a young soldier asks him why he is against the purchase of positions in the legal or military fields. After all, he tells Babouc, he paid "forty thousand gold dar-ics" to command 2,000 men, "to sleep on the ground thirty nights in a row in a red uniform and then receive two good arrow wounds which I still feel" (*World*, 197).

Babouc pursues his course, observing and questioning people from all walks of society: royalty, writers, journalists, merchants, and others. What he hears at times moves him to tears, particularly episodes involving great kindnesses, love, and virtue in the face of adversity, sorrow, and pain. Other incidents shock him for their ignominiousness. At the end of his trajectory, Babouc, weighing both extremes, comes to realize that good cohabits with evil in this world—one does not exist without the other.

Prior to presenting his findings to Ithuriel, Babouc approaches the best metal worker in Persepolis, asking him to cast a statue composed of the most precious and the basest of metals, of stones, and of earth. Upon bringing it to Ithuriel, he asks: "Will you break this pretty statue because it is not all gold and diamonds?" (*World*, 207).

Ithuriel immediately understands the analogy: certain inequities in Persepolis could never be rectified; the only thing to do is to "leave *the world as it is*." He thinks that "*if all is not well, all is passable*" (*World*, 207).

Similarly, Voltaire concluded that life has to be accepted as a blend of contradictions—good and evil, hatred and love, beauty and ugliness, success and failure. To seek only harmony and order by obliterating contention and unpredictability would be like "giving wings to dogs and horns to eagles."

Zadig, or Destiny (1747)

Zadig was written during a relatively happy and fulfilling period in Voltaire's life. In 1745 he was made court historiographer; a year later he was elected to the French Academy, not without behind the scenes intrigue both on Mme Du Châtelet's part and on his (his dedication of his play *Mohammed* to the pope), and was named Gentleman Ordinary of the King's Chamber. Nonetheless, as implicit in *The World as It Is,* unpleasant events were never far off. During Mme Du Châtelet's gambling sessions, as has been mentioned, Voltaire informed her in English and in what he thought was a sotto voce tone that cheats at the table were despoiling her of her winnings. Apprised that the influential culprits to whom he had been alluding had overheard his words, he decided that for reasons of safety he would "flee" to the Duchess Du Maine's estate at Sceaux. It was there that he composed a good part of *Zadig.*

Although written with Voltaire's typical levity and ebullient satiric innuendoes, *Zadig* was all but facile. Trenchant themes—free will, intolerance, fanaticism, arbitrary powers of rulers, scholastic nonsense, clerical abuses, and the ignominies of war—were dealt with even more openly and incisively than in *The World as It Is.* Never maudlin, the tale immediately dispelled any glimmer of emotionality by ironies and sarcasms, thereby injecting a certain bitterness. Was this wistfully saddened mood in *Zadig* perhaps due in part to Voltaire's discovery of Mme Du Châtelet's passion for Saint-Lambert?

As indicated by *Zadig's* subtitle, *Destiny,* the notion of free will was central. Although Voltaire showed himself to be a partisan of the concept of free will in his *Treatise on Metaphysics,* his position during the later 1730s and 1740s stood midway between the rational theology of Samuel Clarke (1675–1729)—a view of absolute liberty for humankind as adumbrated in the *Treatise on the Existence of God*—and Leibniz's belief in the relative nature of free will. Although not himself a Deist, Clarke supported some Deistic ideas, including Newtonianism. For Leibniz, however, free will not only remained subordinate to a general order but also took on meaning only with respect to it. In his *Theodicy, Essay on God's Goodness, Liberty of Humankind, and the Origin of Evil* (1710) and his *Monadology* (1714) Leibniz listed three types of evil: metaphysical, as manifested in the imperfection of God's creatures; physical, represented by suffering; and moral, as in sin. Providence, however, was generally looked upon by him as beneficial, conciliating individual free will and universal harmony.

By 1745 such complex metaphysical arguments as set forth by Leibniz and his popularizer, Christian Wolff, were considered by Voltaire to be anti-Newtonian, prolix, obscure, faulty, confused, and outmodedly scholastic. Thanks to Mme Du Châtelet, Voltaire had acquired a relatively solid—although for some critics flawed—grounding in Leibniz's work, leading him if not to a complete rejection of his thought, at least to a change with respect to it. Voltaire could not, for example, believe in a destiny—the focus of *Zadig*—that conciliated, as understood by Leibniz, individual freedom and universal order.

The Good and the Moral

Voltaire's "oriental tale" opens in ancient Babylonia. Its hero, Zadig (Arabic, "just"), is young, handsome, rich, generous, thoughtful, and in full possession of the highest of moral and intellectual qualities. Injecting a bit of the picaresque into his tale, Voltaire thrusts his protagonist from one area of the globe to another so that he may learn from experience and not from abstract systems or dogmatic theoretical disquisitions.

Seeking only to do good, the naive Zadig believes unequivocally that he is destined to be happy. Early on, however, fate—in the form of human envy, selfishness, jealousy, and acquisitiveness—deals him a series of excoriating blows. Soon, however, the pendulum swings his way. His integrity and high moral standards are appreciated by those in power, and he receives abundant rewards. No sooner do feelings of safety and security lull him into a condition of complacency than he is shunted into slavery and further suffering. Pain, oases of relative joy, and wretchedness alternate in swift succession, accelerating the momentum of Zadig's suspenseful life experience.

Zadig finally realizes that his fine character is not "sufficient reason"—a mockery of Leibniz's words—to ward off pain and suffering or to earn joy and redemption. Only at the tale's conclusion, and thanks to an old sage who appears in the form of an angel, is Zadig enlightened as to the vagaries of fortune. They are not fortuitous, as he had once believed, but are part of Providence's overall design, to which humankind has not been made privy, but which, nonetheless, works in universal terms in its favor despite interludes of suffering. The enlightened Zadig now understands and accepts the existence of evil and its place in life.

Zadig the Unenlightened

At the beginning of his journey through life, the naive Zadig equates happiness with morality. He believes that he who lives a righteous life, whose nature is generous, who adheres to moral integrity, and whose scientific and philosophical learning are paramount will experience joy during his earthly trajectory. No sooner are these concepts articulated than adversity ensues. Zadig is abandoned by his beautiful fiancée. Shocked and despairing, he decides to marry another, only to be deceived by her. Finally discarding all thought of marriage, Zadig decides to find a safe haven by devoting his energies to the study of nature. "No one is happier," says he, "than a philosopher who reads in this great book that God set before our eyes. The truths he discovers belong to him. He nourishes and ennobles his soul. He lives in peace, fearing nothing from men."[5]

Zadig believes beatitude finally to be his, and his scientific learning and powers of deduction increase immeasurably. Following the disappearance of the queen's dog and the king's horse, he offers his services to help retrieve them, even though he was not a witness to the incident and never saw the animals. Proffering impressively logical and precise descriptions of them, as well as practical and opportune directives, Zadig succeeds in restoring the animals to the monarchs. Rather than receive a reward for his help, however, he is accused of theft and fined. Pleading his case so brilliantly that he is exonerated by the judges, Zadig concludes that "it is difficult to be happy in this life!" and resolves to learn from his errors (*Zadig* 1977, 338). Now that he has realized that great knowledge does not lead to happiness, he decides that henceforth he will remain silent in the face of problematic situations.

Just as his vast learning has served him ill, so will his mutism almost cost him his life. Failing to defend himself against an envious man who accuses him of writing verses satirizing the king and queen, Zadig is condemned to death. Envy, having become synonymous with evil, is a progressively powerful agent for destroying individual happiness. Nonetheless, the fickle finger of destiny works in such strange ways that Zadig is saved by the ruler's miraculous parrot, and even wins a royal prize. So impressed are the king and queen by the young man's gentle ways that they appoint him prime minister. His happiness now causes Zadig to have a change of heart. He "began to think that it was not so difficult to be happy" (*Zadig* 1977, 343).

Lulled into a state of contentment, Zadig falls in love with the queen, Astarte, earns the wrath of the king, flees, and is sold into slavery on his way to Egypt. There, too, extremes dominate his world. Veering from immense joy to horrendous sorrow, Zadig takes to reviling the world. He has not yet learned that his definition, as a mortal, of bad or good luck stems from anthropocentrism, his limited understanding of humankind's place within Providence's infinite chain of events.

Zadig the Wanderer

As Zadig wanders through the Arab world in search of enlightenment, his journey, or pilgrimage, leads him to further questioning and to an increased understanding of life's perplexities. The inner chaos he has been suffering—the result of being jolted from infernal to paradisiacal experiences—will henceforth be assessed by him within a broader frame of reference, and his conclusions integrated into the whole of his life experience.

As a slave, Zadig so impresses his master, Sétoc, with his wisdom and goodness that he considers him his friend and becomes dependent upon him for advice. Zadig, however, is disappointed because his master worships constellations of the sun, moon, and stars. These heavenly bodies, he maintains, are no more deserving of adoration than a tree or a rock. In reply, Sétoc speaks these words:

> "But they are the Eternal Beings whence we draw all our blessings. They give life to nature and regulate the seasons, and besides, they are so far away one can barely help holding them in veneration."
>
> "You receive more blessings from the waters of the Red Sea," replied Zadig, "on which is borne your merchandise from the Indies. Why should not they be as old as the stars? And if you worship what is distant you should worship the people of the Ganges, which is at the end of the earth."
>
> "No," answered Sétoc, "the stars shine too brightly for me not to worship them."
>
> When night came Zadig lit a large number of tapers in the tent where he was to sup with Sétoc, and as soon as his patron appeared threw himself on his knees before them and cried: "Eternal and Radiant Lights, grant me always your favors!"—after which he sat down to table without looking at Sétoc.

"What are you doing?" asked Sétoc, astonished.

"I do as you do," replied Zadig. "I worship these candles, and neglect their master and mine." (*Zadig* 1977, 365)

Such are Zadig's attempts at teaching Deism.

In time, Zadig leaves his master under amicable circumstances to pursue his wanderings through Arabia, devoting his energies, as always, to remedying social and spiritual ills. He succeeds, for example, in abolishing the ancient custom of suttee (burning widows at the stake) and in spreading harmony in religious circles where there has been dissension. As recompense for his efforts, he earns the wrath and hatred of priests who try unsuccessfully to murder him, concluding that there must be some mysterious logic directing his destiny.

During the course of his trajectories, he learns with sorrow that his native city of Babylon has been destroyed, that its king has been killed, and that his beloved queen, Astarte, has been captured. Once again bemoaning his fate, he blames destiny for its lack of compassion and rebels against what he judges to be unethical situations. Little by little, Zadig begins to understand that the cleavage between happiness and sorrow varies according to whether it is viewed on an individual and human scale or approached from a cosmic, Deistic point of view—that is, in terms of a well-ordered and infinite universe. Although humans, imprisoned for the most part in their minute worlds, are like so many "insects devouring each other on a little atom of mud," each time Zadig begins focusing on his own pain, the larger universal picture comes forward. For a moment, then, he floats happily about, existing in his mind's eye within the immensities of space. Seconds later this abstract notion vanishes, and Zadig finds himself again alone, and at a loss. Nor do comparisons between his atomlike size and the infinite cosmos help him better to assess or accept the reasons for Destiny's apparent design to reward human vice, on the one hand, and punish virtuous deeds, on the other.

Returning to Babylonia, Zadig continues his adventures: he escapes the clutches of brigands, saves a fisherman from committing suicide and, incredibly enough, discovers his beautiful Astarte amid a group of maidens. Has his fate altered its course? Thanks to Zadig's skill, wit, and perseverance, he and Astarte are finally reunited and return safely to Babylon. After Astarte is received triumphantly as the people's queen, it is determined that she will marry the man able to defeat his adversaries in armed combat. Wearing the white armor given him by

Astarte, Zadig easily wins the contests. During his well-earned sleep, however, his chief adversary steals his white armor, replacing it with the loser's green one. Upon awakening the next morning, Zadig has no choice but to wear the loser's armor, and no sooner does he step outside than he is greeted with hoots, insults, and humiliations. Unable as yet to consistently consider human situations from a cosmic point of view, Zadig, still myopic in his assessment of personal events, once again despairs, concluding that good people are oppressed, whereas evil ones are rewarded.

Meditating on the cruelty of Providence, Zadig walks toward the banks of the Euphrates River trying to find a way of escaping the cyclical recurrences of pain and joy. A hermit endowed with a white beard happens to come by and begins instructing Zadig as to the mysteries of Providence.

Well versed in the Book of Destinies, the hermit opens it and invites the young man to read it. Although multilingual, Zadig cannot decipher a single character in the text. Taken aback, he realizes, perhaps for the first time, that Providence is *mystery.* He listens in awe as the venerable old man speaks eloquently "of destiny, justice, morality, the sovereign good, human frailty, virtues, and vices," and feels irresistibly drawn to him.[6]

The sage will accompany Zadig if he swears that no matter how challenging the ordeal, he will remain with him for the next few days—until enlightenment is experienced. The two go to a magnificent castle, where they are hosted in splendor. Once again on their way, Zadig notices a golden basin studded with emeralds and rubies in the hermit's pouch. Why has he stolen it from one who has entertained them so lavishly? he wonders.

They soon come upon the home of a miser who gives them the bare minimum to eat. To Zadig's surprise, it is to him that the hermit gives the bowl, later explaining that the lordly man who has received strangers most unstintingly has done so out of vanity. The theft of the golden basin will teach him to lessen his materialism and thus make him wiser. The miser, by receiving the golden basin, will learn to be more hospitable. Further on, Zadig questions why, after visiting a wise and virtuous philosopher who had so graciously opened his home to them, the hermit burned down his house. "You monster! You wickedest of all men!" Zadig cries out (*Zadig* 1961, 168).

The hermit, reminding him that he has promised to wait until he learns the workings of Providence, explains that now that the philosopher's house is no longer standing he will be able to discover the immense treasure buried beneath it. But why, Zadig questions, did the hermit drown the widow's beloved 14-year-old nephew, who had shown them such hospitality? Because later on in life he would have murdered his aunt and Zadig as well.

Just as he begins explaining the overall picture or infinite cosmic design of the universe, the hermit is suddenly transformed into the radiant angel Jesrad ("God-given," in ancient Persian).

> "O Envoy from Heaven! O divine angel!" cried Zadig, falling on his face. "So you have come down from the empyrean to teach a frail mortal to submit to the eternal commands?"
>
> "Men," said the angel Jesrad, "pass judgment on everything without knowing anything; of all men you were the one who most deserved to be enlightened." (*Zadig* 1961, 169)

Dissatisfied by what he considers to be a series of coldly conceived rational explanations, Zadig nonetheless decides to continue to devote his life to assuaging the plight of the suffering. Although the hermit has found justification for his acts by reading the Book of Destinies, this does not give him the right to drown a child. In retort, the hermit maintains that people are wrong to judge something about which they perceived only a small segment.

Admitting a lack of confidence in his judgment, Zadig asks Jesrad whether it might not have been wiser to correct the child rather than to drown him. Even if he had been programmed to live, the angel answers, "his destiny was to be assassinated himself, together with the wife he was to marry and the child that was to be born to them" (*Zadig* 1961, 169). Unappeased, Zadig questions: must there always be crimes and misfortunes? and must these befall good people so frequently?

> "The wicked," replied Jesrad, "are always unhappy. They serve to test a small number of just men scattered over the earth, and there is no evil out of which some good is not born."
>
> "But," said Zadig, "what if there were nothing but good, and no evil?"
>
> "Then," replied Jesrad, "this earth would be another earth; the chain of events would be another order of wisdom; and that other order, which would be perfect, can exist only in the eternal abode of the Supreme Being, whom evil cannot approach. He has created millions of worlds not one of which can resemble another. This immense variety is an attribute of his immense power. There are not two leaves of a tree on earth, or two globes in the infinite fields of the heavens, that are alike; and everything

you see on the little atom on which you were born had to be, in its appointed place and time, according to the immutable orders of him who embraces all. Men think this child who has just perished fell into the water by chance, that it was by a similar chance that that house burned down; but there is no chance; all is test, or punishment, or reward, or foreseeing. . . . Frail mortal! cease to argue against what you must worship." (*Zadig* 1961, 169)

Throughout the angel's reply, Zadig interpolates what was to become Voltaire's famous philosophical byword: "*But* . . . ," which encourages humankind always to doubt in its quest for enlightenment. And indeed, even if all is predetermined, the question as to the meaning of free will still remains unanswered!

Zadig the Enlightened

Upon returning to Babylon—after the angel soars into the air, and Zadig prostrates himself, adoring Providence—Zadig faces a contest of riddles, which, if correctly answered, will restore his reputation in his native city. The following is one of them:

> What of all things in the world, is the longest and the shortest, the swiftest and the slowest, the most divisible and the most extensive, the most neglected and the most regretted, without which nothing can be done, which devours everything that is small and gives life to everything that is great? (*Zadig* 1961, 170)

An adversary answers "Light"; another, "The world"; Zadig, "Time."

> "Nothing is longer," he add[s], "since it is the measure of eternity, nothing is shorter, since it is lacking for all our plans; nothing is slower to him who waits, nothing swifter for him who enjoys; it extends right to infinity in greatness; it is divisible right down to infinity in smallness; all men neglect it, all regret its loss, nothing is done without it; it brings oblivion to all that is unworthy of posterity, and it makes great things immortal." (*Zadig* 1961, 171)

Having solved all the riddles with ease, Zadig draws his sword, salutes the queen, and disarms his enemy, Itobad, who had stolen his white armor. Like the great heroes of yesteryear, Zadig marries his beloved queen, knows happiness, becomes a good king, and enjoys a beneficial Providence, which awards them both more joy than sorrow.

During all the days to come, Zadig neither forgets the angel's wise advice nor ignores the counsel of an Arabian brigand he had met on the frontier that separated Arabia Petraea from Syria:

> "My son, do not despair; once upon a time there was a grain of sand which lamented that it was an unknown atom in the deserts; after a few years it became a diamond; and now it is the fairest ornament in the crown of the King of India."
>
> "These words made an impression on me: I was the grain of sand, I resolved to become a diamond." (*Zadig* 1977, 383)

Zadig, like Voltaire, has learned the hard way, through experience, that people are motivated by self-interest, that there is neither reward nor punishment for good or for evil deeds, and that the wise do not necessarily find any more happiness than the ignorant, nor the generous more than the selfish. No longer is it a question of free will for Zadig, but rather of finding a way of reconciling freedom with a certain order in Providence (Van Den Heuvel, 62). The seemingly incoherent events produced by destiny are to be understood as illusions, since the mind of mortals apprehends successive happenings only fragmentarily and on a human, not a cosmic, plane. In *Zadig* we still have the impression that individual lives are geared to hoping for the greatest good, or at least, the least possible evil. Even though at the tale's conclusion Zadig finds the kind of happiness he had hardly ever dared to dream about, Voltaire seemingly had not yet obtained a satisfactory answer to his philosophical questions, particularly those about free will. His fluid approach to them kept open possibilities of continuous reevaluation, even as he attempted all the while to balance out oppressive extremes.

Memnon, or Human Wisdom (1749)

Ten years after the publication of Voltaire's *Elements of Newton's Philosophy* (1738), for which in large measure he had been elected a fellow of the Royal Society of London and its counterpart of Edinburgh, he was still preoccupied with the question of free will. He had now reduced the concept to the power of an individual "to accomplish that which has been dictated to him by an invincible force," and any other affirmation of the notion of individual freedom, Voltaire now asserted, "would interfere with the order of the universe" (Van Den Heuvel, 206). In a letter to his friend Pierre Robert Le Cormier de Cideville, he wrote that his life neither measured up to his desires nor to his expectations, and besides, "what man directs his own destiny?" Humans are simply marionettes unaware of the fact that they are being led around.[7] To Frederick II, he wrote on this same matter: "I had greatly wanted us to be free; I did everything I could to believe it."[8]

Voltaire's protagonist, Memnon, mirrors the author's painful frame of mind at a time when he was attempting to cope not only with the discovery of Mme Du Châtelet's betrayal, but with the French queen's hatred of him, with his virtual exclusion from Versailles, and with the failure of his play *Sémiramis*. Added to his concerns were his severe intestinal problems. Indeed, they were so severe that he was convinced they preluded his death.

Despite his sorrows, Voltaire still rejected facile ways of alleviating his anxieties. Ridicule, as in Zadig and *The World as It Is,* and now in *Memnon,* would continue to be his verbal weapon. Debunking the so-called healing recipes of religious fanatics—austerity, divestiture of passions and desires, and detachment from the outside world—that were the order of the day, Voltaire upheld passions, which often give impetus to humankind's creative powers. Nor did he accept illusory answers based on hubristic anthropocentrism—such as credos linking individual moral attitudes with cosmic happenings. Following in the footsteps of Montaigne, Mandeville, and La Fontaine, and in sharp contrast to Pascal's intransigent self-abnegation and self-mortification, Voltaire favored a modern form of Epicureanism.

Although thematic and structural similarities between *Zadig* and *Memnon* are apparent, dichotomies between the two tales are also evident. The former hero's credos are deprecated because he arrogantly believes in the equation of human goodness and destiny's own determinations for the individual. Equally absurd is Memnon's presumption that stoicism, *unwisely* applied, might alleviate his personal sorrows. As Voltaire calls into question the philosophical errors of both Zadig and Memnon, structural relationships between the two tales also become apparent. The protagonists' lack of vision and understanding is to blame for their betrayal by women, and for their loss of worldly possessions. In both tales, when despair risks overwhelming the heroes, a supernatural being appears on the scene to guide them toward a new understanding of life.

A Commedia Dell'arte Absurdity

At the outset of *Memnon,* the reader is informed in a detached manner of the great sorrows Memnon has suffered. Like the caricature of the absurd Doctor in the Italian *commedia dell'arte,* so Memnon is made to look equally ridiculous in his attempt to protect himself from life's inequities by hiding behind a rigid credo. Spiritually and empirically blind, and the victim of faulty logic as well, Memnon is convinced that by redirecting his ways and thoughts and living the extremes of asceticism, he will without question attain a condition of perfect wisdom and no longer experience earthly adversities.

The "perfectly wise" Memnon, like the contemporary pill taker, outlines his simplistic agenda as follows. First, he will divest himself of all passions in order to eliminate any desire to fall in love. A relatively simple ascesis, he reasons, is not to see the lady of his fancy in her present beauty, but to picture her as she will be in her old age: wrinkled and decrepit. Equally facile is his second law, aimed at controlling his intake of food and drink and his partygoing: imagine himself as he will be in 10 years, debauched, dull-witted, obese, and sickly. Nor will he any longer obsess about money matters. To live frugally and invest wisely will be his goal. Such a lifestyle will neither draw the envy of others nor encourage him to be other than he is.

Shortly thereafter, looking out of his window, Memnon sees two ladies, one old and the other young. Drawn to the latter, perhaps not only because of her weeping and moaning, he inquires why she is so distraught. The young lady confesses being the victim of an uncle who has artfully deprived her of some property, and she claims to live in dread of his violent manner. "You seem to me a man of such good counsel . . . that if you were to condescend to come all the way to my house and examine my affairs, I am sure you would pull me out of the cruel embarrassment I am in."[9] Convinced he can save this damsel in distress, he arrives at her home, and while she continues her charming tale of woe, they draw closer and closer to each other. Indeed, "Memnon advised her so closely, and gave her counsels so tender, that neither of them could talk business, and they no longer knew what point they were at" (*Memnon,* 208). As to be expected, the uncle makes his entrance at the propitious moment, threatening to kill them both unless Memnon hands over a large sum of money. Shamefacedly, Memnon acquiesces, then returns home.

What happens next? An invitation to dinner awaits him. He reasons that if he remains home alone after this horrific experience he will dwell on his own foolishness. If he accepts the invitation from his "intimate friends," he will eat and drink in moderation. Upon his arrival at dinner, his friends find him sorrowful. They ply him with food and offer him glass upon glass of alcoholic beverage to alleviate his chagrin, and then suggest a brief game—"a harmless pastime," Memnon reasons—which he accepts. After he loses all of his money and more, a quarrel arises, during which one of his "intimate friends" throws a dice-box at his head, blinding him in one eye. Memnon is carried home drunk, penniless, and minus an eye.

More misfortunes befall Memnon, including his banker's fraudulent bankruptcy. He fails to obtain justice and redress from his Royal Highness. Returning home, he is even more despairing upon finding his belongings being moved out of his house by his creditors. That night, while he is sleeping feverishly on some straw near the walls of his house, a celestial winged creature appears to him in a dream. "He had six wings, but neither feet nor head nor tail, and he bore no resemblance to anything" (*Memnon,* 211). He is a "good genius," the spirit tells Memnon. He comes from the small planet Sirius, 500 million leagues from the sun. Although Memnon begs him to return his eyesight in one eye, the celestial creature claims his inability to do so. Nonetheless, he does tell him about others, including his older brother, Hassan, who have suffered worse fates. Although Memnon will remain one-eyed the rest of his life, the creature assures him that he will enjoy relative happiness "provided you never form the stupid plan of being perfectly wise" (*Memnon,* 212).

Contrary to the declarations of certain poets, Pope, for example, and noted philosophers, such as Leibniz and Wolff, who claim that "all is well" on earth, Memnon's dream figure asserts that such words are applicable only in terms of cosmic spheres. No earthly being can determine to be completely strong, or completely powerful, or completely happy, or completely anything.

That not one of Memnon's intimate friends took responsibility for the loss of his eye, or even showed him some compassion, not only reveals Voltaire's hostility to the outside world but also discloses the importance of the symbology of the eye in general in Voltaire's writings. Zadig's eye, for example, is healed only after recovery of his inner sight—or the development of a reasonable, nonanthropocentric attitude toward life and cosmic order. In *Candide,* as we shall see, Dr. Pangloss, the spokesperson for Leibnizian optimism, was referred to as "the one-eyed doctor" because of his lack of insight (Van Den Heuvel, 206). In *Memnon,* although the protagonist never recovers his sight, the winged creature at the tale's conclusion inculcates in him a relativistic attitude and promises him enough happiness to deal with his sorrow. Like Zadig, who, at the outset of Voltaire's tale, equated moral virtue with a beneficial destiny, Memnon in his own foolishness initially sought happiness and solace by believing in the unequivocal promises of stoicism.

Micromégas (1752)

Although Voltaire sent an earlier version of one of his most extraordinary tales, *Micromégas* (entitled at the time *Voyage of Baron Gangan*), to Frederick the Great in 1739, the final text was composed during his stay at the Prussian court. Focusing on ways of diminishing the current anthropocentric belief that God created the universe for humankind's benefit, which Voltaire considered hubristic, he expanded his field of vision to include space travel. In so doing, he introduced his readers to two interplanetary voyagers and to a world of relativity where absolutes were either nonexistent or derided. His sense of irony and mockery and his techniques of exaggeration were at times used to denounce what Descartes and his followers had virtually glorified: that highest of powers, *reason.* For them, it was an instrument with the capacity at some future date of divining nature's secrets.

Genesis of Interplanetary Travel and Life

Voltaire was not the first to conceive of the idea of interplanetary travel, as has been mentioned. Lucretius (509 B.C.E.) in *De Rerum Natura* and Plutarch (50–125) in *De Facie in Orbe Lunae* declared that planets and stars were inhabited. The picturesque wanderings of the giants Gargantua and Pantagruel, in the book bearing their names by François Rabelais (1454–1553), also stirred Voltaire's imagination. Cyrano de Bergerac (1619–1655) narrated the joys and terrors of his imaginary visits to the moon and sun in *Comical History of the States and Empires of the Moon* (1656) and *Comical History of the States and Empires of the Sun* (1661). Christian Huygens (1629–1695), one of the best-known astronomers of the time, whom Voltaire mentions in *Micromégas,* suggested in his *Cosmotheoros* that other worlds were inhabited by creatures who resembled humans in size and were also endowed with five senses. *Gulliver's Travels* by Jonathan Swift (1667–1745), featuring giants and dwarfs, satirizes the application of human reason in political, social, and academic institutions. In his *Essay on Cosmology* (1756), Pierre-Louis Maupertuis asserted that other globes were inhabited. In *Elementa Matheseos Universae,* Christian Wolff (1679–1754) indicated a way of measuring the size of beings on other planets, especially Jupiter.[10] Both the notion of a plurality of worlds and the possibility of their being inhabited were very popular in the seventeenth and eighteenth centuries. Following discoveries made by astronomers such as Kepler, Galileo, and Kirchner, the theme of interplanetary travel assumed even greater excitement.

One of the greatest popularizers of interplanetary travel was Bernard le Bovier de Fontenelle (1657–1757), who took it upon himself to explain difficult scientific and astronomical concepts to laypeople, thus furthering their knowledge of Copernican, Galilean, and Keplerian theories. Although Voltaire chidingly took him as a model for the "dwarf" from Saturn in *Micromégas,* and derided Fontenelle's flowery language, he nonetheless recognized Fontenelle's contributions. In *Conversations on the Plurality of the Worlds* (1686), Fontenelle had already explored the notion of relativity, the earth being a small segment of the cosmos and man an insignificant part of a constantly expanding universe.[11] Though Fontenelle believed that the planets were peopled, he was loath to depict their inhabitants. "I don't know anything about them," he wrote. His rejection of the Ptolemaic and adoption of the Copernican and Galilean system not only demonstrated great courage on his part, since the latter veered sharply from papal decree, but paved the way for his later scientific observations as well. Let us recall that Descartes stopped writing what was purported to be his great work, *On the Earth,* when apprised of Galileo's condemnation by the Inquisition. Even the philosopher Pierre Gassendi (1592–1655), adversary of the much-touted Aristotle and Descartes, did not choose outright between the Copernican and Ptolemaic systems. As for Pascal (1623–1662), he felt it wiser not to enter into these matters. Fontenelle, hero that he was, wrote with admiration about Copernicus "for having reduced man's vanity to its proper size" (Fellows and Torrey, 54).

Relativism

Voltaire established the theme of relativity at the outset of his tale by naming his protagonist Micromégas—*micro* (Greek, "small") and *macro* (Greek, "large"). A composite of opposites, his hero represents the smallness of the microcosm and the hugeness of the macrocosm.

Micromégas, an inhabitant of the star Sirius (the Dog Star), measures 120,000 "royal feet" in height. Readers learn that he has left his abode because "the mufti of his country, a hair-splitter of great ignorance, found in [the book he had written] assertions that were suspicious, rash, offensive, unorthodox, and savoring of heresy." On what did his allegedly heretical ideas center? "Whether the bodies of Sirian fleas were made of the same substance as the bodies of Sirian slugs."[12] The mufti, judging the volume irreverent, had it condemned by jurists who had not read it, and Micromégas was banished from court for 800 years. Rather than vegetate, Micromégas decided to increase his knowledge, not by plunging into thoughtful abstractions, but rather, empirically, by living an interplanetary journey. The autobiographical elements in Voltaire's *Micromégas* will not escape the reader.

Micromégas, like Voltaire, felt that the better part of wisdom was to leave his habitat. Having great knowledge of "the laws of gravitation, and of the forces of repulsion and attraction," he traverses the Milky Way, and upon arriving on the planet Saturn, comments both on the absurd smallness of its globe, which is "hardly more than nine hundred times bigger than the earth," and its citizens, who are "dwarfs only about a thousand fathoms tall" (*Micromégas*, 415). After making friends with the secretary of Saturn's Academy of Sciences—a takeoff on Fontenelle—he notes that although the secretary is not an original thinker, he is, nonetheless, an excellent popularizer of science. Referring to him as "the dwarf from Saturn" because he is only 6,000 feet tall, Micromégas accepts nature's astonishing variety. He also learns that whereas Saturnians have been endowed with 72 senses and live 15,000 years, Sirians have nearly 1,000 senses but live 700 times longer than Saturnians. Reason guides Micromégas; he notes that "our existence is a point, our duration a flash, our globe an atom" (*Micromégas*, 418).

Micromégas's gigantic height, as compared with that of his diminutive companion from Saturn, serves to further underscore the notion of relativity. Additional resemblances and divergences become apparent. Sirius, the brightest star in the sky, is twice as large as the sun, and its light is twice as intense. The description of Saturn, a planet identified since Greek days with time, introduces such notions as change and evolution.

After some philosophical discussions between the Saturnian and the Sirian, these lucid observers decide to take a cosmic voyage to Jupiter, then to Mars. They find the latter so small that they fear that "they might not have room enough to lay themselves down," and so they continue (*Micromégas*, 421). After circling the earth in 36 hours on July 5, 1737, they comment on its poor construction and add, subjectively, that no sane person would ever want to live on this "heap of mud." Rather than investigate the globe scientifically, the dwarf bases his judgments on appearances, hastily and erroneously concluding that since he is unable to observe any life on Earth, there is none. Micromégas remonstrates: "With your little eyes you do not see certain stars of the fiftieth magnitude, which I perceive very distinctly. Do you conclude from your blindness that these stars do not exist?" (*Micromégas*, 423). The discussion becomes so heated that Micromégas breaks the string of his diamond necklace. As the dwarf picks up each stone individually, he selects one or two of them and perceives when he put them to his eye "that from the way they were cut they [make] first-rate magnifying glasses" (*Micromégas*, 424). Looking through a cut diamond, the travelers see an almost imperceptible spot, which they judge to be a whale. Micromégas lifts it with his hand and places it on his fingernail. Observing it more closely, they see that the object placed on his two fingers, then on the palm of his hands, is a ship. From its passengers, who are scientists and philosophers—"atoms talking to each other"—the travelers and the reader learn that the ship is returning from the North Pole: a true historical event. The ship's passengers and their leader, the French mathematician Maupertuis, had, in reality, just completed an expedition to Lapland undertaken to determine whether Newton's mathematical computations concerning the flattening of the polar regions were exact.

A conversation between the cosmic voyagers and the earthlings ensues. Micromégas and the Saturnian are shocked to learn that at that very moment 100,000 madmen are killing 100,000 others to determine whether a piece of mud belongs to a group headed by a Sultan or to another ruled by a Caesar. Concomitantly, they are astounded to hear that scientists are calculating the distance between the Dog Star and Gemini, the earth and the moon, and the weight of air. "Since you are so well acquainted with what is outside of you," Micromégas says, "you doubtless know still better what is inside. Tell me what your soul is, and how you form your ideas" (*Micromégas*, 433). At this point, a deafening cacophony breaks out as each passenger verbalizes his thoughts on the subject of the soul, God, and other metaphysical notions. One quotes Aristotle; another, Saint Thomas Aquinas; another, Descartes, Leibniz, Locke, and so forth. "Why do you quote Aristotle in Greek?" Micromégas inquires. "Because," the scholar replies, "one should always quote what one does not comprehend at all in the language one understands least" (*Micromégas*, 434). The wisest of the philosophers is, of course, the humble partisan of Locke:

I do not know how I think, but I do know that I have never thought save
by virtue of my senses. That there are immaterial and intelligent beings I
do not doubt: but that it is impossible for God to endow matter with
mind I doubt very much. I hold the power of God in veneration: I am
not free to set bounds to it: I predicate nothing: I am content to believe
that more things are possible than we think. (*Micromégas*, 435)

Upon hearing the heteroclite conclusions forwarded by these atomlike creatures, the space travelers cannot help but laugh, wondering how
such tiny entities could be so arrogant. But though they are possessed of
minuscule theological, philosophical, and metaphysical knowledge,
their ability to measure, calculate, and observe is impressive. The cosmic
voyagers thereupon declare them to be extraordinary in their scientific
and mathematical acumen.

Before departing, Micromégas and his companion give the "insignificant atoms" a large book from which the secrets of nature and destiny
may be gleaned. The volume is brought to Paris to the Academy of Science, where the aged secretary opens it and finds nothing but blank
pages. "Ah! I thought as much," he says, suggesting that humans must
accept their limitations and not decree what is beyond their capacities
(*Micromégas*, 435).

Anthropocentrism versus Heliocentrism

Judging from the happenings in *Micromégas,* one may affirm that
Voltaire (Micromégas) and Fontenelle (the Saturnian) believed that the
universe was heliocentric and that planetary worlds were inhabited by
creatures varying in size and intelligence. If the earth were not the center of the universe, as Copernicus and Galileo had maintained and as
Micromégas affirmed, then perhaps no center existed. If such were the
case, then comparisons and analogies would be in order, and the establishing of some common denominators between one planet and another
would be equally feasible.

By comparing the sizes of Saturn, the Dog Star, Jupiter, Mars, and
Earth, Voltaire not only underscored the concept of relativity but
derided the Ptolemaic system as well. The latter considered the earth to
be immobile and at the center of the universe, and to be surrounded by
seven "immutable and incorruptible" heavens inhabited by angels.
While the Ptolemaic system was sanctioned by the Roman Catholic
Church, all other doctrines were declared "heretical" until 1822, when
the Vatican finally accepted the Copernican view.

Throughout *Micromégas* Voltaire alluded to groundbreaking experiments and explorations upon which he based his scientific suppositions. His tale used the microscope and the telescope (early models of which were constructed by Galileo) to assert what Pascal and other mathematicians and scientists would also affirm: that there were two extremes within the universe, the infinitely small and the infinitely large.

Voltaire's text is star-studded with references to the achievements of the Dutch naturalist Anton van Leeuwenhoek, who constructed a simple microscope that brought animalcules into view; the Dutch physicist and histologist Niklaas Hartsoeker, who perfected the microscope and discovered spermatozoa in seminal liquid; René-Antoine Réaumur, naturalist and physicist who invented the thermometer; discovered instincts in ants, bees, and other tiny creatures; and was a partisan of relativism. About Jan Swammerdam, the Dutch naturalist who founded the science of entomology, one of the philosophers on the ship noted:

> He made him understand in short, that there are animals which to the bee are what the bee is to man, what the Sirian himself was to the prodigious animals he had mentioned, and what these animals are to other things compared with which they seem but atoms. (*Micromégas*, 430)

Locke, Voltaire's favorite philosopher, suggested the existence of a variety of cosmic beings, some larger and superior to humankind, others smaller and inferior.[13] Even Leibniz, whom Voltaire derided mercilessly, subscribed to the relativistic belief (Wade 1950, 116). Rejected in *Micromégas* were extremists, whether they belonged to the Enlightenment movement or not: to be convinced that nothing can be understood or explained save by means of "the light of reason," or maintain the opposite, that faith is almighty and reason can fathom nothing, was declared to be false. The over- or undervaluation of reason, Voltaire posited, was as destructive as full-fledged dogmatism. Since both lead to blindness, vulnerability increases either way. To assume that reason can also dictate one's emotions, instincts, and desires and that humankind's will can control them all is not only an impossibility but utter madness, as Voltaire had demonstrated so convincingly in *Memnon*.

Voltaire realized that the human mind had its limitations; to think otherwise would not serve humanity's purpose. The relativization of intelligence, as well as religious, philosophical, and political ideations and humankind's place in the cosmos, was clearly forwarded in *Micromégas*. With Locke, Voltaire was convinced that answers to general or specific problems were not possible. Locke "dared to doubt," wrote Voltaire, as did his own two travelers.

Regaling his readers with a giant's enthusiastic but circumspect approach to existence, Voltaire also opened them up to interplanetary journeys vicariously experienced through his cosmic travelers—but without the fear the universe inspired in such a one as Pascal.

Plato's Dream (Songe de Platon) (1756)

At the time of his composition of the *Philosophical Letters,* Voltaire was not knowledgeable about Plato's philosophy. Like his friends Lord Bolingbroke and Alexander Pope, he had lampooned this ancient Greek philosopher/metaphysician, referring to him as a "dreamer." At Cirey in 1737, however, while preparing his *Elements of Newton's Philosophy,* he and Mme Du Châtelet spent long hours reading and discussing Plato's dialogues, and especially the giant cosmological myth related in *Timaeus.* Voltaire admitted that "the first time I read Plato, and I saw this gradation of beings rising from the slightest atom, to the Supreme Being, this ladder struck me with admiration" (Van Den Heuvel, 60). Although the date of publication originally ascribed to *Plato's Dream* was 1756, contemporary scholars believe it was written at Cirey between 1737 and 1738 (Van Den Heuvel, 64).

Plato's Dream was based on the Greek philosopher's image, as adumbrated in *Timaeus,* that of the Demiurgos, the eternal and sovereign God who guaranteed cosmic harmony throughout the universe, and who was "responsible for the main structure and ordered movements of the world's soul and body, and for the creation of the heavenly gods: stars, planets, and Earth."[14] Having delegated some of his creative powers to inferior gods, the Demiurgos proceeded to fashion humans and animals. Plato not only made the distinction between the world of Forms and of Becoming but explored as well the function of the Demiurgos.

In *Plato's Dream,* Voltaire turns his winsome mockery of the Greek philosopher's Idea/Ideals into a delightful minidrama that reveals his own cosmological fantasy. By borrowing from Samuel Clarke's interpretation of Newton's findings, Voltaire expanded on the ancient myth of a spherical world with the earth as its center and the seven planets revolving around it in a circular and perfectly regular movement. In time, after many millions of years, it was said that this movement would diminish, and the irregularities of the planets would increase, thus bringing the universe to an end.

At the outset of his philosophical tale, Voltaire's jocular voice is heard relating one of Plato's dreams:

> It seemed to him that the great Demiurge, the eternal Geometrician, having populated infinite space with innumerable globes, decided to test the knowledge of the genii who had been witnesses of his works. He gave each of them a little piece of matter to arrange, much as Phidias and Zeuxis might have given their disciples statues and pictures to make, if it is permissible to compare small things with great.
>
> Demogorgon had as his share the bit of mud that is called *Earth;* and, having arranged it in the manner that we see today, he claimed to have made a masterpiece. He thought he had triumphed over envy, and was expecting praise, even from his colleagues; he was quite surprised to be received by them with hoots.[15]

A particularly disagreeable genius criticized the Demogorgon for having divided the earth into two parts, separating the hemispheres by large expanses of water and thereby preventing any possible communication between them, and for having permitted people to freeze on the poles, to die of heat at the equinoctial line, and to hunger and thirst in large deserts. Although the disagreeable genius was relatively satisfied with the creation of sheep, cows, chickens, and vegetables that the Demogorgon brought into existence, he was not so with his serpents, spiders, and poisonous plants. What were the reasons for the fashioning of such entities? The Demogorgon had indeed endowed two-footed animals with reason, but even this verged on the ridiculous. Why did he give them so many enemies (thus fomenting wars), illnesses that wiped out multitudes, devastating passions without defense mechanisms for protection, and so little wisdom?

Taken aback by such criticisms, the Demogorgon argued that while moral and physical evil were implicit in his creation, a preponderance of good nonetheless prevailed. "It is easy to criticize, but do you think it is so easy to make an animal that is always reasonable, that is free, and that never abuses its liberty?" (*Plato's Dream*, 226). Counterattacking, the Demogorgon derogated the fashioner of Mars, with its two great bands and moonless nights. Saturn, Jupiter, Mercury, and Venus were all censured for one or another reason. The discussions were long, each genius chiming in to derogate the other's seeming achievements, but always in a very human manner—with humor and witty repartees.

There followed the composition of lengthy volumes, pamphlets, and songs, after which the Demiurgos told the genii that because their creations were a composite of good and evil, they were imperfect. He also informed them that the world would be destroyed in some hundreds of millions of years, after which the two-legged animals would evolve and do better. Meanwhile, "it belongs to me alone to make things perfect and immortal" (*Plato's Dream*, 227). And following this powerful conclusion, Plato awoke!

What was significant in *Plato's Dream* was not the fashioning of the world per se, nor the thought that it was governed by a rational and intelligent principle. Rather, the novelty of the tale lay in the irreverent and contentious means by which Voltaire broached notions such as moral and physical evil with regard to the Creator's organizational plan. Fascinating as well was his view that geniuses—poets, creative people in general—were not, as some contended, superior to others. They, too, proved to be vulnerable to envy, jealousy, rage, and other passions. How naive was Demogorgon, then, to think that he could abolish envy.

Voltaire had again poured his own philosophical doubts, questions, and frustrations into the twists and turns of his realistic and timely tale. And Voltaire knew whereof he spoke, having himself been the butt of jealousy, cupidity, and calumny by poets as well as by fanatics. Unlike Plato, who worked in abstract concepts, Voltaire reviled them.

The notion of relativity implicit in *Plato's Dream* allowed greater argumentative flexibility on the author's part, notably with regard to an individual's identity and his place within the All. For Voltaire, as we know, learning permitted continuous comparisons to be drawn between the whole and its parts—the minute, the atom, or the human being—as juxtaposed to the totality; the earth in proportion to the great All; the imperfect as measured against the perfect; mortality balanced against immortality. As for the notion of duration:

> Experience had made it only too clear that God made machines to be destroyed. We are the product of his wisdom and we perish; why then wouldn't the world experience a similar fate? Leibniz wants this world to be perfect; but if God fashioned it to last only a certain period of time, its perfection consists then in lasting only until the instant ordered for its dissolution."[16]

Voltaire was not so much interested in the origin of the world or other abstract speculations as he was in its condition. The question of good and evil was his main preoccupation; the actuality of the real world was always what triggered his concern.

Candide, or Optimism (1759)

By 1755, Voltaire's years of wandering had concluu⌣⌣ of Les Délices, a property in Geneva. His dream of owning a garu⌣⌣, enjoying country living, and of having the leisure to pursue his writings had been finally fulfilled. Or had it? As for finding a beloved to warm his old age, he settled on his niece, Mme Denis, his paramour for many years. As the days wore on, however, he found her to be dumpy, greedy, loud, and foolish—at least for the time being. Had he anyone else in mind? Did he consciously or unconsciously nourish the thought that Countess Charlotte, Sophie de Beinck, whom he had met during his stay in Prussia, would charm his later years? Disappointment greeted him on this score. Although she settled in Switzerland, she was capricious by nature and remained aloof.

Voltaire's biggest disappointment, however, resulted not from the female quarter but from what he considered to be the "insularity" of the Swiss. Their rejection of new ideas, their Calvinism—especially their ban on theater—was anathema to Voltaire. Was he perhaps trying to duplicate that happy time he had spent with Mme Du Châtelet at Cirey? If so, he no doubt must have eventually realized the harsh differences existing between the lifestyle at Les Délices and that in the Garden of Eden with his great mentor and friend Mme Du Châtelet (Van Den Heuvel, 238).

Unlike *Zadig* and *Micromégas,* with their still relatively positive modus vivendi, *Candide* is, understandably, pessimistic on the subject of collective problems such as war, fanaticism, intolerance, persecution, clericalism, and the exploitation of the weak and the ignorant. Nonetheless, Voltaire's struggle against the ills of society took on even greater momentum. Nor did his belief in relativism, moderation, and heliocentrism diminish in intensity. Although Voltaire knew moments of despair, he was never one to yield to it.

Voltaire's Diminishing Optimism

Because *Candide*'s message so consistently denigrated the optimistic philosophy of both Pope and Leibniz, let us briefly review Voltaire's own stand.

An early partisan of optimism in his poem *Man of the World* (1736), Voltaire contented himself in his younger days with relatively superficial arguments as a means of confronting the great adversities befalling humanity. He depicted life in glowing terms—"Terrestrial paradise is where I am"—sidestepping the dicta of those who preached frugality and asceticism. In time, however, he could no longer reconcile his own mechanistic interpretation of the universe with Leibniz's notion of a solely good God (Bolingbroke called Leibniz a "chimerical quack," and metaphysicians "learned lunatics"). Life's vagaries, however, taught Voltaire to be more circumspect. Instead of criticizing unwelcome ideas directly, he used various subterfuges to communicate his disenchantment, as is evident in the ironic choice of the word *Optimism* as a subtitle for *Candide.*

What had attracted the young Voltaire to Pope was the English poet-philosopher's adherence to many of Newton's theories, such as his Deism and his repudiation of the doctrine of Original Sin. Indeed, Voltaire's own belief in the divine harmony existing in nature had once bellowed forth in his *Discourses in Verse on Man* (1738). But in time, he lost his conviction that all was well on Earth in its present form and that an infinitely perfect being had created the earth, as enunciated by Pope in his *Essay on Man.* He came to dislike Pope's optimism because he felt it encouraged a state of passivity in humans.

> Then say not Man's imperfect, Heaven in fault;
> Say rather, Man's as perfect as he ought. . . .
> Who finds not Providence all good and wise,
> Alike in what it gives and what it denies?

Nor did Voltaire accept Pope's concept that what appears to be an evil, which is beyond humans' comprehension, may be part of a universal good, thus fitting into the harmony of God's plan.

In Voltaire's *Treatise on Metaphysics* (1734), he suggested that the concepts of good and evil had nothing to do with God. They were finite—as was man who created them—and could not be applied to Deity, an infinite being. Humankind, not God, was responsible for good and for evil acts. Therefore, humankind was the propagator of evil in the form of wars, fanaticism, and intolerance: "It is the fault of men if such abominable pillaging takes place, which they frequently honor with the name of virtue; the blame is theirs, the poor laws they made, or their lack of courage which prevents them from executing the good ones" (Brooks, 77).

Good and evil being coeval, Voltaire affirmed that people were free to create their own happiness within the framework of virtue and moderation. Under the tutelage of Mme Du Châtelet, a partisan of Leibniz's optimism, Voltaire came to know the German philosopher's concepts more thoroughly. After her death (1749), and following his own humiliating dispute with Frederick the Great (1752), Voltaire became increasingly disenchanted with life. The bloody carnage during the wars that had engulfed and still were engulfing Europe (the Succession of Poland, the Succession of Austria, the Seven Years' War), as well as the 1755 Lisbon earthquake, tidal wave, and fire that killed 30,000 to 40,000 people, added to his disillusionment. Voltaire finally discarded optimism.

The disparities between Leibniz's idealism and the sordid realities Voltaire faced daily seemed irremedially opposed. Although he considered Leibniz one of the most brilliant philosophers of the day, Voltaire frequently and willfully misunderstood or exaggerated his ideas to suit his own purposes. Particularly demonstrable is the leitmotiv of *Candide,* "this is the best of all possible worlds." But the German metaphysician had never stated that the world was perfect. He was well aware that evil existed as part of the scheme of things: "an expression of an indifferent and all-powerful Will, but of an all-powerful Will which knows and decrees the best." Leibniz pronounced himself on matter as well, defining it as an indivisible entity composed of "monads" and possessing a consciousness, similar to but greater than the atom. Rising in an ascending hierarchy, as in a "chain of being," the highest monad, he concluded, was God. Body and mind functioned according to a "preestablished harmony," and thus everything has its cause, or, in Leibnizian terms, its "sufficient reason."[17]

Voltaire rejected Leibniz's metaphysical premises: that God is good; that he created this world over all the others he could have created, and that although evil exists, it has moral value, given the goodness of God. Voltaire at this juncture found Leibniz's point of view objectionable for the same reason he disapproved of Pope's: their beliefs inspired an attitude of complacency. To accept poverty and stupidity as part of God's "preestablished harmony," Voltaire subsumed, was to destroy humankind's sense of growth, evolution, and accomplishment. "I owe my precious happiness to myself alone," Voltaire affirmed. To believe on the one hand in an infinite, perfect God that transcends finite humanity and on the other hand to suggest that he enters into worldly affairs is to degrade him.

Voltaire's antioptimism, basic to *Candide,* evidently coalesced after the Lisbon earthquake. The disaster was the catalyst that caused him to write the following to his friend Elie Bertrand concerning the doctrine of optimism: "It's a cruel philosophy under a consoling name." Now more than ever Voltaire questioned the ways of Providence. How did God care for his creatures? Rousseau's blithe statement concerning the Lisbon earthquake—had people been living in the country rather than in the city, fewer would have been killed—could only displease him. Other rationalizations were equally anathema to Voltaire: the Portuguese Jesuit Malgrida's claim that the quake was God's punishment for a vice-ridden Lisbon; and the Moslems' proclamation that it was Allah's revenge for the Inquisition.

All in all, the Lisbon disaster disproved the philosophies of both Pope and Leibniz: the world is neither stable nor benign. It is up to human-kind to rectify both personal and social ills, Voltaire affirmed under the rubric "Liberty," in his *Philosophical Dictionary*: "Your will is not free but your actions are. You are free to act when you have the power to act." Individual and collective action are the only means of improving humankind's lot (*PD,* 178).

To say that Voltaire, in *Candide,* made satirical mincemeat of Pope's, but mostly of Leibniz's cosmic plan, is an understatement. He accom-plished his goal via philosophical disquisitions and satiric innuendos, and by means of rapid accumulation of contrasting episodes, each of which either injected a false sense of well-being into the protagonists or forced them to face catastrophic fallouts. Seeking refuge neither in Pas-calian despair nor in a convoluted world of illusions, Voltaire opens his tale with a parody of Genesis leading to Candide's Fall from Paradise.

The Archetypal Candide

No longer an outlandish creature, such as Babouc or Zadig, or a giant, like Micromégas, Voltaire's new hero, although exaggerated, nonethe-less seems more plausible. His name, Candide, from the Latin *candidus* (honest, straightforward), underscores his salient characteristics: unprej-udiced, unbiased, impartial, honest, and sincere. Such a universal and eternal type lives and reacts humanly to concatenations of all kinds.

One might allude to Candide as a metaphor of Locke's tabula rasa: born pure and unblemished by life's many imprints. Candide's adventures unfold within a picaresque format—a genre whose intent was to deride the prototype of the so-called great heroes of the past, who realized their noble dreams and ideals through slaughter and the usurpation of lands. Candide differed from his predecessors, in that he neither achieved wealth or fame nor inflicted suffering upon others—only upon himself. Nonetheless, each time he was hurt, physically or emotionally, rather than stagnate, he went on to increase his understanding of life, striving to know how best to construct a personality capable of coping with real terrors and how best to avoid being caught up in a dazzling hope syndrome, which would lead inevitably to the deepest of depressive states. Candide's wise reasonings at the conclusion of his life amounted to living life honorably, as nobly and as simply as he could, given the options.

Voltaire, as was his way, offered no theories, no plans, no systems or credos. The individual must seek his or her way, learn from past mistakes, and proceed under the banner of truth and virtue, no matter the pain and difficulties confronted.

The Divestiture of Optimism

To face reality and divest oneself of palliatives—religious, philosophical, or other—was for Voltaire the only way to evolve, to find one's direction, and to strengthen oneself during life's arduous journey. Like such heroes as Tristan and Parzival, Candide would learn to observe and to see clearly through adversity, calamity, and suffering. Although victimized by a series of catastrophes, including wars and the Inquisition, Candide not only endured his ordeals, he never strayed from the path of kindness and stalwartness he had chartered for himself early in his quest.

Candide may be said to be structured around a series of falls—catastrophes—and renewals. Readers are admonished not to fall prey to easy doctrines that promise this and that on earth or in heaven, according to one's behavior in the here and now. They are encouraged to determine, on an individual basis, the most productive way of life for themselves, and to make that life as bearable as possible.

Candide's first ordeal involved shedding the lessons taught him by the great philosopher Dr. Pangloss (Greek, *pan,* all; *glossa,* tongue, i.e., "Windbag"), a caricature of Leibniz. To accomplish such a feat, however, required that he begin thinking for himself, and thus reject Leibniz's pat slogan: "All is for the best in the best of all possible worlds," or Pope's "Whatever is, is right." He must learn to live his ordeals, his experiences, for these are better teachers than abstract hypothesizing.

We are told that Candide was brought up in the west German province of Westphalia, and more precisely in the castle of the baron of

Thunderten-Tronckh, the name being a metaphor for Frederick II, and a mockery of long, convoluted, and guttural German-sounding appellations. Although Candide was said to be an orphan, the older servants suspected he was the son of the baron's sister and a gentleman of the vicinity. So absurd were the traditions of the petty German princes that the baron's sister refused to marry the father of her child because his coat of arms, under the rigorous code of heraldry, did not meet her family's "quarterings."[18]

The baron's family was imposing. His wife, weighing 350 pounds, commanded great consideration. The son was worthy of his father. Cunégonde, the 17-year-old "plump" and "appetizing" daughter, became Candide's heartthrob. Dr. Pangloss, the castle's "oracle," presided over the intellectual evolution of the family. His sphere of expertise was "metaphysical-theological-cosmolonigology" (the last word, of Voltaire's manufacture, includes the homonym *nigaud,* "simpleton, foolish, blockhead," and thus the author's derision for Pangloss's philosophy (*Candide* 1977, 231).

> He proved admirably that there is no effect without a cause . . . in this best of all possible worlds. . . . Tis demonstrated . . . that things cannot be otherwise; for, since everything is made for an end, everything is necessarily for the best end. Observe that noses were made to wear spectacles; and so we have spectacles. Legs were visibly instituted to be breeched, and we have breeches. Stones were formed to be quarried and to build castles; and My Lord has a very noble castle; the greatest Baron in the province should have the best house; and as pigs were made to be eaten, we eat pork, all the year round; consequently, those who have asserted that all is well talk nonsense; they ought to have said that all is for the best. (*Candide* 1977, 230)

While the entire family listened intently to Dr. Pangloss's discourses, Candide reasoned most innocently that he was living in the happiest of all possible worlds.

One day, while Cunégonde happened to be passing through a wooded area she *chanced* upon Dr. Pangloss, who was in the process of giving her mother's chambermaid a lesson in experimental physics. "Breathlessly" and "excitedly," she observed the Doctor's "sufficient reason" and "the effects and the causes" and was "filled with the desire of learning." The following day,

> Cunégonde and Candide happened to find themselves behind a screen; she most innocently dropped her handkerchief, and he most innocently

picked it up; she most innocently held his hand; the young man most innocently kissed it with remarkable vivacity, tenderness and grace, whereupon their lips met, their eyes sparkled, their knees trembled, their hands wandered. (*Candide* 1977, 231)

The baron, who chanced to pass near the screen, "observing this cause and effect," banished Candide from the Edenic kingdom (*Candide* 1977, 231).

Candide's Wanderings: Theory versus Reality

Although still a firm believer in Dr. Pangloss's reasonings, once on his own Candide began to experience the chasm separating theory from reality.

In the Bulgarian Army

Alone, without a sou, shivering in a snowbound land, Candide, a proto-type of the contemporary antihero, wandered about. Every now and then he looked up to heaven for counsel, then looked back to the castle with yearning.

Happening upon the town of Waldberghoff-trarbk-dikdorf, after a series of humorous incidents, he was forcibly inducted into the Bulgar-ian (Prussian) army. No sooner had the two recruiting soldiers taken his measurements, declaring that his height met their standards and pre-dicting that fortune and glory would be his, than they "put irons on his legs and [took] him to the regiment." So poorly did Candide perform during his drills, that to improve his execution, educational standards required that he be beaten.

On a beautiful spring day, Candide decided to take a walk in the countryside, reasoning that to use "his legs as he pleased [was] a privi-lege of the human species as well as of animals." Hardly had he gone two leagues than he was caught, bound, dragged back to the barracks, and put into a cell. He was given his *choice* of punishments: he could either be "thrashed thirty-six times by the whole regiment or receive a dozen lead bullets at once in his brain" (*Candide* 1977, 233). Although neither alternative appealed to Candide, he realized that he had to com-ply with the court order "by virtue of that gift of God [free will] which is called *liberty*." He therefore "determined to run the gauntlet thirty-six times and actually did so twice" (*Candide* 1977, 233). Since there were 2,000 men in the regiment, it meant receiving 4,000 strokes, thus lay-ing "bare his muscles and nerves from his neck to his backside." So excruciating was the pain that Candide begged to have his "head smashed." His wish was granted. They bound his eyes and forced him to kneel down, at which point the king of the Bulgarians happened to pass by. After talking with Candide, he realized that he was "very ignorant in worldly matters" and pardoned him. An "honest surgeon"—a rarity for the time—healed the wounds he had incurred from three weeks of beatings. No sooner had Candide's skin begun to heal and his legs to function, than the Bulgarian king declared war on the Abarians. (The blood-soaked war that was now to be depicted by Voltaire is a reference to the Seven Years' War [1756–1763], in which Prussia was allied with England against the French, Austrians, and Russians.)

The conflagration having erupted, Candide, trembling "like a philosopher," hid during the "heroic butchery." An archenemy of war, Voltaire described his battle scenes in purposefully gory terms:

> Old men dazed with blows watched the dying agonies of their murdered wives who clutched their children to their bleeding breasts; there, disem-boweled girls who had been made to satisfy the natural appetites of heroes gasped their last sighs; others, half burned, begged to be put to death. Brains were scattered on the ground among dismembered arms and legs. (*Candide* 1977, 234)

Because the bayonet was the "sufficient reason" for about 30,000 deaths, the two kings commanded a Te Deum to be performed to thank God for victory, or to ask God for his blessing in defeat. Recourse to God under such beastly circumstances was a religious custom Voltaire found more than obnoxious.

Holland: Religious Zeal

Once out of the war zone, Candide walked on until he reached Holland. He had heard that the citizens of this land were rich and Christian, and he looked forward to being well treated by them. Aware that he had not a sou, he asked for alms virtually upon arrival. Much to his surprise, he was told that should he continue to beg he would be put into a house of correction. After speaking with an orator who had been lecturing for one hour to a large group of people on the meaning of charity, he asked him for alms, thinking he would be well received. "What are you doing here?" the orator asked Candide. Had he come here for the Church? Upon repeating Dr. Pangloss's credo—"There is no effect without a cause"—the orator asked: "Do you believe the Pope is the Anti-Christ?" Naively, Candide replied: "I had never heard so before, but whether he is or not, I am starving." Angered by his answer, the orator told him that he did not deserve to eat, nor should he ever come near him again. As for the orator's wife, who had listened to the conversation from her upstairs window, she settled the matter by pouring the contents of a slop pail on Candide's head. "O, heavens!" Candide cried out, "to what excess religious zeal is carried by ladies!" (*Candide* 1977, 235).

Since "there is no effect without a cause" and all "is necessarily linked up and arranged for the best," it stands to reason that Candide should meet a man who had never been baptized (*Candide* 1977, 235). And he did: Jacques, an honest Anabaptist, who took Candide to his home, washed and fed him, gave him money, and taught him bookkeeping. Out of gratitude, Candide threw himself at Jacques's feet, then said: "Dr. Pangloss was right in telling me that all is for the best in this world" (*Candide* 1977, 236).

Dr. Pangloss

To degrade a protagonist, Voltaire freely used the literary technique of commenting ironically on his or her fate. Candide happened upon a beggar "covered with sores, [one-eyed], with the end of his nose fallen away, his mouth awry, his teeth black, who talked huskily, was tormented with a violent cough and spat out a tooth at every cough" (*Candide* 1977, 236). This ghastly specimen threw his arms around Candide. Didn't he recognize his "dear Pangloss"? Aghast, Candide asked him what misfortunes had befallen him. His love for Paquette—and for many other women—had brought him syphilis. Candide asked about Cunégonde, "the pearl of young ladies, the masterpiece of Nature" (*Candide* 1977, 236). Before receiving Dr. Pangloss's answer, Candide took him to Jacques's stable to give him food. Only then was he informed of Cunégonde's demise, and he fainted. She was raped and her belly slit. The Baron, rushing to his daughter's rescue, had his head smashed. The baroness was cut into pieces. The castle was destroyed. But Dr. Pangloss added—in one of Voltaire's memorable ironies—that the family's side had been avenged, for the Abarians did the same to a Bulgarian lord. Where, then, is the best of all possible worlds? Candide queried.

Lisbon: The Inquisition, the Tidal Wave, the Fire

Jacques, called to Lisbon for business reasons, invited Candide and Dr. Pangloss to join him. Aboard ship, Dr. Pangloss philosophized anew. The evils that had befallen them were for the best and "indispensable," inasmuch as "private misfortunes [made for] public good, so that the more private misfortunes there are, the more everything is well" (*Candide* 1977, 239).

As they approached the port of Lisbon, darkness covered the world. A tempest raged. Some of the sick passengers screamed, others prayed. As for the good Anabaptist, he was cast into the waves and drowned after preventing a sailor from falling overboard. Paradoxically, the brutal sailor whose life he had saved not only made no attempt to save him but never even looked his way. Instinctively, Candide wanted to jump into the sea to rescue his benefactor, but he was prevented by Dr. Pangloss, who reasoned that the Lisbon harbor had been created expressly for the Anabaptist to drown in. Moments later the ship split in two, and all aboard were drowned except for Dr. Pangloss, Candide, and the brutish sailor.

No sooner had the group arrived in Lisbon than "the sea rose in foaming masses in the port . . . whirlwinds of flame and ashes covered the streets and squares, the houses collapsed" (*Candide* 1977, 240). Meanwhile, Pangloss wondered what the sufficient reason could have been to have provoked this phenomenon. Having perhaps read the Apocalypse, the last book in the Bible, Candide reasoned: "It is the last day!" (*Candide* 1977, 240). While they philosophized, the brutal sailor ran among the corpses, picked their pockets, got drunk, and enjoyed the favors of a prostitute. As for Candide, he was struck by falling stones from a building, fell to the ground, and, believing himself to be dying, begged Dr. Pangloss to get him a little wine and oil. Too busy philosophizing to respond, only after Candide had lost consciousness did Pangloss bring him water from a nearby fountain.

After receiving some food, the group wandered through the ruins, helping the wretched as best they could. Pangloss consoled them with the thought that "all this is for the best; for, if there is a volcano at Lisbon, it cannot be anywhere else; for it is impossible that things should not be where they are; for all is well" (*Candide* 1977, 241).

A member of the Inquisition, having heard Pangloss's discourse, replied: "Apparently, you do not believe in Original Sin; for, if everything is for the best, there was neither fall nor punishment" (*Candide* 1977, 242). Pangloss begged to be heard: "The fall of man and the curse necessarily entered into the best of all possible worlds" (*Candide* 1977, 242). The Inquisitor retorted: "Then you do not believe in free will?" But of course he did, he affirmed, and then discoursed on the subject: "Free will can exist with absolute necessity; for it was necessary that we should be free; for, in short, limited will . . ." (*Candide* 1977, 242).

Lisbon's wise men decided that there was no better way of allaying the trauma suffered by a people after their city's destruction than by giving them "a splendid *auto-da-fé*" (act of faith; burning at the stake). The great teachers at the University of Coimbre maintained that "the sight of several persons being slowly burned in great ceremony is an infallible secret for preventing earthquakes" (*Candide* 1977, 242). Understandably, they arrested some people on trumped-up charges, bound Pangloss for having spoken, and Candide for having listened, and took them to an area where they would feel no "discomfort from the sun." At the end of the week, they dressed them in a san benito and on their heads, put paper mitres, and marched them in procession to the accompaniment of a sermon and plainsong. Although contrary to custom, Candide was flogged in rhythm to the music, and Pangloss was hanged; the others were burned at the stake, in keeping with tradition.

While Candide was still questioning Pangloss's reasonings—"If this is the best of all possible worlds, what are the others?"—an old woman approached him. "Courage, my son, follow me" (*Candide* 1977, 243). He obeyed. Once in her hovel, she gave him an ointment for his wounds, food, drink, and clothing. The following day, she took him to an isolated house surrounded by gardens and canals. Leading him up a back stairway, he entered a gilded apartment where he met a veiled woman adorned with precious stones. No sooner did she lift her veil than Candide recognized her as Cunégonde and fainted. After Candide came to, Cunégonde told him that her parents and brother were dead; that she had been raped by a Bulgarian soldier, saved by a Bulgarian captain who forced her to do his washing and cooking; that after tiring of her, he sold her to a Jew, Don Issachar, who took her to Holland, then to Portugal, where he gave her a gorgeous country home. One day, however, the Grand Inquisitor noticed her at mass, "ogled her," and told her that it was beneath her rank to belong to a Jew. Only by threatening Don Issachar with an auto-da-fé, did he obtain that the two should divide her favors: she belonged to the Jew on Mondays, Wednesdays, and the Sabbath; and to the Grand Inquisitor the other days. The Grand Inquisitor did her the honor of inviting her to an auto-da-fé. Her seat was excellent. It was after having been offered refreshments "between the Mass and the execution" that she recognized Pangloss and Candide (*Candide* 1977, 247).

In time, Don Issachar, annoyed at the thought of having to share Cunégonde with the Grand Inquisitor, and now with Candide, drew his long dagger to slay the latter. No longer the gullible lad he had once been, Candide, having learned from experience—in this case from the Bulgarian soldiers—slew Don Issachar and the Grand Inquisitor as well. The latter's body was buried in a splendid church, while Don Issachar's was thrown into a sewer. Cunégonde and Candide fled to Cadiz, then took a ship to Buenos Aires.[19]

Buenos Aires and the Jesuits of Paraguay

Upon landing, the three called on the governor of Buenos Aires, Don Fernando d'Ibaraa y Figueora y Mascarenes y Lampourdos y Souza, a spoof on Portuguese and Spanish names. He fell in love with Cunégonde and offered to marry her. Complications arose when Candide learned that he was wanted for the murder of the Grand Inquisitor. It was decided that Cunégonde would remain with the governor and Candide would flee. Though heartbroken at having to be separated from his beloved, Candide and his sensible valet, Cacambo, whom he had brought from Spain, left full speed ahead on Andalusian horses.

Having once been a servitor in the College of the Assumption, Cacambo was familiar with *Los Padres* land, and its admirable government—"a masterpiece of reason and justice"—for it is *"los padres* who own everything, and the people nothing" (*Candide* 1977, 263). Upon their arrival, Cacambo tried to arrange for Candide to see the reverend provincial father (the commandant) but was told that after saying mass, he was out on parade. Candide would have to wait three hours before being given permission to kiss his spurs (*Candide* 1977, 263). When finally the commandant learned that the visitors were not Spanish but German, he met Candide. They all sat down to a copious breakfast served in gold dishes, in contrast to the Paraguayan people, who ate maize in wooden bowls in the heat of the sun.

No sooner did their conversation grow animated than Candide recognized the commandant as the baron's son, "embraced [him] and shed rivers of tears" (*Candide* 1977, 265). He informed him that his sister had not been "disemboweled" but was in fine health, and that he intended to marry her. "Insolent wretch," the Jesuit priest responded, striking him with the flat of his sword. No longer the passive and tender young man, Candide struck him a deadly blow, then wept in disbelief at the thought that he had actually killed three people—two of whom had been priests.

Cacambo and Candide fled on horseback, shouting in Spanish, "Way, way for the Reverend Father Colonel!" and arriving at the land of the naked "savages," the Oreillons, only to pursue their course to Eldorado.

Eldorado: Land of Plenty

No sooner had they set foot in the land of plenty, Eldorado (in Peru), than they saw children dressed in torn brocade playing with glimmering red, yellow, and green quoits. Curious about these gorgeous stones, they picked some up and were overwhelmed when they realized they were chunks of gold, emeralds, and rubies. Those children, Candide reasoned, surely belonged to the nobility and were very well brought up since they had been taught to "despise gold and precious stones" (*Candide* 1977, 274). Wherever they went, people were dressed in gold, and, upon being served the finest delicacies at an inn, Candide paid for his meal with the gold he had picked up from the streets. The host and hostess could not refrain from laughing, explaining that everything in Eldorado being geared to helping commerce, hotels were subsidized by the government.

Unlike all other countries they had visited, Eldorado was devoid of wretched and suffering creatures. A country of wonder in every sense of the word, materially as well as spiritually, it had a population that lived in harmony and serenity. The homes, for example, although lavish, were tastefully decorated. Neither rancor, nor bitterness, nor envy, nor pretentiousness corroded the population. Upon questioning an old sage as to what religion the Eldoradians professed, he answered: "Can there be two religions? . . . We have, I think, the religion of everyone else; we adore God from evening until morning" (*Candide* 1977, 277). When asked whether they worshiped one or more gods, the sage answered "One," but was taken aback by the question. Did they pray? "We do not pray, we have nothing to ask from him; he has given us everything necessary and we continually give him thanks." Did they have priests? "We are all priests; the King and all the heads of families solemnly sing praises every morning, accompanied by five or six thousand musicians" (*Candide* 1977, 277). Nor did they have or need monks "to dispute, to govern, to intrigue and to burn people who do not agree with them" (*Candide* 1977, 277).

Having bathed prior to their audience with the king in his incredibly magnificent palace, Candide and Cacambo were ushered into the throne room. They asked what protocol should be followed: should they "fall on their knees or flat on their faces . . . put their hands on their heads or on their backsides . . . lick the dust of the throne-room"? (*Candide* 1977, 278). Eldorado was a land of sincere and simple mores, Candide was told: "to embrace the King and to kiss him on either cheek" was the custom. After being received with great warmth and dignity, Cacambo

184

VOLTAIRE REVISITED

and Candide were taken to see the town's marvels, the most impressive being the palace of sciences. Candide was more than surprised to learn that there were neither law courts nor prisons. How could it be otherwise? There was no corruption, no poverty, no envy, no crime. With every yearning gratified, everyone basked in happiness and contentment. Was something missing?

Despite the beauty, comfort, and peaceful surroundings, and against the king's advice, Candide and Cacambo opted to leave. The former was intent on rescuing Cunégonde, the latter, on following his master. Since high mountains surrounded Eldorado, access to the outside world was extremely difficult.

No longer able to cope with a world of extreme purity, light, goodness, and innocence, Candide rejected the very notion of perfect happiness. How could it have been otherwise? Hadn't Adam and Eve also opted to leave their idyllic state in the Garden of Eden? Voltaire must have mused. Only in a world of contrasts does life take on meaning, motivation becoming a factor and a means of working toward an ideal.

Candide asked the king for a few sheep laden with pebbles and mud from his land to help him survive in his own world—a den of virtual iniquity. "I cannot understand the taste you people of Europe have for our yellow mud; but take as much as you wish and much good may it do you," the king retorted, ordering 3,000 of his learned scientists to design and construct machinery to hoist his visitors over the high perpendicular mountains surrounding his kingdom (*Candide* 1977, 280).

Exiting Paradise by Choice
Following the Eldorado respite, more eviscerating adventures awaited Candide and Cacambo, including the loss of their sheep. Thus they were deprived of their gold and jewels, except for the stones and nuggets hidden in their pockets. Not only had Candide lost faith in humanity; he had come to accept evil as a fact of life and had even learned to deal with it.

He reasoned that since Cacambo had killed neither a Jesuit nor a Grand Inquisitor, he should be the one to rescue Cunégonde in Buenos Aires and take her to Venice, where they would meet. Before embarking for Europe, Candide met Martin, a former Amsterdam bookseller who had fallen on hard times. Deciding to invite him to travel with him, he reasoned that Martin's ability to discuss philosophy, religion, government, and other important matters would distract, entertain, and enrich him. Although both men were disgusted with the evils they had endured, they were both drawn to, as well as revulsed by, the very notion of culture, civilization, and mental gymnastics.

Finally, after innumerable adventures, including an instance of infidelity to Cunégonde, they went to Venice via England and were reunited with the faithful Cacambo. After learning that Cunégonde was living in Constantinople, they took a ship to that city. On board, they happened to notice two galley slaves who, because they rowed so badly, were being whipped by the Levantine captain. Despite the cruelties, the duplicities, and the injustices he had experienced, Candide's heart had retained his innate generosity and sensitivity. Feeling great pity for the less fortunate, he approached the galley slaves, and recognized one of them as Cunégonde's brother, the Jesuit/baron he thought he had killed, and the other, as his dear Dr. Pangloss, who had supposedly been hanged in Lisbon. After Candide had bought them both, the group sailed on to Constantinople.

Candide and Cunégonde
Relating their adventures to one another, "reasoning upon contingent or noncontingent events of the universe, arguing about effects and causes, moral and physical evil, free will and necessity," the group arrived at the home of a Transylvanian prince on the shores of the Propontis, where they happened upon Cunégonde and an old woman hanging their master's laundry on a line (*Candide* 1977, 322).

The baron grew pale at the sight of his sister, and Candide recoiled three paces in horror. His beloved was "sun-burned, bleary-eyed, flat-breasted, with wrinkles round her eyes and red, chapped arms" (*Candide* 1977, 322). Although shorn of all happiness, he still retained his compassionate and kind ways, so he embraced Cunégonde and the old woman. With his few remaining precious stones he bought them both. Tragically, or perhaps mercifully, since no one had told Cunégonde of her ugliness, she was completely unaware of the physical change she had undergone. Her youthful illusions intact, she reminded Candide that he had promised to marry her. Gentle as always, he agreed, and would inform the baron of his decision.

Still living in his own fantasy world, the baron answered with a categorical "Never." Lashing out at Candide, he made it clear that he would not "endure such baseness on [Cunégonde's] part and such insolence on [Candide's]; nobody shall ever reproach me with this infamy; my sister's children could never enter the chapters of Germany. No, my sister shall never marry anyone but a Baron of the Empire" (*Candide* 1977, 323).

Although Cunégonde fell to her feet before her brother and wept loudly, he was unmoved. As for the adamant Candide, he spoke his mind. "Madman, I rescued you from the galleys, I paid your ransom and your sister's; she was washing dishes here, she is ugly, I am so kind as to make her my wife, and you pretend to oppose me! I should kill you again if I listened to my anger" (*Candide* 1977, 323).

Equally adamant, the baron informed Candide that he was free to kill him once again, but that as long as he was alive, no marriage between him and his sister would take place. Candide, who no longer had any desire to marry Cunégonde, consulted with Dr. Pangloss, Martin, and Cacambo. Acting upon the latter's advice, Candide summarily returned the baron to the Levantine captain, who would take him to the vicar-general in Rome.

Meanwhile, Candide had bought a small farm for the group. Each in his own way was unhappy: Cunégonde was growing uglier each day; the old woman, sicker and crankier; Cacambo was overworked planting, caring for, and selling vegetables; Pangloss, despairing because he did not hold a post in one of the great German universities. Martin, perhaps the wisest of them all, remarked that because "people were equally uncomfortable everywhere, he accepte[d] things patiently," later concluding that "man was born to live in the convulsions of distress or in the lethargy of boredom" (*Candide* 1977, 324).

The small group spent their time working and talking, each in his or her own way pondering solutions to unsolvable problems. Candide, perhaps the most reasonable of them all, spoke simply and directly about the activities in which he and his friends should indulge: "We should cultivate our garden." Pangloss agreed: "for when man was placed in the Garden of Eden, he was placed there *ut operaretur eum,* to dress it and to keep it; which proves that man was not born for idleness." And Martin added: "Let us work without theorizing, 'tis the only way to make life endurable" (*Candide* 1977, 327). And each time Pangloss reverted to his old ratiocinations, Candide interjected: " 'Tis well said, but we must cultivate our garden" (*Candide* 1977, 328).

Although their plot of land and small garden may not have been a Garden of Eden, their world was neither illusory nor sterile. When all was said and done, a conglomerate of different types, classes, sexes, and nationalities were able to live peacefully in the same house; each was given the opportunity to explicate his or her philosophies of life; each worked, thereby fulfilling a function. The admirable fact that the farm yielded food—for thought and for nourishment—was also a wondrous achievement!

Candide was an instant success. Twenty editions were published in 1759. Its condemnation, as of necessity, followed. The volume was ordered destroyed in Geneva, and put on the Index in Rome.

The Story of a Good Brahmin (L'histoire Du Bon Bramin) (1761)

As the years passed, Voltaire's philosophical meditations took on increasing urgency. Although never altering his concept of God as sovereign Being and ruler of the cosmos in keeping with its general laws, he more and more emphasized his belief that God was responsible "for making humans feel and think" (Pomeau 1969, 415). Adding a caveat, Voltaire explained that humans were no more masters of their thought than they were of their will. Free will was an illusion, as was free thought. If humans were free, the very notion of God would be unnecessary.

Interestingly, Pascal's pessimistic beliefs, which Voltaire had denigrated in his *Philosophical Letters,* seemed with age to take on greater appeal for him. For example, he came to agree to some extent with Pascal's opinion that humans were the unhappiest of creatures; that they were a prey to "disquietude and boredom, resulting from self-disgust." Although humans experience "passing pleasures for which they thank Providence, they [also know] they are born to innumerable sufferings and to be eaten by worms; they know it, animals do not. . . . Outside of a few wise people, most humans are but an assemblage of unfortunate horrible criminals, and the globe contains nothing but cadavers."[20]

A resounding Pascalian note reverberated likewise throughout *The Story of a Good Brahmin.* During his travels, the narrator/Voltaire informed his readers, he had met a rich, wise, and brilliant old Brahmin who spent his days in study, meditation, and speculation. He needed nothing. Indeed, the three women tending his household did their utmost to please him in every way. Nearby there lived an old Indian woman, bigoted, ignorant, and poor.

One day the Brahmin told Voltaire that he wished he had never been born. Why? Because after 40 years of continuous study, he considered himself as ignorant now as he had been when he began his investigations. Moreover, people constantly came to consult him, seeking help to

resolve their doubts and fears. That he could give them no ready-made
answer made his life unbearable.

> I was born, I live in time, and I do not know what time is; I find myself
> in a point between two eternities, as our sages say, and I have no idea of
> eternity. I am composed of matter; I think, and I have never been able to
> find out what produces thought. I do not know whether my understand-
> ing is a simple faculty in me like that of walking or of digesting, and
> whether I think with my head, as I take with my hands.[21]

Humiliation overcame him still more egregiously whenever a person
asked him why evil permeated the earth. How could he possibly tell
those who had undergone the horrors of war "that all is for the best"?
(*Good Brahmin*, 241). In despair, the Brahmin wondered whether his
years of thoughtful probings had led to any kind of valid ontological
and/or empirical conclusions. He neither knew where he had come from
nor where he was going, nor what would become of him.

Voltaire could not but feel compassion for this noble being. "I perceived that the greater the lights of his understanding and the sensibility
of his heart, the more unhappy he was" (*Good Brahmin*, 241).

That very day Voltaire went to visit the old woman living nearby. He
asked her if she felt any qualms about the fact that she knew nothing
about the nature of her soul. Not only did she not answer his query, but
she did not even understand the question. "She had never reflected a single moment of her life over a single one of the points that tormented the
Brahmin" (*Good Brahmin*, 241). She practiced the rituals of her faith and
considered herself the happiest of women.

Upon returning to the Brahmin, Voltaire asked him whether he did
not feel a sense of shame each time he tormented himself with problems
of such great profundity. After all, the old woman nearby not only spent
her days thinking of absolutely nothing but laughed from morning until
night. "You are right," he answered. "I have told myself a hundred times
that I would be happy if I was as stupid as my neighbor, and yet I would
want no part of such a happiness" (*Good Brahmin*, 241).

Impressed with the Brahmin's answer, Voltaire probed the question
of happiness and concluded, like the wise man, that he would not want
to experience felicity if it meant being an imbecile. Following some speculation on his own and with friends, he argued that if the problem posed
is how to be happy, what difference does it make if one is imbecilic or
not? But then: "Those who are content with their being are quite sure of
being content; those who reason are not so sure of reasoning well" (*Good*

Brahmin, 242). It was quite clear, Voltaire responded, "that we should choose not to have common sense, if ever that common sense contributes to our ill-being" (*Good Brahmin*, 242). Although his friends agreed with his argument, not one was willing to pay the high price of divesting himself of reason in order to be happy. "But, upon reflection, it appears that to prefer reason to felicity is to be very mad. Then how can this contradiction be explained? Like all the others. There is much to be said about it" (*Good Brahmin*, 242). Still in a quandary, Voltaire must have concluded that insoluble questions are food for cogitation, speculation, communication, and talkathons!

The Ingénu or The Huron (L'Ingénu) (1767)

The Ingénu, composed at Ferney, was less episodic and more compact than *Zadig* or *Candide.* It focused on the rise of political repression and religious injustice in France after the revocation of the Edict of Nantes in 1685. Like Zadig and Candide, Voltaire's protagonist in *The Ingénu* was handsome, good, naive, and young. Highlighted more overtly than in Voltaire's previous philosophical tales was a topic that fascinated philosophers such as Diderot, Rousseau, and Helvetius: the various implications of such concepts as moderation and progress. What were the attributes of an up-to-date person? Is country or city living more salubrious? *The Ingénu* was also instrumental in popularizing—derisively—Rousseau's myth of the "noble savage," who advocated living in a state of nature, that is, in accordance with natural law and allowing intuitive religious feeling rather than philosophical abstractions or rigid dogmatic beliefs to dictate his approach to God and to Providence.

Far from being an extremist, Voltaire considered all excesses to be illusory. He rejected the extremes of the ideal, beautiful, and free forest existence where goodness supposedly always reigned, and the constraining and onerous citified environment, where only fanaticism, injustice, and cruelty supposedly dictated comportment. That an Edenic and virtually beatific life could be experienced in the forest in North America was, for Voltaire, completely far-fetched. Nor did he lend credence to the contention of some European travelers, that certain "savages" from these regions were anthropophagous. Voltaire chose a more accommodating approach to the issues. Balanced and objective, he was aware of the inequities and positive aspects implicit in both types of society. On a personal and humorous note, Voltaire confessed that he could not live in a state of nature since he was dependent on both his doctor and his medicines to maintain his health. Despite its evils, therefore, Voltaire opted for civilization and worked consistently toward its betterment.

As in his other tales, Voltaire uses his hero, the Ingénu, a so-called savage brought up by the Huron Indians in the New World, to make a point. Seeking to debunk the myth of the noble savage, he maintains that the kind, naive, honorable, and loving youth to whom he introduces his readers is good not because he is a savage and has been raised in a forest but because these characteristics are inborn. In fact, the reader learns in time that the Ingénu is not a Huron, but French by birth; orphaned, he has been brought up by this tribe. Its chief had him taught French, and upon his arrival in Brittany, readers learn he speaks the language fluently.

At the outset of the tale, the Ingénu meets Father de Kerkabon, prior of Our Lady of the Mountains, and his unmarried sister, Mlle de Kerkabon. He then has the pleasure of being introduced to Father de Saint-Yves and Mlle de Saint-Yves, his delightfully pretty and well-bred sister from Lower Brittany. In the course of conversation, Mlle de Saint-Yves's curiosity encourages her to ask a rather piquant question: how do the Hurons make love? She observes with no lack of pleasure that the physically strong Ingénu has been endowed with a body that was designed to please any and all women. The reader soon discovers that the two young people have fallen in love and that the supposedly young savage Huron is none other than the nephew of Father de Kerkabon's brother and sister-in-law, who had traveled in the New World 20 years ago. Had the parents been eaten by the Hurons? they wondered.

Not a dissimulator of his thought, nor hypocritical in his conversations with others, the Ingénu, referred to as the Savage at times, says what he thinks, and thus is looked upon as an aberration in French society. Some sidesplitting passages revolving around the Ingénu's sincerity in all matters—considered by the French in the tale to be a lack of manners, and by Voltaire, a divestiture of hypocrisy—touch on religion, his conversion to Christianity, and his literal interpretation of biblical passages dealing with confession and baptism. Because the Ingénu's understanding of the Scriptures varies from that of Father de Kerkabon's reasoned interpretations, a Recollect, a Jesuit from lower Brittany, is called in to perform the ceremony when the Ingénu becomes a Christian. The Ingénu/Savage, well versed in biblical dicta, readily complies with the commandment "Confess your sins (faults) one to another" (James 5:16). Having done so, however, he expects the Jesuit to do likewise. When no words are forthcoming, the Ingénu pulls the Recollect from the confessional, forcing him down on his knees to confess his sins. Still no words of confession. A farcical tussle ensues: "the Huron fixe[s] his great knee against his adversary's stomach." The church echoes and reechoes from the Recollect's roars and groans, and people come to his assistance. Finding "the catechumen cuffing the monk in the name of St. James the Minor," they put an end to the havoc.[22]

The same contentions occur when it comes to the Ingénu's baptism. Quoting the Scriptures, he says adamantly, "I either will not be baptized at all, or the ceremony shall be performed in the river" (*Ingénu*, 84). The "civilized" Europeans, having rejected the idea of total immersion, call upon Mlle de Saint-Yves, the Ingénu's future godmother, to convince him to agree to a church ceremony. After all, Voltaire adds on a satiric note, great care has been taken in pompously decorating the church for the occasion. Docilely Mlle de Saint-Yves asks the Ingénu whether he is willing to do her a favor. "Ah! anything you command," he replies with tender grace. He will refuse her nothing, "be baptized in water, fire, or blood" (*Ingénu*, 85). The ceremony proceeds as planned, but later, when he makes known his intent to marry his beloved immediately afterward, in keeping with the dictates of "natural law," the family resorts to insidious means to prevent the event. Their excuse? Because Mlle de Saint-Yves is the Ingénu's godmother, such a wedding cannot take place! To ensure the girl's safety, the king's unsympathetic administrator advises that she be locked up in a convent, and so she is.

Meanwhile, war being imminent, the despairing Ingénu proves his mettle and his fidelity to France by repulsing British troops attempting to land on the coast of Brittany. His heroic deeds accomplished, he makes his way to Versailles, where he expects the king to award him a great honor. On his way, however, he stops at Saumur, a city that had been virtually devastated by religious conflict after the revocation of the Edict of Nantes. A Jesuit spy, overhearing the Ingénu's derogatory comments on the forced conversion of Protestants in France, and on the subject of religious intolerance in general, denounces him to a friend of the king's confessor. After the Ingénu's arrival at Versailles in search of Mlle de Saint-Yves, he is arrested in the middle of the night and summarily imprisoned in the Bastille.

Perhaps the most insightful part of the tale takes place within those confines. It is in prison that the Ingénu/Savage meets an old and sympathetic Jansenist, Father Gordon, also a victim of religious fanaticism. This "civilized" man takes it upon himself to teach the prisoner physics, geometry, history, astronomy, Malebranche's philosophy, and literature.

Endowed with a fine memory and nobility of character, the Huron prisoner learns rapidly, proving not only that savages have brainpower but also that they may be acculturated.

The Ingénu also has much to offer the Jansenist, especially his commonsense approach to dogma. By inculcating into the man of cloth the notion of free thought, he teaches him how to reasonably investigate the tenets of his sect instead of approaching them in rigid and blind belief. Enlightened by the Ingénu/Savage's understanding of spiritual and earthly matters, the civilized Jansenist is dumbfounded to realize that he has been studying for 50 years and has never once questioned the implications or the veracity of his beliefs. Because of his uninsightful approach to the dogmas he has professed, he has unwittingly been instrumental in fomenting prejudice and fanaticism. Could he ever hope to learn *common sense,* he wonders, a quality that comes so naturally to the Huron?

The Jansenist's concept of love, too, is altered through his dialogues with the Huron prisoner. He has formerly considered love to be a sin, of which one accuses oneself during confession. Now, however, it has been transformed into a noble and tender feeling that "can elevate the soul as well as soften it, and can at times produce virtues" (*Ingénu,* 131). The last miracle that their discussions produces, and for Voltaire perhaps the most outstanding, is that a Huron converts a Jansenist.

Meanwhile, Mlle de Saint-Yves, having been released from the convent, returns to her family and friends at the priory, after which she sets out to earn the release of her beloved Ingénu. Making the most of her connections, she is received by M. de Saint-Pouange, a cousin to and favorite of Louvois (appointed by Louis XIV to rout out Protestants), and pleads her case. Although she achieves her goal, the French system of justice—or injustice—is far from vindicated. Her success is not dependent on the integrity of the legal system, but on the whims and fancies of the minister in question. He demands nothing less than sexual gratification from Mlle de Saint-Yves for having intervened in the case. The Jesuit priest, Father Tout à Tous (All Things to All Men), basing his arguments on casuistic reasoning (Jesuit reasoning of case-study processes), convinces Mlle de Saint-Yves to yield to the lecher. She acquiesces for the greater cause. Sickened by remorse, by a sense of culpability over her lost virginity, and by the medicines given to her by the physicians called into the case, she dies at the very moment the Ingénu/Savage receives a letter releasing him from prison and promising him a brilliant career.

The Jansenist, whose transformation has taken on a most radical, noble form, consoles the Ingénu after the loss of his beloved and encourages him to choose a military career. Ironically, the so-called acculturated savage, really a naive and untutored Frenchman, distinguishes himself as one of Louvois's officers. Voltaire concludes his tale with an anti-Leibnizian motto: *"Misfortunes are of some use.* How many honorable people are there in the world who may justly say: *Misfortunes are good for nothing?"* (*Ingénu*, 163).

The Ingénu gave Voltaire free rein to depict Jesuits as unprincipled intrigants, as muzzlers of free thought, and as propagators of religious fanaticism. Nor were Jansenism, Calvinism, or any dogmatic religious creeds spared. Their repressive teachings and blind assertions had gone a long way in destroying the lives of naive and honest believers. Is there, then, a conclusion to be drawn?

> We are under the power of the eternal Being like the stars and the elements . . . we are little wheels of the immense machine of which he is the soul; he acts by general laws, and not by particular views.[23]

The Story of Johnny, or the Sage and the Atheist (L'histoire de Jenni) (1775)

Unlike the previous narratives, *The Story of Johnny* is a conversation-tale that promotes Deism by satirizing atheism and fanaticism. The hero, Johnny, a 20-year-old Englishman described as "strange," "young," and "unhappy," bears some resemblance to Candide, Zadig, and the Ingénu for his amiable and engaging disposition. Aware that his son is unhappy at the thought of taking up the ministry, Johnny's father, Freind, a respected Quaker/Deist army chaplain, takes his son to Spain. After opting for army life, and participating in some skirmishes, Johnny is wounded, imprisoned by the fanatic Spanish inquisitor Reverend Father Don Jeronimo Bueno Caracurador and his confrère, the theologian Papalamiendo. Johnny is condemned to be ceremoniously burned alive the following Sunday despite the pleadings of Boca Vermeja, the reverend father's mistress, who had wanted to see how an "English animal and heretic" was made and thus observed him in his bath. Serendipitously, the town is taken by the English, and Johnny is rescued by his father. No sooner does Johnny return to London than he falls under the influence of a debauched and evil atheist, Mrs. Clive-Hart, and her lover, the highly intelligent but cynical Birton, who introduce him to a society of godless libertines. Attempting to detach him from Mrs. Clive-Hart, Johnny's father introduces him to the adorable young, witty, highly born, and rich Lady Primrose. In true melodramatic style, Mrs. Clive-Hart poisons her rival, whereupon she and her atheist friends take Johnny to America. Chaplain Freind leaves England in quick pursuit of his son only to discover that he has been captured by a tribe of Indians and that Mrs. Clive-Hart has been killed and scalped by them, thus receiving her due. As for Johnny, he is brought safely back to England, along with Birton, who, after being converted to right thinking—Deism—by Freind's astute philosophical arguments, is determined to lead a clean life. Lady Primrose, having miraculously survived her poisoning, weds the now-virtuous Johnny, and all live a beautiful Deistic life.

Although less dramatic than either *Candide* or *Zadig, The Story of Johnny* is more prescriptive, indicating Voltaire's attempt to win his readers over to a world of Deistic virtue. Not only did Voltaire take issue with fanaticism, as identified with the Spanish Inquisitor and his Jesuit colleague in the tale, he likewise targeted atheism as subscribed to by Diderot, Holbach, and La Mettrie. Deism was the one form of worship, according to Voltaire, that safeguarded the notion of a morally useful God.

The calamitous events depicted in *The Story of Johnny* were designed to prepare the reader for the four "educational" dialogical chapters inserted within the framework of the tale. These were devoted to convincing the reader of the pros of Deism and the cons of atheism and dogmatism. The dialogue form chosen by Voltaire in many of his works to illustrate his point is in this instance somewhat reminiscent of Diderot's own dramatic literary device. In Voltaire's case, the discussions between a man of faith, Chaplain Freind, and a fanatic, the Spanish theologian Papalamiendo who is also the accomplice of the inquisitor, as well as Birton, Johnny's friend, who had at the outset helped Mrs. Clive-Hart lead the young Johnny astray, are both pithy and insightful. Needless to add, because of the conversion of the latter two to Deism, all were redeemed.

What sets *The Story of Johnny* apart from such tales as *Candide* or *Zadig* are, as already mentioned, the four fascinating dialogic chapters revealing Voltaire, the proselytizer, at work. Unwilling to allow himself the luxury of being bogged down in casuistic, hubristic argumentation by the fanatic, the chaplain always returns to his main argument: his respect for the Scriptures. Unwilling to delve into the nitty-gritty of dogma, which is the Jesuit's direction, he veers toward humility: God and his way are "too far above our weak human reason" to allow mortals to determine his direction.[24] When, however, an advanced Jesuit student in his discussions with the chaplain insists upon focusing on certain doctrinal points, namely, whether the "Holy Virgin" is the "Mother of God" or not, the chaplain reveals his expertise in these matters:

> We revere and cherish her. But we think she cares very little for the titles given her in this world. She is never styled the Mother of God in the gospel. In the year 431 there was a great dispute at the council of Ephesus to ascertain if Mary was Theo[d]toc[k]os; and if Jesus Christ, being at the same time God and the son of Mary, Mary could at the same time be mother of God the Father and God the Son. We do not enter into these disputes of Ephesus. The Royal Society at London does not concern itself with such controversies. (*Johnny*, 130)

What amazes readers is the vastness of Voltaire's knowledge of early Church history and dogma. For example, he was well versed in the facts concerning the Church's council of bishops held at Ephesus, at which Cyril of Alexandria presided, when the heresy promulgated by Nestorius, the patriarch of Constantinople, was condemned. He had claimed that "Jesus was two separate persons, one human and one divine, and that Mary was the mother of the human person only and, consequently, could not be called the Mother of God."[25]

During a discussion of Christ's human/divine nature, when the Jesuit student admits to not knowing the word *theodokos,* the pastor is stunned: "What, are you a student at Salamanca, and you don't understand Greek?" Peeved, the student responds:

> But Greek! Of what use can Greek be to a Spaniard? But, sir, do you believe that Jesus Christ has one nature, one person, and one will; or two natures, two persons and two wills; or, one will, one nature, and two persons; or, two wills, two persons and one nature; or—? (*Johnny*, 131)

When the chaplain replies that these matters don't concern him in the least, the student is aghast:

> But what does concern you? Do you suppose there are only three persons in God, or that there are three Gods in one person? Does the second person proceed from the first person, and the third from the two others, or from the second *intrinsecus,* or only from the first? Has the father all the

attributes of the son except paternity? And does the third person proceed
by infusion, by identification, or by spiration? (*Johnny,* 131)

In the preceding discussions, Voltaire is referring to the doctrine of
monophytism forwarded by certain Eastern Churches that claimed that
Christ had two natures (human and divine) and that these were
absorbed into one nature (the divine). Monophytism was condemned as
a heresy at the Council of Chalcedon in 451, when it was declared that
Christ's two natures were "unmixed and unchangeable even though
indistinguishable and inseparable."[26] The chaplain remonstrates: "This
question is not mooted in the gospel. St. Paul never wrote the name of
the Trinity" (*Johnny,* 131). The student is notably annoyed because the
chaplain consistently refers to the gospel rather than mention Saint
Bonaventura, Albert the Great, Tambourini, Grillandus, or Escobar.
The chaplain replies: "Because I do not call myself a Dominican, a Fran-
ciscan or a Jesuit, I am satisfied with being a Christian" (*Johnny,* 131).
The disputations continue, giving the Deist ample opportunity to state
and restate his beliefs: to adore God, to be just and well intentioned.

The Story of Johnny heralds perhaps more explicitly than Voltaire's
other tales his impatience with doctrinal disputes and with atheists' lack
of discernment into the impenetrable nature of the cosmos, of existence,
and of the very existence of God as the Supreme Artisan.

Lord Chesterfield's Ears (1775)

In *Lord Chesterfield's Ears,* Voltaire, still seeking to educate his reader,
reverts to his well-tried theme of fate as the all-powerful factor in directing human destiny.

A humorous interlude is introduced at the very outset of the tale as
Chaplain Goudman and his longtime friend and patron, Lord Chesterfield, begin their discussions. The latter's deafness causes him to mis-
understand the chaplain's request that he recommend him for a well-
paid clerical post. Instead, he thinks the chaplain is having a gall
bladder attack, is in great pain, and needs an operation. Only when he
finds himself in the office of the surgeon Sidrac does Goudman realize
the error his patron made. Not long after, he also learns that his com-
petitor has been granted the curacy he had craved, and has also
acquired Miss Fidler, the young lady he, Goudman, was to marry following reception of his new post. Lord Chesterfield dies before the
error can be rectified.

To make life bearable, the chaplain spends his time studying the science of nature—much like Zadig—under Sidrac's tutelage. Reminiscent as well of Micromégas and the Saturnian, Goudman avails himself of his spectacles, his telescope, and his five senses to pursue his examinations. The knowledge he gains, however, instead of pacifying him increases his frustrations. He concludes that there is no "trace of what the world calls nature." To the contrary, "everything seems to me to be the result of art. By art the planets are made to revolve around the sun, while the sun revolves on its own axis."[27] Humorous speculations follow, regarding the animal, vegetal, mineral, and human worlds—and love as well. Sidrac convinces the chaplain not to wallow in despondency, but to deepen his philosophical acumen, to withdraw from the world, and to live on his meager pension.

While the two discuss the nature of the soul, spirit, and reason as conceived by the Greeks and Latins, and the more up-to-date thinkers such as Rabelais, Newton, Berkeley, and Locke, they realize how little they know. Although certain facts are known to humankind, Sidrac states, the governance of the universe remains a mystery:

> You grant that the Supreme Being has given you the faculties of feeling and thinking; he has in the same manner given your feet the faculty of walking, your hands their wonderful dexterity, your stomach the capability of digesting food, and your heart the power of throwing arterial blood into all parts of your body. Everything you enjoy is derived from God, and yet we are totally ignorant of the means by which He governs and conducts the universe. (*Lord*, 23)

Veering toward the question of destiny, they agree with those who refer to humans as "the puppets of Providence" (*Lord*, 23). Had Goudman received his lucrative post and kept Miss Fidler, Sidrac asserts, the world would be completely different. The events regulating Goudman's life, however, are in keeping with the laws of cause and effect, all being a part of the chain of being. The interlocutors realize that dangerous notions—the role played by God and Providence—are being probed. Nonetheless, Goudman argues that if God, like humankind, is a slave of divine will, and of the very laws he has himself promulgated, then why pray to him? At pains to answer the query, both men seemingly agree that it is wiser to behave in a moral manner, to fulfill one's obligations to people justly and humanely, and to forever thank and praise the eternal one. To adore God and be just are the only meaningful ways humans may truly sing his praises in prayer.

As their conversations continue, they reaffirm what Voltaire had stated in *Micromégas*: that only in mathematics and in the sciences may theories be affirmed. To even attempt to prove metaphysical speculations is to reveal one's ignorance. During their concluding discussions, a friend, Dr. Grou, a world traveler, joins them for dinner. Having just returned from a visit to Tahiti, he interjects some piquant details concerning the nature of the fertility rites he witnessed among aboriginals. The mores of New Zealanders, as well as the Hottentots, the French, and syphilis, are also fare for their discussions. Then the three turn to the question of human motivations. The chaplain wonders whether love or ambition catalyzes humans into action. Grou believes money to be that energetic power. Sidrac gets down to basics and opts for the toilet stool as being the greatest inducement to activity.

A master at scatology, Voltaire now allows his Rabelaisian side to overwhelm his characters' relatively sedate philosophical discussions. No longer does a world revolving around Deity and ethical and psychological problems take center stage. The flesh to which humans are enslaved comes into focus, adding zest and humor to what might otherwise have simply been a dull didactic discussion. The topic of dysentery, which dominates the dialogue at the tale's conclusion, seems not only to delight the gentlemen's intellect, but takes precedence in helping them make some historical determinations. There were times in centuries past, the conversationalists note, when dysentery was said to have altered the course of history, as in the battle of Azincourt during the Hundred Years' War, when the troops won their victory pants down. Forwarded as well is the belief that Charles IX's extreme constipation was one of the principal causes of the Saint Bartholomew's Day Massacre (1572). Life in winter time was intolerable for Henry III (reigned 1574–1589) because during these months he went to the toilet with great difficulty.

At the conclusion of this hilarious tale, we are told that Goudman's rival has lost both his well-paying post and Miss Fidler, while ironically Goudman now finds himself in a strange predicament. He will be given the curacy, he learns, if he agrees to give up Miss Fidler. Sidrac and Grou persuade him to accept the offer. With all the money given to him by the parish, they reason, he can have Miss Fidler or any other girl he wants. And so it goes. Providence or fate governs all worldly matters. . . .

By denigrating the simplistic answers offered by the optimists of his day, Voltaire, the empiricist, recommended in his philosophical tales that humans work diligently and live virtuously. Only in so doing may they improve their earthly conditions, and perhaps those of others as well! Crucial in all of Voltaire's writings, and especially in his philosophical tales, is his injunction to always *question and think, and never conclude.* Among the imponderables humans will never understand, he asserts throughout, are the nature of the soul and of God's universal law. As light emerges from the sun, so a general Providence regulates all things for all eternity. To even toy with the belief that Providence is an individual affair is puerile. Humankind's personal existence is of no concern to God, who is remote, immanent, and transcendental.

Who but Voltaire, with his enormous energy, his thirst for knowledge, and his pertinent diatribes, humorous ironies, satiric ventures, and lean style, could sum up life's problematics in such arresting terms as he did in *Candide, Zadig, Micromégas, The Ingénu,* and his other tales?

One of the most salient dialogic questions concerning the human personality takes place between Candide and Martin as they approach the coast of France. Will human behavioral patterns change in time? Will life take a turn for the better? Candide wonders:

> Do you think that men have always massacred each other, as they do today? Have they always been liars, cheats, traitors, brigands, weak, flighty, cowardly, envious, gluttonous, drunken, grasping, and vicious, bloody, backbiting, debauched, fanatical, hypocritical and silly?

Martin responds:

> Do you think that sparrow-hawks have always eaten the pigeons they came across?

Candide answers:

> Yes, of course.

Martin reasons:

> Well, if sparrow-hawks have always possessed the same nature, why should you expect men to change theirs?

Candide retorts:

> Oh! there is a great difference; free will. . . .
> Arguing thus, they arrived at Bordeaux. (Candide 1977, 290)

May we not pose the same questions in our century that Candide did in Voltaire's time? Have humans changed their ways? Are they capable of doing so?

Conclusion: *"We Are Balloons That the Hand of Fate Pushes about Blindly"*

Voltaire—the Promethean—traveled, learned, experienced, and believed in evolution and progress through human reason. The issues with which he dealt throughout his life were for the most part moral in nature and empirically based, thus universal and eternal in breadth and scope.

Although Voltaire cherished freedom of thought and freedom of expression, he not only was very much aware of opposing views on these subjects but also fought for his beliefs actively wherever possible. Since he believed that openness of thought catalyzed objectivity and independence of spirit, he also understood that conservative factions feared intellectual explorations into unknown territories. It could, they were convinced, set dangerous precedents. New directions, therefore, had to be obliterated. Understandably, heads of state and Church institutions did their utmost—with some exceptions—to maintain the status quo. Indeed, maximization of constraint prevented new concepts, foreign philosophies, and a variety of trends from destabilizing tried and true organizations. Shutting out fresh air encouraged the spread of well-worn and frequently abusive modes of behavior and beliefs. It also paved the way for mold, decay, and putrescence.

Voltaire's answer to regressiveness frequently took the form of satire. In *The Horrible Danger of Reading* (1765), a hilarious mockery of censorship of the press, he chose the form of a pastoral mandate to label printing in general "pernicious" and "infernal," because it tended "to dissipate ignorance," which, of course, would be a catastrophe for individuals as well as for societies. Wasn't it easier to rule the ignorant with an iron hand? How best could one prevent the introduction of new concepts into a society? Prohibit the publication of books, articles, and all other reading material that might undermine government and Church. Muzzle speech! Forbid learning! Teach by rote! Parrot! Never dare to *think* or to play with thoughts, or allow ideas to wander or circulate into *chancy or uncertain* territories!

Hazardous as well, Voltaire maintained, was an overevaluation of reason, which could instill arrogance—*hubris*—in humans, thus paving the

way for intellectual and spiritual blindness and for psychological vulnerability. Descartes's dictum that held that by perfecting reason people
would expand their knowledge and eventually dominate nature was neither realistic nor appropriate. Aware of the pitfalls of both extremes, as a
partisan of the Enlightenment Voltaire suggested a balanced use of reason: to encourage its growth and depth and to *accept its limitations*. The
thought that one could ever dominate nature was folly, and to believe
that a state of perfection could be experienced on Earth was equally
absurd. In that perfection was and is an ideal, thus an abstract notion,
the moment it purports to be real, it can no longer be ideal.

Imbued with the skeptical tradition of Montaigne, Bayle, Saint-Evremond, Fontenelle, and the English empiricists, Voltaire, although working toward alleviating people's suffering, nonetheless accepted the ills of
humanity, believing that no amount of human activity would or could
cure them all. He lived with a sense of doubt, which he considered beneficial. Doubt, he said, fostered wisdom and action; to reject doubt was
to accept placebos.

Voltaire also understood that an attitude of relativity must be forwarded if intellectual and spiritual growth was to be forthcoming. A relative point of view in life—if properly channeled and applied to scientific,
humanistic, and empirical spheres—could go a long way in alleviating
persecution, repression, and other social ills. Like Prometheus, Voltaire
was a committed man.

As a Deist, he adroitly expressed his distaste for a theocratic state,
organized religion, and an anthropomorphic conception of deity. In his
philosophical opera *Pandora* (originally entitled *Prometheus*), composed
most probably around 1740, the hero, Prometheus ("forethought"), was
rebellion incarnate—a man who fought against the status quo—
Jupiter's religious and governmental dogmatism and authority. His
anti-Jupiter exploits were incisive. As to the punishments received for
his infractions, Prometheus responded:

> Away then, ye destroyers, ye are not
> The deities Prometheus shall adore;
> Hence to your gloomy seats, ye hateful powers,
> And leave the world in peace.[1]

In hateful retribution for what he considered to be Prometheus's
heinous act of stealing fire from God, Jupiter sent Pandora ("all-gifts")

to earth. On her way, she succumbed to her curiosity and opened the box she carried with her, releasing in so doing the evils contained inside. Diseases and other noxious misfortunes would henceforth come to plague humanity. Hope alone chose to remain in her box. In time, Prometheus and Pandora not only fell in love but discovered that together, and with humanity as well, they could live without the gods. "Now earth, defend thyself and combat heaven," Prometheus cried out (*Pandora*, act 4, line 304). No longer fearful of heaven's interdicts, he realized that humankind had liberated itself from an appalling weight. Thus did he consider himself, along with mortals in general, ready and able to begin the great task of working toward their own evolution. One of the goals was "Let us teach mankind / To succor the unhappy" (*Pandora*, act 5, line 308).

Voltaire knew that he had to combat the despot on his own terrain, as his hero Prometheus had done. He ridiculed the concepts of Original Sin, guilt, and paradise. He believed that evil stemmed not from the Fall, as Pascal, and many of the devout Christians had maintained, but from the phantasms humans created around the image or concept of God and the dogmas they erected around this cosmic power. As an earthly happening, evil had to be combated by each individual, inwardly as well as outwardly, wherever it is confronted. Rather than having recourse to God to save them, people had to take it upon themselves to better their own lot and humankind's in general. "Adore a God, and be just," Voltaire wrote in his *Poem on Natural Law*.

Voltaire, the Deist, felt suffocated when he met with religious fanaticism. "I am like Cato, *Deleatur Carthago*," he wrote to d'Alembert, "free from cult and ritual"[2] As a Deist, he believed that organized religion created a haven for impostors, that the very notion of heaven and hell had been invented for lucre, and that dogma was an ossification of thought and feeling. Since youth Voltaire had believed neither in a "particular revelation" nor in "intercessory prayer." Hence he did not hesitate to satirize Sister Fessue, who had accused a metaphysician of heresy for believing "in a general Providence" instead of a particular or individual Providence capable of altering "the economy of the world for [her] sparrow or [her] cat" (Torrey 1938, 99). God, the Supreme and Infinite Artisan—or Clockmaker—ruled and rules in terms of universal or general laws and not specific ones. As for free will, a meaningless term for Voltaire, it indicated that humans were free to act, but here, too, within the limitations placed on them by destiny. Thus humankind could not lay claim to omnipotence via their actions, prayers, or any other way.

Lest anyone forget, humans were finite! God alone was infinite! Voltaire
repeated multiple times in his poetry, theater pieces, historical writings,
essays, and correspondence.

"Victory is mine!" Prometheus clamored at the opera's conclusion.
Indeed, but with victory there existed responsibility for one's acts and
for one's happiness—all, of course, within limitations (*Pandora*, act 5,
line 308). Voltaire's rebellion, like Prometheus's, resulted from a human
need for compassion and love, and a spirit of inquiry, from a desire to
free thought that would liberate people from tyrannical intellectual and
spiritual constraints.

Although Voltaire's optimism and idealism in later years were tempered
by an increasingly realistic attitude, he never despaired. Unlike Pascal,
who believed that humankind and nature were corrupt and that God
had created mortals imperfect to punish them for their sins, Voltaire felt
no blame or shame for anyone. Nor was he a partisan of Pascal's notion
that people were predestined to be saved or damned, or that a person's
sole dignity was in his ability to think. What was of import to Voltaire
was the fight for justice and morality. One must be grateful to God,
Voltaire maintained, for endowing humankind with extraordinary qualities. Although he wept—and sometimes became physically sick—over
the ills that befell humanity, Voltaire was also endowed with that
remarkable capacity for laughter. His humor healed, at least temporarily, the bitterness he felt, and dispelled the agonizing tension that at
times overwhelmed him.

In his *Treaty on Tolerance* (1763), he concluded with "A prayer to
God":

> May all men remember that they are brethren! May they alike abhor that
> tyranny which seeks to subject the freedom of the will, as they do the
> rapine which tears from the arms of industry the fruits of its peaceful
> labors! And if the scourge of war is not to be avoided, let us not mutually
> hate and destroy each other in the midst of peace: but rather make use of
> the few moments of our existence to join in praising, in a thousand differ-
> ent languages, from one extremity of the world to the other, Thy good-
> ness, O all-merciful Creator, to whom we are indebted for that exis-
> tence![3]

205

Gentlemen, great men rarely come alone; large trees seem larger when they dominate a forest; there they are at home. There was a forest of minds around Voltaire; that forest was the eighteenth century. Among those minds there were summits: Montesquieu, Buffon, Beaumarchais, and among others, two, the highest after Voltaire, Rousseau and Diderot. Those thinkers taught men to reason; reasoning well leads to acting well; justness in the mind becomes justice in the heart. Those toilers for progress labored usefully.

—Victor Hugo, "Oration on Voltaire"

Notes and References

Unless otherwise noted, all translations are my own.

Introduction

1. *Oeuvres complètes de Voltaire,* ed. Louis Moland (Paris: Garnier Frères, 1883; reprint, Nendeln, Lichtenstein: Kraus Reprint, 1967), 34:249; hereafter cited in text as Moland by volume and page.
2. Voltaire, *Philosophical Dictionary,* ed. and trans. Theodore Besterman (London: Penguin, 1972), 281; hereafter cited in text as *PD* 1972.
3. Voltaire, *History of Charles XII,* in *Oeuvres historiques,* ed. René Pomeau (Paris: Pléiade, 1957), 272.
4. Norman L. Torrey, *The Spirit of Voltaire* (New York: Columbia University Press, 1938), 213; hereafter cited in text as Torrey 1938.

Chapter One

1. Raymond Naves, *Voltaire: L'homme et l'oeuvre* (Paris: Boivin, 1942), 25; hereafter cited in text as Naves 1942.
2. The group had been so named because its members gathered in the meeting place of the religious order of the Knights Templars, founded in 1119.
3. Jean Orieux, *Voltaire ou la Royauté de l'esprit* (Paris: Flammarion, 1966), 94; hereafter cited in text.
4. Ira O. Wade, *The Intellectual Development of Voltaire* (Princeton, N. J.: Princeton University Press, 1969), 271; hereafter cited in text as Wade 1969.
5. Voltaire to Frederick the Great, 27 May 1737, *Voltaire's Correspondence,* ed. Theodore Besterman (Paris: Gallimard, 1977), no. 1331; this collection hereafter cited as *Correspondence.*
6. Haydn Mason, *Voltaire* (Baltimore, Md.: Johns Hopkins University Press, 1981), 60; hereafter cited in text as Mason 1981.
7. Voltaire to Mme Denis, 24 July 1752, *The Portable Voltaire,* trans. S. G. Tallentyre, ed. Ben Ray Redman (New York: Penguin, 1977), 483.
8. Voltaire, *Poem on Natural Law,* in *A Treatise on Toleration and Other Essays,* trans. Joseph McCabe (Amherst, N.Y.: Prometheus Books, 1994), 1; hereafter cited in text as *Natural Law* 1994.
9. Gladys S. Thomson, *Catherine the Great and the Expansion of Russia* (New York: Collier Books, 1947), 165.
10. The marquis de Saint Marc to the advocate Linquet, April 1778, in Theodore Besterman, *Voltaire* (New York: Harcourt, Brace and World, 1969), 526; Besterman hereafter cited in text.

11. René Pomeau, *La Religion de Voltaire* (Paris: Nizet, 1969), 453; hereafter cited in text as Pomeau 1969.

Chapter Two

1. Gustave Lanson, *Voltaire*, trans. Robert A. Wagoner (New York: John Wiley and Sons, 1966), 48; hereafter cited in text.
2. Voltaire to N. C. Thiériot, 12 August 1726, *Correspondence*, no. 299.
3. Voltaire admired Descartes as a geometer, but not as a theologian or as a metaphysician.
4. Voltaire, *Philosophical Letters*, trans. Ernest Dilworth (New York: Macmillan, 1989), 55; hereafter cited in text as *PL*.
5. Richard A. Brooks, *Voltaire and Leibniz* (Geneva: Librairie Droz, 1964), 77; hereafter cited in text.
6. Georg Brandes, *Voltaire* (New York: Tudor Publishing Co., 1936), 204.
7. After becoming the butt of political and religious condemnation and persecution, especially after the publication of his *Poem on the Lisbon Earthquake*, Voltaire altered his concept of a beneficial Providence to a more realistic outlook on life. Never, however, was he plagued with despair.
8. The honor of having first staged Shakespeare's works as they should have been went to the twentieth-century Jacques Copeau, director of his Théâtre du Vieux-Colombier.
9. Voltaire, *Mélanges*, texte établi et annoté par J. Van Den Heuvel (Paris: Pléiade, 1961), 162; hereafter cited in text as *Mélanges*.
10. Raymond Naves, *Voltaire et l'Encyclopédie* (Paris: Les Editions des presses modernes, 1938), 91; hereafter cited in text as Naves 1938.
11. Voltaire, *Philosophical Dictionary*, trans. Peter Gay, 2 vols. (New York: Basic Books, 1962), 1:311; hereafter cited in text as *PD* 1962.
12. Voltaire, *Philosophical Dictionary*, in *The Works of Voltaire*, trans. William F. Fleming and others, 22 vols. (New York: The St. Hubert Guild, 1901; reprint, New York: Howard Fertig, 1988), 4.1:54; hereafter cited in text as *PD* 1988 by volume, part, and page numbers.

Chapter Three

1. Voltaire, *The Henriade*, in *The Works of Voltaire*, trans. William F. Fleming and others, 22 vols. (New York: The St. Hubert Guild, 1901; reprint, New York: Howard Fertig, (1988), 15.2:62; hereafter cited in text as *Henriade* by volume, part, and page numbers.
2. Raymond Naves, *Le Goût de Voltaire* (Geneva: Slatkin Reprints, 1967), 192; hereafter cited in text as Naves 1967.

3. Voltaire, *The Temple of Taste,* in *The Works of Voltaire,* trans. William F. Fleming and others, 22 vols. (New York: The St. Hubert Guild, 1901; reprint, New York: Howard Fertig, 1988), 10.2:47–48; hereafter cited in text as *Taste* by volume, part, and page numbers.

4. Voltaire to Pierre Robert Le Cormier de Cideville, 18 February 1737, *Correspondence,* no. 720; Naves 1967, 185.

5. Naves refers to the article "Taste" in Voltaire's *Philosophical Dictionary.*

6. Voltaire, *The Man of the World,* in *The Works of Voltaire,* trans. William F. Fleming and others, 22 vols. (New York: The St. Hubert Guild, 1901; reprint, New York: Howard Fertig, 1988), 2:293.

7. Voltaire, *Discourses in Verse on Man,* in *The Works of Voltaire,* trans. William F. Fleming and others, 22 vols. (New York: The St. Hubert Guild, 1901; reprint, New York: Howard Fertig, 1988), 1.2:289; hereafter cited in text as *Verse on Man* by volume, part, and page numbers.

8. R. S. Ridgway, *Voltaire and Sensibility* (Montreal: McGill-Queen's University Press, 1973), 67; hereafter cited in text.

9. Voltaire, *Poem on Natural Law,* in *The Works of Voltaire,* trans. William F. Fleming and others, 22 vols. (New York: The St. Hubert Guild, 1901; reprint, New York: Howard Fertig, 1988), 10.2:23; hereafter cited in text as *Natural Law* 1988 by volume, part, and page numbers.

10. To explain Voltaire's conflictual feelings on the subject, Torrey writes: "Belief in the social and political utility of divine moral sanctions has been more powerful than has personal intellectual persuasion from Cicero to the present day" (Torrey 1938, 240).

11. Voltaire, *Poem on the Lisbon Disaster,* in *A Treatise on Toleration and Other Essays,* trans. Joseph McCabe (Amherst, N.Y.: Prometheus Books, 1994), 4; hereafter cited in text as *Lisbon.*)

Chapter Four

1. Voltaire, "Dissertation on Ancient and Modern Tragedy," in Moland, 4:499; hereafter cited in text as "Tragedy."

2. With some exceptions—*The Scotsman, The Prodigal,* and *Nanine*—Voltaire's social comedies, farces, and satires are not sufficiently noteworthy to be mentioned in this book. One of the earliest comedies, however, *The Indiscreet* (1725), although performed only six times, was produced at Fontainebleau at the marriage of Louis XV and Marie Leszczyńska. Some time later, Voltaire participated in his own light satire, *Belebat's Feast,* performed at the Castle of Belebat.

The Scotswoman (1760), a comic satire, was written by Voltaire to avenge himself against the despised Fréron, editor of the infamous defamatory sheet *L'Année littéraire.* Using all of his art and artfice to persuade the censors to allow his play to be performed, he finally won his case on the grounds that permission had been granted for Palissot's brutal satire *Les Philosophes* (1760).

The year 1736 saw the production of *The Child Prodigy,* a *comédie larmoyante.* The actress Mlle Quinault, who had happened upon the theme of the prodigal son at the Théâtre de la Foire St. Germain, was about to suggest it to the playwright, Philippe Néricault Destouches, when Voltaire asked her to allow him to use it. After 30 consecutive performances, one was given at court with Mme de Pompadour playing the role of Lise, the virtuous lover of the prodigal son.

Voltaire's *Nanine ou le préjugé vaincu* (1749) was his second foray into the sentimental comedy. His defense of this kind of comedy in his preface was made all the more palatable by his inclusion of a cluster of witticisms. Although Voltaire made no mention of the work that had inspired his play's theme, it was seemingly drawn from Richardson's *Pamela* (1740). In Voltaire's adaptation, however, the emotional outbreaks and freethinking teachings were rendered virtually innocuous to fit the standards of French taste. Rather than allow the play to drag, he used his dramatic skills to create a sense of urgency and excitement, and 10-syllable verse rather than the alexandrines, to accentuate plot and movement.

3.   Toby Cole and Helen Krich Chinoy, *Actors on Acting* (New York: Crown Publishers, 1949), 148; hereafter cited in text.

4.   Voltaire, "Discourse on Tragedy," in Moland, 2:323; hereafter cited in text as "Discourse."

5.   Although a playwright of no consequence, Jean-François Ducis (1733–1816) was one of the earliest to adapt, basing his work on very poor French translations, some of Shakespeare's well-known tragedies. His script of *Hamlet* (1769) was used for the first production of this play in France.

6.   Voltaire is referring to a castle, 10 kilometers from Versailles, constructed by Mansart for Louis XIV.

7.   Voltaire, "Essay on Epic Poetry," in Moland, 8:307.

8.   Voltaire, "Letters on Oedipus," in Moland, 2:26.

9.   Voltaire, *Oedipus,* in vol. 8, pt. 2 of *The Works of Voltaire,* trans. William F. Fleming and others, 22 vols. (New York: The St. Hubert Guild, 1901; reprint, New York: Howard Fertig, 1988), act 4, scene 3, line 195; hereafter cited in text as *Oedipus* by act, scene, and line numbers.

10.   Voltaire, *Zaïre,* in vol. 10, pt. 1 of *The Works of Voltaire,* trans. William F. Fleming and others, 22 vols. (New York: The St. Hubert Guild, 1901; reprint, New York: Howard Fertig, 1988), act 1, scene 1, line 27; hereafter cited in text as *Zaïre* by act, scene, and line numbers.

11.   Voltaire, "An Epistle Dedicatory to Mr. Falkener," in *The Works of Voltaire,* trans. William F. Fleming and others, 22 vols. (New York: The St. Hubert Guild, 1901; reprint, New York: Howard Fertig, 1988), 10:7.

12.   Colbert Searles, ed., *Seven French Plays* (New York: Henry Holt, 1935), 70.

13. Voltaire, *Alzire,* in vol. 9, pt. 1 of *The Works of Voltaire,* trans. William F. Fleming and others, 22 vols. (New York: The St. Hubert Guild, 1901; reprint, New York: Howard Fertig, 1988), act 1, scene 1, line 9; hereafter cited in text as *Alzire* by act, scene, and line numbers.

14. Henry C. Lancaster, *French Tragedy in the Time of Louis XV and Voltaire, 1715–1774,* 2 vols. (Baltimore, Md.: The Johns Hopkins University Press, 1950), 2:422; hereafter cited in text.

15. Virgil W. Topazio, *Voltaire: A Critical Study of His Major Works* (New York: Random House, 1967), 92.

16. Voltaire, *Brutus,* in vol. 8, pt. 1 of *The Works of Voltaire,* trans. William F. Fleming and others, 22 vols. (New York: The St. Hubert Guild, 1901; reprint, New York: Howard Fertig, 1988), act 1, scene 1, line 240; hereafter cited in text as *Brutus* by act, scene, and line numbers.

17. Voltaire, *The Death of Caesar,* in vol. 10, pt. 1 of *The Works of Voltaire,* trans. William F. Fleming and others, 22 vols. (New York: The St. Hubert Guild, 1901; reprint, New York: Howard Fertig, 1988), act 2, scene 2, line 112.

18. Crébillon believed that impetuous passions were "capable of driving people to the greatest of crimes and to the most virtuous of actions" (Crébillon, Preface to *Oeuvres,* quoted in Jacques Morel, *La Tragedie,* Paris: Armand Colin, 1964, 72).

19. Voltaire, *Mérope,* in vol. 8, pt. 1 of *The Works of Voltaire,* trans. William F. Fleming and others, 22 vols. (New York: The St. Hubert Guild, 1901; reprint, New York: Howard Fertig, 1988), act 4, scene 2, line 78; hereafter cited in text as *Mérope* by act, scene, and line numbers.

20. Voltaire, *Eriphyle,* in Moland, 2:465.

21. Voltaire, *Sémiramis,* in vol. 9, pt. 1 of *The Works of Voltaire,* trans. William F. Fleming and others, 22 vols. (New York: The St. Hubert Guild, 1901; reprint, New York: Howard Fertig, l988), act 1, scene 1, line 148; hereafter cited in text as *Sémiramis* by act, scene, and line numbers.

22. Voltaire, *Mohammed, or Fanaticism,* in vol. 8, pt. 2 of *The Works of Voltaire,* trans. William F. Fleming and others, 22 vols. (New York: The St. Hubert Guild, 1901; reprint, New York: Howard Fertig, 1988), act 5, scene 4, line 85; hereafter cited in text as *Mohammed* by act, scene, and line numbers.

23. As censor, Crébillon refused approval for *Mohammed* to be performed, not for religious reasons, but because it could be considered as rivaling his own *Atreus.* Upon referral to d'Alembert, it was approved and performed in Paris in 1742.

24. In *The Works of Voltaire,* trans. William F. Fleming and others, 22 vols. (New York: The St. Hubert Guild, 1901; reprint, New York: Howard Fertig, 1988), vol. 8, p. 14.

25. Voltaire, *Tancred,* in Moland, vol. 5, act 5, scene 4, line 561.

26. Voltaire, *The Scythians,* in Moland, 6:270.

27. Arthur Pougin, *Dictionnaire du théâtre* (Var, France: Editions D'aujourd'hui, 1985), 245–47.

Chapter Five

1. John H. Brumfitt, *Voltaire Historian* (Oxford: Oxford University Press, 1958), 2–4; hereafter cited in text.
2. Voltaire, *History of Charles XII,* in *The Works of Voltaire,* trans. William F. Fleming and others, 22 vols. (New York: The St. Hubert Guild, 1901; reprint, New York: Howard Fertig, 1988), 20:7; hereafter cited in text as *Charles XII* by volume and page.
3. Because so few named sources appeared in the first edition, Voltaire answered his critics, Des Roches de Parthenay in particular, by mentioning the names of those who had supplied him with memoirs, eyewitness accounts, and other types of materials in the 1733 edition (Brumfitt, 18). H. P. Limiers's *History of Sweden Under the Reign of Charles XII* (1720), although not always accurate, but to which Voltaire owed much, was omitted from his text. The Swedish historian J. A. Nordberg, author of a *History of Charles XII* (1748), took special joy in underscoring errors made by both Limiers and Voltaire.
Impressive was Voltaire's willingness, even eagerness, to rectify the errors pointed out to him by his derogators. Whenever he could, Voltaire took what he deemed to be valid criticism to heart. Always on the alert for ways of improving his documentation, of probing the accuracy of his sources, he found himself continuously altering his texts. When he felt criticism to be unjustified, however, even if it meant attacking so-called authorities, he spoke out overtly in his own favor. Nor did he stay criticism of his enemies, especially, the historian A. de La Mottraye, for his *Historical and Critical Remarks on the History of Charles XII, King of Sweden, by Mr. de Voltaire* (1732). Much is to be said for Voltaire's restraint in indulging in overromanticization or even fabrication of incidents and characters, as was the practice of V. de Saint-Réal and Courtilz de Sandras.
4. Voltaire, *The Age of Louis XIV,* trans. Maartyrn P. Pollack (New York: Dutton, 1961), 1; hereafter cited in text as *Louis XIV.*
5. Voltaire, *Essay on the Customs and the Spirit of Nations,* in *The Works of Voltaire,* trans. William F. Fleming and others, 22 vols. (New York: The St. Hubert Guild, 1901; reprint, New York: Howard Fertig, 1988), 16.2:144; hereafter cited in text as *Customs* by volume, part, and page.
6. René Pomeau, introduction to *Essai sur les moeurs,* in *Oeuvres historiques,* ed. René Pomeau (Paris, Pléiade, 1957), xxiv.

Chapter Six

1. Jacques Van Den Heuvel, *Voltaire dans ses contes* (Paris: Colin, 1967), 123–139; hereafter cited in text.
2. Voltaire to Count Caylus, 7 January 1739, *Correspondence,* no. 1675.
3. Ithuriel, according to Van Den Heuvel in *Voltaire dans ses contes* (127), may be a composite of Ithiel (Prov. 29:30) and the land of Ithuree, northeast of Palestine (Gen. 25:15).

4. Voltaire, *The World as It Is* in *Candide, Zadig, and Selected Stories,* trans. Donald M. Frame (New York: New American Library, 1961), 192; hereafter cited in text as *World.*

5. Voltaire, *Zadig,* trans. H. I. Woolf, in *The Portable Voltaire,* ed. Ben Ray Redman (New York: Penguin, 1977), 334; hereafter cited in text as *Zadig* 1977.

6. Voltaire, *Zadig,* in *Candide, Zadig, and Selected Stories,* trans. Donald M. Frame (New York: New American Library, 1961), 165; hereafter cited in text as *Zadig* 1961.

7. Voltaire to Pierre Robert de Cideville, 2 January 1748, *Correspondence,* no. 3221.

8. Voltaire to Frederick II, 26 January 1749, *Correspondence,* no. 3349; also see Van Den Heuvel, 206.

9. Voltaire, *Memnon,* in *Candide, Zadig and Selected Stories,* trans. Donald M. Frame (New York: New American Library, 1961), 209; hereafter cited in text as *Memnon.*

10. Peter Gay, *Voltaire's Politics: The Poet as Realist* (Princeton: Princeton University Press, 1988), 23.

11. Otis Fellows and Norman L. Torrey, eds., *The Age of Enlightenment,* 2d ed. (New York: Meredith Corporation, 1971), 58; hereafter cited in text.

12. Voltaire, *Micromégas,* trans. H. I. Woolf, in *The Portable Voltaire,* ed. Ben Ray Redman (New York: Penguin, 1977), 334; hereafter cited in text as *Micromégas.*

13. Ira O. Wade, *Voltaire's Micromégas* (Princeton: Princeton University Press, 1950), 68; hereafter cited in text as Wade 1950.

14. Plato, *Timaeus,* trans. Francis M. Cornford (New York: Bobbs-Merrill, 1959), 18.

15. Voltaire, *Plato's Dream,* in *Candide, Zadig and Selected Stories,* trans. Donald M. Frame (New York: New American Library, 1961), 225; hereafter cited in text as *Plato's Dream.*

16. Van Den Heuvel 64; see also Voltaire, *Elements of Newton's Philosophy,* in Moland, 22:419.

17. George R. Havens, introduction, in *Candide, ou l'Optimisme,* ed. George R. Havens (New York: Henry Holt, 1959), xxxv.

18. Voltaire, *Candide,* trans. Richard Aldington, in *The Portable Voltaire,* ed. Ben Ray Redman (New York: Penguin, 1977), 231; hereafter cited in text as *Candide* 1977.

19. Voltaire's satire of Judaism throughout his work has led scholars to believe that he was anti-Jewish. He was, however, no more so than most French people from the Middle Ages on. As Rabbi Arthur Hertzberg wrote: "Voltaire complained of the Inquisition all his life. He denounced the persecutions of the Jews many times as evidence of the unworthiness of the Church. In the *Sermon du Rabbin Akib* .... Voltaire even went so far in that passage as to absolve the

Jews of murdering Jesus, although he was not always so generous to the Jews on this point." In the *The Henriade* he also took their side once again: Jews were burned at the stake "for not having abandoned the faith of their ancestors" (Arthur Hertzberg, *The French Enlightenment and the Jews* [New York: Columbia University Press, 1968], 280).

Peter Gay maintained that Voltaire "struck at the Jews to strike at the Christians" (Hertzberg, 284). Pierre Aubéry suggested that "all of Voltaire's charges against Jews were meant for the ancient Jews and that the only attack he repeated on those of the present was his dislike for their absurd attachment to their tradition" (Hertzberg, 284). The conclusion for Aubéry would be that they give up their traditions and become "enlightened." When accused of hating the Jews because he had experienced bankruptcies at their hands, Voltaire retorted that he had also lost money with Christian moneylenders. Although the entire question is ambiguous, Hertzberg concludes that "for the next century [Voltaire] provided the fundamentals of the rhetoric of secular anti-Semitism" (Hertzberg, 286).

20. Voltaire, *Les Adorateurs,* in Moland, 28:322.

21. Voltaire, *Story of a Good Brahmin,* in *Candide, Zadig and Selected Stories,* trans. Donald M. Frame (New York: New American Library, 1961), 240; hereafter cited in text as *Good Brahmin.*

22. Voltaire, *The Ingénu,* in *The Works of Voltaire,* trans. William F. Fleming and others, 22 vols. (New York: The St. Hubert Guild, 1901; reprint, New York: Howard Fertig, 1988), 2.1:81; hereafter cited in text as *Ingénu.*

23. Trans. Lester Crocker in *An Age of Crisis. Man and World in Eighteenth Centruy French Thought* (Baltimore, Md.: The Johns Hopkins University Press, 1959), 78.

24. Voltaire, *The Story of Johnny,* in *The Works of Voltaire,* trans. William F. Fleming and others, 22 vols. (New York: The St. Hubert Guild, 1901; reprint, New York: Howard Fertig, 1988), 1.2:131; hereafter cited in text as *Johnny.*

25. Bernard McDonagh, *Turkey* (New York: W. W. Norton, 1995), 202.

26. Michael Haag, *Syria and Lebanon* (London: Cadogan Books, 1995), 376.

27. Voltaire, *Lord Chesterfield's Ears,* in *The Works of Voltaire,* trans. William F. Fleming and others, 22 vols. (New York: The St. Hubert Guild, 1901; reprint, New York: Howard Fertig, 1988), 2.2:17; hereafter cited in text as *Lord.*

Conclusion

Quote used as subtitle in the conclusion is from a letter to the duke de Richelieu written in 1752 from Potsdam (Moland 37:437).

1. Voltaire, *Pandora,* in vol. 9 of *The Works of Voltaire,* trans. William F. Fleming and others, 22 vols. (New York: The St. Hubert Guild, 1901; reprint,

New York: Howard Fertig, 1988), act 1 and lines 293–96; hereafter cited in text by act and line.

2. Voltaire to Jean Le Rond d'Alembert, 6 December 1757, *Correspondence*, no. 4953.

3. Voltaire, *Treaty on Tolerance*, in *The Works of Voltaire*, trans. William F. Fleming and others, 22 vols. (New York: The St. Hubert Guild, 1901; reprint, New York: Howard Fertig, 1988), 12:378.

Selected Bibliography

PRIMARY SOURCES

Voltaire's Notebooks. Ed. Theodore Besterman. Geneva: Institut et Musée Voltaire, 1952.

Oeuvres complètes de Voltaire. Ed. Louis Moland. 52 vols. Paris: Garnier Frères, 1883. Nendeln/Lichtenstein, Kraus Reprint Limited, 1967.

The Works of Voltaire. Trans. William F. Fleming and others. 22 vols. New York: The St. Hubert Guild, 1901. Reprinted by Howard Fertig, New York: 1988.

Candide, ou l'Optimisme. Ed. George R. Havens. New York: Holt, Rinehart & Winston, 1934.

Oeuvres historiques. Texte établi et annoté par René Pomeau. Paris: Pléiade, 1957.

Studies on Voltaire and the Eighteenth Century. Les Délices, Geneva: Institut et Musée Voltaire, 1959.

The Age of Louis XIV. Trans. Maartyrn P. Pollack. New York: Dutton, 1961.

Candide, Zadig, and Selected Stories. Trans. with an Introduction by Donald M. Frame. New York: New American Library, 1961.

Mélanges. Texte établi et annoté par J. Van Den Heuvel. Paris: Pléiade, 1961.

Voltaire. The Age of Louis XIV. Trans. F. C. Green. New York: Dutton, 1961.

Philosophical Dictionary. Trans. Peter Gay. 2 vols. With a Preface by André Maurois. New York: Basic Books, 1962.

Voltaire. The Age of Louis XIV and Other Selected Writings. Trans. and ed. John H. Brumfitt. New York: Washington Square Press, 1963.

The Complete Works of Voltaire [*Oeuvres complètes de Voltaire.*] Ed. Theodore Besterman and others. Geneva, Toronto: Institut et Musée Voltaire. University of Toronto Press, 1968 –.

Selections from Voltaire. Ed. George R. Havens. Rev. ed. New York: Holt, Rinehart & Winston, 1969.

Voltaire's Essay on Epic Poetry: A Study and an Edition. Ed. Florence D. White. New York: Phaeton Press, 1970.

Philosophical Dictionary. Ed. and trans. Theodore Besterman. London: Penguin Books, 1972.

The Selected Letters of Voltaire. Ed. and trans. Richard A. Brooks. New York: New York University Press, 1973.

The Portable Voltaire. Ed. Ben Ray Redman. New York: Penguin Books, 1977.

Voltaire's Correspondence. Edition de Theodore Besterman. 1–7. Paris: Gallimard, 1977.

Candide ou l'Optimisme. Ed. René Pomeau. Paris: Nizet, 1980.

Seven Plays. [*Mérope, Olympia, Alzire, Orestes, Oedipus, Zaïre, Caesar*]. Trans. William F. Fleming. New York: Howard Fertig, 1988.

Philosophical Letters. Trans. Ernest Dilworth. New York: Macmillan, 1989.

A Treatise on Toleration and Other Essays. Trans. Joseph McCabe. Amherst, N.Y.: Prometheus Books, 1994.

Letters Concerning the English Nation. Ed. Nicholas Cronk. Oxford: Oxford University Press, 1994.

Voltaire's Philosophical Dictionary. Trans. H. I. Woolf. New York: Alfred A. Knopf, n.d.

SECONDARY SOURCES

Ages, Arnold. "Tainted Greatness: The Case of Voltaire's Anti-Semitism: The Testimony of Correspondence." *Neohelicon: Acta Comparationis Litterarum Universarum* (Amsterdam, Netherlands), 1994, 21:2. 357–67. An important pinpointing of Voltaire's views on anti-Semitism.

Badinter, Elisabeth. *Emilie, Emilie.* Paris: Flammarion, 1983. What fascinates in this highly readable and well-researched volume is Voltaire's relationship with Emilie Du Châtelet.

Besterman, Theodore. *Voltaire.* New York: Harcourt, Brace & World, 1969. A thought-provoking volume by one of the foremost Voltaire scholars.

Brandes, Georg. *Voltaire.* New York: Tudor, 1936. A valuable and in-depth analysis of Voltaire's creative ideas by a well-known Danish critic.

Brooks, Richard A. *Voltaire and Leibniz.* Genève: Librairie Droz, 1964. A brilliant and clearly written volume treating complex ideas.

Brumfitt, John H. *Voltaire Historian.* Oxford: Oxford University Press, 1958. A significant analysis of Voltaire's works and philosophy of history.

Cole, Toby, and Helen Krich Chinoy. *Actors on Acting.* New York: Crown, 1949. A wonderful history of performers writing on their art.

Coulet, Henri. "L'érotisme des contes voltairiens." *Travaux de littérature* (Boulogne, France), 10 (1997): 195–201. Interesting asides on Voltaire's literary eroticism.

Crocker, Lester. *An Age of Crisis. Man and World in Eighteenth Century French Thought.* Baltimore: The Johns Hopkins Press, 1959. A sage in the field of eighteenth-century studies.

Dédéyan, Charles. *Le Retour de Salente, ou, Voltaire et l'Angleterre.* Paris: Nizet, 1988. Voltaire's English relationships are treated with understanding.

Deloffre, Frédéric. "Aux origines de *Candide*: Une économie de roman." *Revue d'histoire littéraire de la France* (Paris), (Jan.–Feb. 1998): 98:1, 63–83. An intriguing genetic criticism of *Candide*.

Epoka-Mwantuali, Joseph. "Désir et transformations dans *L'Homme aux quarante écus de Voltaire*." *Les lettres romanes* (Louvain-la-Neuve, Belgium), (Feb.–May 1996): 50:1–2, 37–52. Interesting treatment of desire and transformation as a narrative technique.

Faudemay, Alain. *Voltaire allégoriste: Essai sur les rapports entre conte et philosophie chez Voltaire.* Fribourg: Ed. Université de Fribourg, 1987. A finely researched work on Voltaire as allegorist.

Fellows, Otis, and Norman L. Torrey, eds. *The Age of Enlightenment.* 2d ed. New York: Meredith Corporation, 1971. Both authors reveal a deeply sensitive and masterful approach to Voltaire's times and his religious and philosophical ideas.

Gay, Peter. *The Enlightenment.* New York: Simon & Schuster, 1973.

————. *Voltaire's Politics: The Poet as Realist.* Princeton: Princeton University Press, 1988. Both of these works must be read to gain a broader understanding of Voltaire and his times.

Goldzink, Jean. "La morale du *Dictionnaire.*" *Revue de littérature française et comparée,* (Pau, France), (Nov. 1994): 3, 99–105. An excellent treatment of ethics in the *Dictionnaire.*

Gouch, G. P. "Catherine the Great and Voltaire," in *Catherine the Great and Other Studies.* London: Longmans, Green, 1954, 55–71. Important for an understanding of eighteenth-century Russia and Voltaire's epistolary relationship with Catherine the Great.

Gunny, Ahmand. *Voltaire and English Literature: A Study of English Literary Influences on Voltaire.* Oxford: Voltaire Foundation, 1979. Most important for an understanding of Voltaire's frequently controversial ideas on English literature.

Haag, Michael. *Syria and Lebanon.* London: Cadogan Books, 1995.

Havens, George R. *Voltaire's Candide, Ou L'Optimisme.* New York: Henry Holt and Company, 1959. Knowledgeable and meticulously researched.

Hertzberg, Arthur. *The French Enlightenment and the Jews.* New York: Columbia University Press, 1968. A scholarly analysis of Voltaire's anti-Semitism and its impact on French thought.

Howells, Robin. "Rousseau and Voltaire: A Literary Comparison of Two 'Professions de foi.' " *French Studies: A Quarterly Review* (Oxford, England), 49, no. 4 (Oct. 1995): 397–409. Sheds new light on the subject.

Lancaster, Henry C. *French Tragedy in the Time of Louis XV and Voltaire. 1715–1774.* 2 vols. Baltimore, Md.: The Johns Hopkins Press, 1950. The most complete discussion of eighteenth-century French theater to date.

Lanson, Gustave. *Voltaire.* Trans. Robert A. Wagoner. Introduction by Peter Gay. New York: John Wiley & Sons, 1966. A classic work on Voltaire.

Magnan, André. *Dossier Voltaire en Prusse: 1750–1753.* Oxford: Voltaire Foundation, 1986. A must for those interested in Voltaire's Prussian venture.

Mason, Haydn. *Voltaire.* Baltimore, Md.: The Johns Hopkins University Press, 1981. A very helpful and meticulously written biography.

————. "Flaubert on Voltaire." In *Essays in Memory of Michael Parkinson and Janine Dakyns,* ed. Christopher Smith. Norwich: School of Modern Languages and European Studies, University of East Anglia, 1996, 101–105. The new insights offered are valuable to Flaubertians.

McDonagh, Bernard. *Turkey*. New York: W. W., Norton, 1995.

McGhee, Dorothy. *Voltairian Narrative Devices*. Menasha, Wis.: George Banta, 1933. Very perceptive insights on Voltaire's literary style.

Menant, Sylvain. *L'Esthétique de Voltaire*. Paris: Sedès, 1995. Interesting perceptions on Voltaire's esthetic concepts.

Mervaud, Christine. *Voltaire et Frederic II: une dramaturgie des lumières 1736–1778*. Oxford: Voltaire Foundation, 1985. Sheds insights on Voltaire's relationship with Frederick II.

————. "Un génie voltairien: Demogorgon." *Revue d'Histoire littéraire de la France* (Vineuil, France), (Nov.–Dec. 1995): 95: 6, 1017–22. Solid treatment of supernatural figures.

Morel, Jacques. *La Tragédie*. Paris: Armand Colin, 1964. An outline-type volume on the philosophy, rules, and regulations of French tragedy.

Morizot, Raymonde. *Voltaire en toutes lumières*. Genève: Editions Aquarius, 1994. A lively volume on Voltaire as precursor to the modern era.

Naves, Raymond. *Voltaire et l'Encyclopédie*. Paris: Les Editions des presses modernes, 1938.

————. *Voltaire: L'homme et l'oeuvre*. Paris: Boivin et Co., 1942.

————. *Le Goût de Voltaire*. Genève: Slatkin reprints, 1967. All of Naves's works on Voltaire are written with sensitivity, knowledge, and passion.

Orieux, Jean. *Voltaire ou La Royauté de l'esprit*. Paris: Flammarion, 1966. An interesting, although at times verbose, biography of Voltaire.

Peyrefitte, Roger. *Voltaire: Sa jeunesse et son temps*. Paris: Albin Michel, 1985. Although a popularizer of Voltaire's youth and times, Peyrefitte's volume makes for an interesting read.

Plato. *Timaeus*. Trans. Francis M. Cornford. New York: Bobbs-Merrill, 1959.

Pomeau, René. *Voltaire par lui même*. Paris: Editions du Seuil, 1956.

————. *La Religion de Voltaire*. Paris: Nizet, 1969. *Voltaire en son temps*. 2 vols. Oxford: Voltaire Foundation, 1985. All of Pomeau's works on Voltaire are first rate and should be consulted.

Raynaud, Jean-Michel. "Rousseau Jean-Jacques, que j'aurais pu aimer . . ." *Magazine littéraire* (Paris), (Sept. 1997): 357, 23–25. Although brief, it sheds interesting insights on the subject.

Richter, Peyton, and Ilona Ricardo. *Voltaire*. Boston: Twayne, 1980. A very thoughtful, pertinent, and well written volume on Voltaire.

Ridgway, R. S. *Voltaire and Sensibility*. Montreal: McGill-Queen's University Press, 1973. A highly poetic volume.

Rivière, M.S. "Voltaire's Concept of Social History." *New AUMLA* (New Zealand), 1, 1966, 86:4, 49–61.

Roulin, Jean-Marie. "Le Grand Siècle au futur: Voltaire, de la prophétie épique à l'écriture de l'histoire." *Revue d'Histoire littéraire de la France* (Vineuil,

France), 96, no. 5 (Sept.–Oct. 1996): 918–33. A fine treatment of Voltaire's prophetic talents with regard to French civilization.

Rusell, Trusten Wheeler. *Voltaire, Dryden and Heroic Tragedy.* New York: AMS Press, 1966. Significant for a broader understanding of Voltaire's ideas on theater.

Russell, W. M. S. "Voltaire, Science and Fiction: A Tercentenary Tribute." *The Review of Science Fiction* (London), 62 (Winter 1994–1995): 31–46. An important article on Voltaire's attitude toward science.

Sandhu, Marcelle. "Le théâtre de Voltaire: Tragédie ou drame?" *Dalhousie French Studies* (Canada), 38 (Spring 1997): 77–84. A good overview of some of Voltaire's plays.

Sareil, Jean. *Essai sur Candide.* Geneva: Librairie Droz, 1967. Always perceptive and knowledgeable.

Searles, Colbert. *Seven French Plays.* New York: Henry Holt, 1935. A well-done anthology.

Sgard, Jean. "Reflexions sur le personnage de Gordon dans *l'Ingénu.*" *Rivista di Letterature Moderne e Comparate* (Florence, Italy), 49, no. 3 (July–Sept. 1996): 285–92. An informative treament of a complex male protagonist.

Sung, Shun-Ching. *Voltaire et la Chine.* Aix-en-Provence: Université de Provence, 1989. Very helpful to those interested in Voltaire and China.

Temmer, Mark J. *Samuel Johnson and Three Infidels: Rousseau, Voltaire, Diderot.* Athens: University of Georgia, 1988. Sheds a variety of insights on three eighteenth-century greats.

Thomson, Gladys S. *Catherine the Great and the Expansion of Russia.* New York: Collier Books, 1947. Important for a historical understanding of eighteenth-century Russia.

Topazio, Virgil W. *Voltaire. A Critical Study of His Major Works.* New York: Random House, 1967. Especially excellent on Voltaire's theater.

Torrey, Norman L. *The Spirit of Voltaire.* New York: Columbia University Press, 1938.

———. *Voltaire and the English Deists.* New York: Archon, 1967. Torrey's writings are brilliant, insightful, and profound.

Van Den Heuvel, Jacques. *Voltaire dans ses contes.* Paris: Colin, 1967. An in-depth analysis of Voltaire's contes.

Vons, Jacqueline. "De la tribune à la scène . . . : Ou comment Voltaire entreprit de mettre en scène *Les Catilinaires* de Cicéron dans la tragédie: *Rome sauvée.*" In *Anniversaire 1994,* ed. Poignault-Rémy. Centre de Recherches: A. Piganio l'Université de Tours, 1996, 43–68. Interesting asides on Voltaire's directing techniques.

Wade, Ira O. *The Intellectual Development of Voltaire.* Princeton: Princeton University Press, 1969.

———. *The Structure and Form of the French Enlightenment.* 2 vols. Princeton: Princeton University Press, 1977.

———. *Voltaire's Micromégas.* Princeton: Princeton University Press, 1950.

————. *Voltaire and Candide*. Princeton: Princeton University Press, 1959. All of Wade's volumes are both scholarly and fascinating to read.

Waldinger, Renée, ed., *Approaches to Teaching Voltaire's Candide*. New York: Modern Language Association of America, 1987. Important for those teaching *Candide*.

Waterman, Mina. *Voltaire, Pascal and Human Destiny*. New York: Octagon Books, 1971. Informative appraisals on human destiny.

Wolff, Larry. "'If I were younger I would make myself Russian': Voltaire's Encounters with the Czar." *New York Times Book Review* 99 (13 Nov. 1994): 14–18. An exciting and lively review depicting Voltaire's views of Russia "emerging from chaos, darkness, and barbarism."

Index

223

The Author

Bettina L. Knapp is professor of Romance and Comparative Literatures at Hunter College and the Graduate Center, City University of New York. She has received a Presidential Award from Hunter College in the area of scholarship/creative activity, a Guggenheim Fellowship, a grant from the American Philosophical Society, and has been made *Chevalier dans l'Ordre des Arts et des Lettres* by the French government. Her works include *Jean Racine, Mythos and Renewal in Modern Theatre; Gérard de Nerval, The Mystic's Dilemma, Theatre and Alchemy; Antonin Artaud, Man of Vision; Gertrude Stein; Anaïs Nin; Exile and the Writer; Emily Dickinson; Women in Myth;* and *Women, Myth, and the Feminine Principle.* Among the books she has written for Twayne are *Jean Genet; Jean Cocteau; Maurice Maeterlinck; Ferdinand Crommelynck;* and *French Theater Since 1968.*

The Editor

David O'Connell is professor of French at Georgia State University. He received his Ph.D. in 1966 from Princeton University, where he was a National Woodrow Wilson Fellow, the Bergen Fellow in Romance Languages, and a National Woodrow Wilson Dissertation Fellow. He is the author of *The Teachings of Saint Louis: A Critical Text* (1972), *Les Propos de Saint Louis* (1974), *Louis-Ferdinand Céline* (1976), *The Instructions of Saint Louis: A Critical Text* (1979), and *Michel de Saint Pierre: A Catholic Novelist at the Crossroads* (1990). He has edited more than 60 books in the Twayne's World Authors Series.